About Me!
Sobre Mí!

Hey! Paste your picture here!

Age?

Write your name.
_____
_____

Date
_____

Greatness!
In this oval, write something that is great about you!
_____
_____
_____

Where do you live?
Your city _____
Your state _____

Top 5 Vacation Spots
List the top 5 places that you would like to visit.
_____
_____
_____
_____
_____

Who is your best friend?
My best friend is:
_____

T5-ACP-904

bridges

Welcome to *Bridges*, where building partnerships between home and school is an important part of ensuring that all children perform at their true academic potential.

Bridges is a unique workbook series developed by classroom teachers and based on national standards in language arts and mathematics. *Bridges* workbooks (available for students in grade/skill levels Pre-K–Grade 5-6) review basic skills in reading, writing, math, and language arts from the grade students are leaving and preview upcoming skills to help prepare students for the grade ahead.

Bridges begins with a pre-assessment test module to help determine student skill level and a parents' guide to help parents become more involved with their children's education. The parents' guide provides tips and on how to encourage interest in reading and a "Blueprint" for success that discusses how to use the workbook most effectively.

Bridges is divided into three sections that progress in difficulty. Each section begins with an incentive contract calendar to help generate excitement and interest in completing assignments and to give parents and teachers a tool to gauge progress. Exercises are typically in half-page increments to give students with shorter attention spans or those who do not yet have a full mastery of the English language a variety of skills and manageable assignments. Exercise instructions are presented in English and Spanish to allow Spanish-speaking parents to become more involved with their children's assignments and overall education.

A post-assessment module is also included to help evaluate student progress. Each *Bridges* workbook includes a certificate of completion that can be awarded by a teacher or parent to recognize and reinforce the student achievement.

We wish you, and your child or students, success this year.

Level Orange = Transition from Grade 4 to Grade 5

All rights reserved.
Copyright 1998, 2004 Federal Education Publishing

Reproduction in any manner, in whole or in part, in English or in other languages, or otherwise without written permission of the publisher is prohibited.

For information, write: Bridges • PO Box 57936 • Salt Lake City, Utah 84157-0936 • 801-313-0332

Please visit our website at www.BridgesProgram.com for supplements, additions, and corrections to this book.

Second Edition 2004
Printed in the United States of America

ISBN: 1-932210-65-2

PRINTED IN THE UNITED STATES OF AMERICA
10 9 8 7 6 5 4 3 2

Table of Contents

Parents' Guide—Getting the Most from *Bridges* iv
Using the Spanish Instructions in *Bridges* vii
How to Encourage Children to Pick Up a Book and Read xi
Bridges Assessment Tests xii
Reading Book List xxvi
Ready for Reading xxviii

1st Section

Incentive Contract Calendar 1
Try Something New 2
Daily Activities in Math, Reading, Writing, and Language 3

2nd Section

Incentive Contract Calendar 33
Try Something New 34
Daily Activities in Math, Reading, Writing, and Language 35

3rd Section

Incentive Contract Calendar 65
Try Something New 66
Daily Activities in Math, Reading, Writing, and Language 67

High-Frequency Word List 97
Words to Sound Out, Read, and Spell 98
Glossary 101
Answer Pages 105

Flashcards 132

© Federal Education Publishing   Level Orange

Parents' Guide

"Getting the Most from Bridges"

You are the most important teacher your child will ever have. *Bridges* is a guided daily workbook to help you succeed in this role.

Studies indicate that basic learning skills are more easily acquired early in life, and small successes can have a lifelong effect on a child's accomplishments. In fact, the more often you tell your children they are intelligent, the more likely they are to become just that. Chances to make such comments present themselves every day, especially during summer or off-track breaks.

You can encourage your children's intellectual development by involving them in things you do. When you cook, point out what ingredients you use and what effect they have on the meal—you've taught vocabulary and science. Take time to explain the newscast—you've taught social studies. Take your child shopping and point out price, brand, and weight differences—you've taught math, economics, and consumer skills.

Of course, you can also encourage your children to learn by getting directly involved in their schoolwork with a book like *Bridges*. This workbook contains:

- Over 200 specially designed, self-motivating activities to keep your child busy, happy, and learning. Each day includes an activity in reading, writing, arithmetic, and language. There are forty-five days in all.
- A Parents' Guide containing ideas for getting the most out of *Bridges*.
- A carefully selected book list full of works children love to read.
- An Incentive Contract to motivate and reward your child's efforts.
- "Try Something New" lists of creative ideas for when your child says: "What can I do? I'm bored."
- High-Frequency Word Lists with vocabulary to sound out, read, and spell.
- A frameable Official Certificate for successfully completing the workbook activities.
- A Spanish Glossary of terms used in the book. (Glossary words are marked with a ‡.)
- Instructions translated into Spanish to help you help your child.

Bridges is packed with ideas for extracurricular activities, as well as fun and challenging math, reading, writing, spelling, and identification exercises that will take your children a step ahead and help them reach for the stars.

Level Orange

Bridges Blueprint for Success

Summer Reading

- There is a suggested reading list on pages xxvi–xxvii.
- Experts recommend that you read to your pre-kindergarten through first grade children 5–10 minutes each day and ask questions about the story. For older children, the recommended daily reading times are—
  Grades 1–2, 10–20 minutes; Grades 2–3, 20–30 minutes; Grades 3–4, 30–45 minutes; Grades 4–5, 45–60 minutes; and Grades 5–6, 45–60 minutes.
- You and your child should decide the length of reading time and fill it in on the Incentive Contract Calendar.

Incentive Contract Calendar

- An Incentive Calendar is located at the beginning of each section.
- You and your child should sign an agreement for an incentive or reward before your child begins each section.
- When your child completes the agreed reading time each day, he/she colors or initials the box below the 📘. When your child completes a day of *Bridges,* he/she colors or initials the box below the 📔.
- Let your child explore and experiment with the "Try Something New" activities lists.

Sections of Bridges

- There are three sections in *Bridges*.
- Each section becomes progressively more challenging.
- There are four activities each day.
- Your child will need a pencil, eraser, ruler, and crayons to complete the activities.

Words to Sound out, Read, and Spell

At the end of each book (except Pre-K and K-1) are lists of words to sound, read, and spell. You can use these for a number of activities and word games you can play with your child:

- Choose you child's favorite words, make two sets of flash cards, and play the matching game (in order to keep the two matching cards, you have to know their meaning or spelling).
- Draw pictures of exciting words.
- Use as many words as you can from the list to make up five questions, statements, or explanations.
- Write a story using as many words as you can from the word list.
- Write a list of words you have a hard time spelling.
- Write a list of action verbs.
- Close your eyes, try to remember as many words as you can from the word list, and write them down.
- Practice writing each word five times.
- Write a list of words you find while traveling to the mountains, on vacation, or on the way to a friend's house.

10 Hints on How to Maximize *Bridges*

1. Let your child explore the book by flipping through the pages and looking at the activities.

2. Help select a good time for reading or working on the activities. Suggest a time before your child has played outside and becomes too tired to do his or her work.

3. Provide any necessary materials. A pencil, ruler, eraser, and crayons are all that are required.

4. Offer positive guidance. Children need a great deal of guidance. Remember, the activities are not meant to be tests. You want to create a relaxed and positive attitude toward learning. Work through at least one example on each page with your child. "Think aloud" and show your child how to solve problems.

5. Give your child plenty of time to think. You may be surprised by how much children can do on their own.

6. Stretch your child's thinking beyond the page. If you are reading a storybook, you might ask, "What do you think will happen next?" or "What would you do if this happened to you?" Encourage your child to name objects that begin with certain letters, or count the number of items in your shopping cart. Also, children often enjoy making up their own stories with illustrations.

7. Reread stories and occasionally flip through completed pages. Completed pages and books will be a source of pride to your child and will help show how much he/she accomplished over the summer.

8. Read and work on activities while outside. Take the workbook out in the back yard, to the park, or to a family camp out. It can be fun wherever you are!

9. Encourage siblings, baby-sitters, and neighborhood children to help with reading and activities. Other children are often perfect for providing the one-on-one attention necessary to reinforce reading skills.

10. Give plenty of approval! Stickers and stamps, or even a hand-drawn funny face are effective for recognizing a job well done. At the end of the summer, your child can feel proud of his/her accomplishments and will be eager for school to start.

Level Orange   Bridges™

Guía para los padres

"Obteniendo el mayor beneficio de Bridges"

Los padres son los maestros más importantes que los niños tendrán en su vida. *Bridges* ofrece un cuaderno guía de ejercicios diarios para que usted tenga éxito en este papel.

Hay estudios que indican que las habilidades básicas de aprendizaje se obtienen con mayor efectividad durante los años formativos de la persona. Los pequeños triunfos pueden producir efectos permanentes en los logros de los niños. Mientras más a menudo les diga usted a sus hijos que son inteligentes, mayores son las posibilidades de que se conviertan justamente en ello.

Las oportunidades para hacerles tales comentarios a sus hijos se presentan a diario, especialmente durante las vacaciones de verano o los descansos entre periodos de estudio.

Puede motivar el desarrollo intelectual de sus niños al permitirles participar en actividades que usted hace. Por ejemplo, muéstreles los ingredientes que use y enséñeles el efecto que tienen en las comidas y les habrá enseñado vocabulario y ciencias. Tome tiempo para explicarles las noticias y les habrá enseñado ciencias sociales. Lleve a sus hijos de compras y enséñeles sobre las diferencias de precios, marcas y medidas, y les habrá enseñado matemáticas, economía y habilidades del consumidor.

Este cuaderno de ejercicios contiene:

- Más de 200 actividades especialmente diseñadas para incentivar a los niños a que se motiven a sí mismos y se mantengan ocupados y felices a medida de que aprenden. Esta guía está dividida en cuatro actividades diarias: lectura, escritura, aritmética y uso del idioma. La guía presenta un programa de 45 días; cada página con el número del día pertinente.
- Una Guía para los padres que contiene pautas útiles sobre cómo usar mejor el libro.
- Una lista de libros cuidadosamente seleccionados de obras que a los niños les encanta leer.
- Un Contrato de Incentivo para motivar y premiar los esfuerzos de los niños.
- Una lista de ideas creativas "Trata Algo Nuevo" para cuando los niños pregunten: "¿Qué puedo hacer?, estoy aburrido".
- Listas de palabras, con vocabulario para pronunciar, leer y escribir.
- Un Certificado Oficial para cuando el niño haya completado exitosamente todas las actividades del libro.
- Un Glosario en español de términos utilizados en el libro. (Las plalbras que se encuentran en el glosario están marcadas con una ‡).
- Instrucciones traducidas al español para ayudarlo a usted y a su niño.

Bridges contiene muchísimas ideas para actividades extracurriculares, así como también divertidos y desafiantes ejercicios de matemáticas, lectura, escritura, ortografía e identificación, que harán progresar a su niño y lo ayudarán a obtener las estrellas.

© Federal Education Publishing — Level Orange

Bridges Blueprint para el éxito

Lectura para el verano

- En la página XXVI encontrará una lista de sugerencias para lectura.
- Los expertos recomiendan que se le lea al niño entre edad preescolar y 1er grado, por 5 a 10 minutos diarios y que se le haga preguntas acerca de la historia. Para niños de mayor edad se recomienda una lectura diaria de:
   Grados 1–2: 10–20 minutos; Grados 2–3: 20–30 minutos; Grados 3–4: 30–45 minutos
   Grados 4–5: 45–60 minutos; Grados 5–6: 45–60 minutos.
- Usted y su niño deberán pactar el tiempo que dedicarán a la lectura y completar el Calendario de Incentivo de Actividades.

Contrato de Incentivo

- Al principio de cada sección se encuentra un Contrato de Incentivo.
- Usted y su niño deberán firmar un acuerdo de incentivo o recompensa antes de que el niño comience cada sección.
- Cuando el niño complete un día de *Bridges*, coloreará o escribirá sus iniciales en la ▢. Cuando su niño complete el tiempo diario de lectura pactado, coloreará o escribirá sus iniciales en el 📘.
- Deje que el niño explore y experimente la lista de actividades <u>Trata Algo Nuevo</u>.

Secciones de Bridges

- *Bridges* contiene 3 secciones.
- Cada sección se torna progresivamente más desafiante.
- Cada día consta de cuatro actividades.
- El niño necesitará un lápiz, una goma, y lápices de colores para completar las actividades.

Palabras para pronunciar, leer y deletrear

Después de la última sección figuran palabras para pronunciar, leer y deletrear. Usted puede utilizar estas palabras para muchas actividades y juegos de palabras que realice con su niño:

- Elija las palabras favoritas de su niño, prepare dos juegos de tarjetas y juegue al *Juego de la Memoria*. Ponga las tarjetas boca abajo y dé vuelta de a dos a la vez, tratando de recordar las coincidencias a medida que avance (para quedarse con las dos tarjetas que coinciden, se debe saber o el significado o cómo se escriben).
- Haga dibujos de las palabras interesantes.
- Utilice la mayor cantidad posible de palabras de la lista para inventar cinco preguntas, oraciones declarativas o explicaciones.
- Escriba una historia utilizando la mayor cantidad posible de palabras de la lista.
- Escriba una lista de las palabras que más le cuesta deletrear.
- Haga una lista de verbos activos.
- Cierre los ojos, trate de recordar la mayor cantidad posible de palabras de la lista y escríbalas.
- Escriba cada palabra cinco veces.
- Haga una lista de palabras que encuentre mientras viaja a las montañas, vacaciona o se dirige a la casa de un amigo.

Level Orange Bridges™

10 sugerencias para obtener el mayor beneficio de *Bridges*

1. Deje que su niño explore el libro, hojeando las páginas y mirando las actividades.

2. Seleccione un buen momento para la lectura y la realización de actividades. Sugiera un momento luego de que su niño haya jugado al aire libre y antes de que se encuentre demasiado cansado.

3. Facilite el material necesario, generalmente todo lo que necesitará será: un lápiz, una regla, una goma y lápices de colores.

4. Ofrezca una guía positiva. Los niños necesitan guía permanente. Recuerde que las actividades no son exámenes. Cree una actitud relajada y positiva hacia el trabajo escolar. Realice con el niño por lo menos un ejemplo de cada página. "Piense en voz alta" y muéstrele al niño cómo resolver los problemas.

5. Dele al niño mucho tiempo para pensar. Se sorprenderá de cuánto pueden realizar los niños por sí solos.

6. Extienda el pensamiento del niño más allá de las actividades de la página. Si está leyendo una historia puede preguntarle: "¿Qué crees que sucederá ahora?" o "¿Qué harías si te sucediera a ti?" Incentive a su niño a nombrar objetos que comiencen con ciertas letras o a que cuente los objetos de su carrito de compras. Muchas veces los niños también disfrutan inventando sus propias historias con ilustraciones.

7. De vez en cuando, revise las páginas ya terminadas. El trabajo hecho y los libros ya leídos serán una fuente de orgullo para su niño y lo ayudarán a demostrar lo mucho que ha logrado a través de las semanas.

8. Lea y realice las actividades al aire libre. Lleve el libro de actividades al aire libre al jardín, al parque o a un campamento. ¡Puede ser divertido!

9. Anime a los hermanos, niñeras y niños del vecindario a que ayuden a su niño en las actividades y la lectura. Muchas veces otros niños son perfectos para proporcionar la atención recíproca que necesitan los lectores principiantes.

10. ¡Muestre aprobación! Las calcomanías, las etiquetas y hasta una cara divertida dibujada por usted son un reconocimiento efectivo de un trabajo realizado satisfactoriamente. Cuando su niño haya completado el libro, cuelgue el certificado de logro en un lugar donde todos puedan verlo.

© Federal Education Publishing   Level Orange

Using the Spanish Instructions in *Bridges*

Basic instructions in Spanish for each activity are provided in red underneath the English instructions. These are to help you as a parent understand the overall nature of the assignment and what tasks your child is supposed to complete. On pages 101–104, *Bridges* also includes a Spanish glossary of grammatical and mathematical terms which may be unfamiliar. All words included in the glossary are marked with a ‡. For example, one instruction reads:

> **Write adjectives in the blanks.**
> **Escribe adjetivos‡ en los espacios en blanco.**

The ‡ tells you that you will find an explanation for the word *adjective* in the glossary:

> **Adjetivo** (adjective)—una palabra que califica a un sustantivo o pronombre. Los adjetivos pueden describir cuántos, de qué tipo o cuál. En la oración "El hombre delgado cepillaba tres perros con un peine azul", *tres*, *delgado* y *azul* son adjetivos.

Note: Once he or she is old enough, your child should read the complete instructions in English. The English paragraphs sometimes contain additional information your child will need to complete the assignment. While this may be challenging at first, it will help your child develop important educational skills. As children work to understand the English instructions, they will not only strengthen their English skills; they will also develop strategies for learning, such as using context clues, a dictionary to look up unfamiliar terms, and a glossary. These are skills all students need, regardless of their native language.

Uso de las instrucciones en español en *Bridges*

Debajo de las instrucciones en inglés para cada actividad, encontrará instrucciones básicas en español escritas en rojo. El objetivo de estas instrucciones es ayudarlo a usted, como padre, a comprender la naturaleza general del trabajo y las tareas que se supone su niño debe realizar. En las páginas 99–100, *Bridges* también incluye un glosario en español de términos gramaticales y matemáticos que podrían resultarle poco comunes. Todas las palabras incluidas en el glosario se encuentran marcadas con una ‡. Por ejemplo, una de las instrucciones dice:

> **Write adjectives in the blanks.**
> **Escribe adjetivos‡ en los espacios en blanco.**

El ‡ le indica que encontrará una explicación de la palabra adjetivo en el glosario:

> **Adjetivo** (adjective) — una palabra que califica a un sustantivo o pronombre. Los adjetivos pueden describir cuántos, de qué tipo o cuál. En la oración "El hombre delgado cepillaba tres perros con un peine azul", tres, delgado y azul son adjetivos.

Nota: Una vez que el niño tenga la edad apropiada, deberá leer las instrucciones solamente en inglés. Muchas veces los párrafos en inglés contienen información adicional que su niño necesitará para completar la tarea. Aunque al principio esto puede resultar un desafío, ayudará a que su niño desarrolle habilidades educativas importantes. Al mismo tiempo que los niños trabajan para comprender las instrucciones en inglés, no solamente refuerzan sus habilidades con respecto al idioma, sino que también desarrollan estrategias de aprendizaje, como por ejemplo, el uso de pistas de contexto, de un glosario y de un diccionario para buscar términos desconocidos. Estas son habilidades que todos los estudiantes necesitan, sin importar cuál sea su lengua nativa.

How to Encourage Children to Pick Up a Book and Read

You can help your child develop good reading habits. Most experts agree that reading with your child is the most important thing you can do. To choose a good book, use *Bridges*' book list.

Set aside time each day to read aloud to your child at bedtime or after lunch or dinner. Read some of the books you enjoyed when you were young.

Visit the library to find books that meet your child's specific interests. Ask a librarian which books are popular among children of your child's grade. Take advantage of storytelling activities at the library. Ask the librarian about other resources, such as stories on cassettes, videotapes, records, and even computers.

Encourage and provide a variety of reading materials. Help your child read house numbers, street signs, signs in store windows, and package labels. Encourage your child to tell stories using pictures.

Best of all, show your child you like to read. Sit down with a good book. After supper, share stories and ideas that might interest your child from the newspapers and magazines you're reading.

Cómo motivar a los niños para que escojan un libro y lo lean

Usted puede ayudar a su niño a desarrollar buenos hábitos de lectura. La mayoría de los expertos coincide en que leer con su niño es lo más importante que usted puede hacer. Para elegir un buen libro, utilice la lista de libros *Bridges*.

Reserve un momento del día para leerle en voz alta a su niño: a la hora de irse a dormir o luego del almuerzo o de la cena. Lea algunos de los libros que a usted le gustaban cuando era niño. Visite la biblioteca para encontrar libros que coincidan con los intereses específicos de su niño.

Pregúntele a un bibliotecario cuáles son los libros populares entre los niños del mismo grado. Aproveche las actividades de narración de cuentos en las bibliotecas. Pregúntele al bibliotecario acerca de otros recursos, como historias en casetes, cintas de video, discos y computadoras.

Fomente y proporcione gran variedad de material de lectura. Ayúdele a su niño a leer los números de las casas, los carteles de las calles, los carteles en los escaparates y las etiquetas de envoltorios. Anime a su niño a relatar historias basándose en dibujos.

Pero, por sobre todo, demuéstrele al niño que a usted le gusta leer. Siéntese con un buen libro. Luego de la comida comparta las historias e ideas del periódico o revistas que usted lee que puedan interesarle al niño.

© Federal Education Publishing   Level Orange

Assessment Tests

A Word about Assessment

The goal of the assessment test is to help you discover what skills your students have acquired and what skills they need to learn. You can use the pretest at the beginning of a new school year or during the course of the school year to give you an idea of where your students are in their development. The post-test can then be used as a follow-up. As you give the assessment, talk with your students about their thinking. Ask questions about the answers they give. If a student cannot complete the assessment, you can use the assessment as a teaching tool. Walk the student through the assessment, teaching as you go.

Keys to Positive Assessment

Your students will need the assessment page and a pencil.
Provide a quiet place free of clutter and distractions.
If parents are administering the test at home, suggest that they try answering questions with a question. For example:

    Student: *"What is this word?"*
    Parent: *"What letters do you see in the word?"* or *"What sound does each letter make?"*

Instruct parents to refrain from immediately correcting their child and to note skills that need to be taught or reinforced. They should have the child move on if he or she is having difficulty.

Assessment Tests

The assessment tests are divided into four parts:

    <u>Assessment 1</u> Assesses reading ability, including comprehension, differentiating between fact and opinion, and vocabulary.
    <u>Assessment 2</u> Assesses language skills and the ability to recognize such things as subjects and predicates, prefixes and suffixes, base words, homophones, synonyms, antonyms, and verb tenses.
    <u>Assessment 3</u> Provides writing practice in cursive and also tests knowledge of basic grammar, punctuation, and sentence logic.
    <u>Assessment 4</u> Assesses math skills, including numeration, time and money values, addition, subtraction, multiplication, division, word problems, fractions, and decimals.

The *Bridges* Assessments Include three Parts:

1. An <u>assessment</u> to test what students already know.
2. A <u>post-assessment</u> to test what students have learned.
3. An <u>assessment analysis</u> to refer you to activity pages in *Bridges* where students can practice specific skills.

Level Orange   *Bridges*™

Assessment Test Analysis

After you review your child's assessment test, match the problems that contain incorrect answers to the *Bridges* pages below. Pay special attention to these pages and ensure that your student receives supervision and extra help if needed. In this way, your child will strengthen skills in these areas.

Reading Skills
Reference Books:	4, 44, 51, 55,
Fact/Opinion:	36, 54
Categorizing:	44, 48, 94

Language Skills
Base Words:	6, 10, 13, 35, 38, 90, 91
Verb Tense:	21, 23, 25
Homonyms/Synonyms:	5, 26, 27, 29, 30, 39, 56, 67, 68, 73, 95
Parts of Speech:	11, 15, 21, 41, 43, 45, 51, 87, 89, 91

Writing Skills
Proofreading/punctuation:	20, 59, 61, 63, 64, 71, 76, 79, 93
Sentence Structure:	3
Abbreviations:	12
Apostrophe:	17, 19
Contractions:	18, 47

Mathematics
Counting & Numeration:	7, 15, 93
Addition & Subtraction:	3, 5, 9, 11, 17, 19, 23, 81
Multiplication & Division:	11, 21, 25, 27, 31, 35, 37, 43, 45, 47, 51, 53, 59, 63, 91, 95
Word Problems:	13, 29
Fractions:	55, 57, 67, 69, 75, 77, 79, 85, 87

© Federal Education Publishing   Level Orange

Assessment 1 — Reading Skills

Choose the reference book you would use to find the answer to the questions. If there is more than one possibility, choose the best answer.

almanac   atlas   dictionary   encyclopedia   telephone book

1. Where would you find a map of the United States? _____
2. Where would you find information about the life of Abraham Lincoln? _____
3. Where would you find the phone number for a plumber? _____
4. Where would you find the definition of *indefatigable*? _____
5. Where would you find information about World War II? _____
6. Where would you find the average temperature for July 4th in your area? _____
7. Where would you look to check the spelling of *independence*? _____
8. Where would you look to find the phone number for a movie theater? _____

Decide if each statement is fact or opinion.

Fact   Opinion
[ ]   [ ]   9. The *Star Wars* movies are the best movies ever made.
[ ]   [ ]   10. A *pigpen* is also called a *sty*.
[ ]   [ ]   11. My neighbor's name is Mr. Jackson.
[ ]   [ ]   12. My dog is the best dog in our neighborhood.
[ ]   [ ]   13. Everyone loves to go to the library.
[ ]   [ ]   14. The White House is where the president lives.

Categorize the words under one of the headings.

15. encyclopedias   stethoscope   seashells   surgeon   scanner
     librarian   produce   gurney   operating rooms   manager
     surfers   study rooms   horizon   gnats   cash registers
     customers   biographies   sunbathers   novels   patients

Things Found on a Beach	Things Found in a Library	Things Found in a Hospital	Things Found at a Grocery Store

Level Orange — Bridges™

Assessment 2 — Language Skills

Look at the sentence. Then follow the directions.

Jake and I baked delicious bread.

1. Draw a line between the subject and the predicate.
2. Underline the proper noun.
3. Circle the pronoun.
4. Draw a box around the noun in the predicate.
5. Draw two lines under the verb.
6. Cross out the adjective.

Use a prefix or suffix to form a new word.

7. one who invents _____
8. not healthy _____
9. able to afford _____
10. to not agree _____
11. full of thanks _____
12. record before _____

Choose the correct verb to complete each sentence.

13. My sister (chose   choosed) the pink shirt.
14. I will (chose   choose) the blue one.
15. My brother has (chose   chosen) the yellow shirt.

Choose the correct homophone to complete the sentence.

16. Tell your _____ not to stare into the _____ .   son   sun
17. Our teacher read a _____ about a rabbit without a _____ .   tail   tale
18. I _____ you would get a _____ bike for your birthday.   knew   new
19. I _____ my bike in the _____ .   road   rode
20. _____ going to _____ grandmother's house.   they're   their

Write S if the words are synonyms, A if the words are antonyms, or H if the words are homophones.

21. weigh—way _____
22. try—attempt _____
23. problem—solution _____
24. stroll—saunter _____
25. their—they're _____
26. gaze—stare _____
27. light—dark _____
28. stair—stare _____
29. problem—answer _____
30. board—bored _____

© Federal Education Publishing — Level Orange

Assessment 3 — Writing Skills

1. **Rewrite the paragraph in cursive, adding the correct punctuation and capitalization.**

   my great grandmother was born may 16 1917 in mexico her name is julia rosa cortez hernandez she married my great grandfather in 1937 three years later they moved to the united states my grandmother was the youngest of their five children she was born in texas in 1948 my grandmother has four brothers named joseph phillip roberto and samuel

   _____
   _____
   _____
   _____
   _____
   _____

2. **Cross out each incomplete sentence.**

   My brother's friend has a cool skateboard.

   My skateboard is.

   Jumping and racing down the street.

   I like to ride my skateboard.

3. **Write the word that each abbreviation stands for.**

   Dr. _____   Mr. _____
   Fri. _____   Ave. _____
   lb. _____   ft. _____
   USA _____   Oct. _____
   St. _____

4. **Use an apostrophe to show the correct possessive form.**

   Marys house is down the street.

   The Joneses house is next door to our house.

   The girls dresses all matched.

   That girls dress is very pretty.

5. **Write the contraction formed by combining the pairs of words.**

   we are _____   I have _____
   she will _____   he is _____
   let us _____   would not _____

Level Orange　　　　　　　　　　xvi　　　　　　　　　　Bridges™

Assessment 4 — Mathematics—Page 1

Solve the problems.

1.
   46   29   36   91   53   85
   + 37   + 87   + 76   - 49   - 37   - 28

2.
   266   723   278   594   642   526
   + 185 - 108 + 369 - 126 - 258 + 59

3.
   4   6   9   5   6   9
   x 8   x 7   x 3   x 9   x 8   x 9

4.
   9)63   8)56   5)130   4)218   7)317   6)579

5.
   225   434   93   71   32   45
   x 8   x 6   x 27   x 69   x 48   x 65

Write each number.

6. 4 thousands, 2 hundreds, 4 tens, and 8 ones _____
7. 5,000 + 400 + 30 + 3 _____
8. 15 thousand, 3 hundred, and 9 _____

Read and solve the problems.

9. The fifth graders were going on a field trip. There were 29 in Mrs. Jensen's class, 28 in Miss Huff's class, and 29 in Miss Rogers's class. The bus cost $210, and cost of admission was $3 per person. How much did the school pay for the field trip? _____

10. Jared has 1 bill and 10 coins totaling $6.52. What bill and coins might Jared have?
    _____

11. School starts at 8:30. It takes Lydia 10 minutes to walk to school, 10 minutes to eat breakfast, and 15 minutes to get dressed and ready for school. What time does Lydia need to wake up to get to school on time? _____

12. There were 18 rows of 54 people at the school performance. How many people attended the performance? _____

Assessment 4 — Mathematics—Page 2

Write the fraction that tells what part is colored.

13. _____

14. _____

15. _____

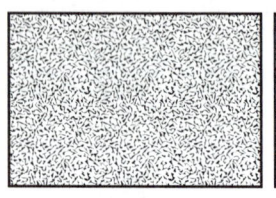

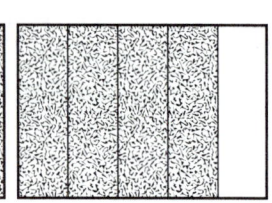

16. _____

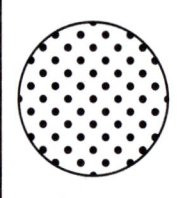

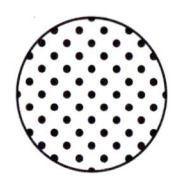

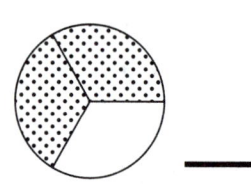

Use <, >, or = to compare the fractions.

17. 4/8 [ ] 3/6
18. 1/5 [ ] 1/8
19. 2/3 [ ] 2/6

20. 1/3 [ ] 4/8
21. 5/6 [ ] 3/4
22. 2/4 [ ] 5/10

Reduce each fraction to its simplest term. Write as a mixed number.

23. 10/4 _____
24. 8/16 _____

25. 9/2 _____
26. 4/6 _____

Rename each mixed number as an improper fraction.

27. 7 1/2 _____
28. 4 3/4 _____

29. 3 2/5 _____
30. 5 1/6 _____

Solve the problems. Write the answer in its simplest form as a mixed number.

31. 1/6 + 5/6 _____
32. 2/7 + 3/7 _____
33. 3/4 + 1/2 _____
34. 1/4 + 3/8 _____

35. 4/8 − 2/8 _____
36. 3/6 − 1/3 _____
37. 3 1/2 − 1 1/4 _____

Write each fraction as a decimal.

38. 3/10 _____
39. 4/10 _____

40. 5/100 _____
41. 24/100 _____

Level Orange xviii Bridges™

Assessment Answers

Assessment 1 • Reading Skills
1. atlas
2. encyclopedia
3. telephone book
4. dictionary
5. encyclopedia
6. almanac
7. dictionary
8. telephone book
9. O
10. F
11. F
12. O
13. O
14. F
15. <u>Things Found on a Beach:</u> surfers, seashells, horizon, sunbathers, gnats
    <u>Things Found in a Library:</u> encyclopedias, librarian, study rooms, biographies, novels
    <u>Things Found in a Hospital:</u> stethoscope, gurney, surgeon, operating rooms, patients
    <u>Things Found at a Grocery Store:</u> customers, produce, scanner, manager, cash registers

Assessment 2 • Language Skills

1–6. <u>Jake</u> and (I) / <u>baked</u> de~~li~~(c)ious [bread.]

7. inventor
8. unhealthy
9. affordable
10. disagree
11. thankful
12. prerecord
13. chose
14. choose
15. chosen
16. son   sun
17. tale   tail
18. knew   new
19. rode   road
20. They're   their
21. H
22. S
23. A
24. S
25. H
26. S
27. A
28. H
29. A
30. H

Assessment 3 • Writing Skills Page xvi
1. My great-grandmother was born May 16, 1917, in Mexico. Her name is Julia Rosa Cortez Hernandez. She married my great-grandfather in 1937. Three years later they moved to the United States. My grandmother was the youngest of their five children. She was born in Texas in 1948. My grandmother has four brothers named Joseph, Phillip, Roberto, and Samuel.
2. ~~My skateboard is.~~
   ~~Jumping and racing down the street.~~

3. Dr.   doctor   Mr.   mister
   Fri. Friday   Ave. avenue
   lb.   pound   ft.   foot / feet
   USA   United States of America
   Oct. October
   St.   street
4. Mary's
   Joneses'
   girls'
   girl's
5. we're   I've
   she'll   he's
   let's   wouldn't

Assessment 4 • Mathematics
1. 83   116   112   42   16   57
2. 451   615   647   468   384   585
3. 32   42   27   45   48   81
4. 7   7   26   54 R2 45 R2 96 R3
5. 1800 2604 2511 4899 1536 2925
6. 4,248
7. 5,433
8. 15,309
9. The school paid $468 for the field trip.
10. Jared may have 1 five-dollar bill, 5 quarters, 2 dimes, 1 nickel, and 2 pennies, OR
    Jared may have 1 five-dollar bill, 2 half-dollars, 4 dimes, 2 nickels, and 2 pennies.
11. Lydia needs to wake up by 7:55.
12. Nine hundred seventy-two people attended the performance.
13. 1 1/2
14. 1 4/5
15. 2 2/3
16. 2 2/3
17. =
18. >
19. >
20. <
21. >
22. =
23. 2 1/2
24. 1/2
25. 4 1/2
26. 2/3
27. 15/2
28. 19/4
29. 17/5
30. 31/6
31. 1
32. 5/7
33. 1 1/4
34. 5/8
35. 1/4
36. 1/6
37. 2 1/4
38. .3
39. .4
40. .05
41. .24

© Federal Education Publishing   Level Orange

Post-Assessment 1 — Reading Skills

Choose the reference book you would use to find the answer to the questions. If there is more than one possibility, choose the best answer.

almanac   atlas   dictionary   encyclopedia   telephone book

1. Where would you find a map of Africa? _____
2. Where would you look to find the phone number of your neighborhood library? _____
3. Where would you find information about the light bulb? _____
4. Where would you find the average rainfall in 1997 in San Diego? _____
5. Where would you find a map of Mexico? _____
6. Where would you look to check the spelling of *cornucopia*? _____
7. Where would you find information about the life of Albert Einstein? _____
8. Where would you find the definition of *rudimentary*? _____

Decide if each statement is fact or opinion.

Fact   Opinion
[ ]   [ ]   9. Pepperoni is the best pizza topping.
[ ]   [ ]   10. Mrs. Jensen is the best fourth grade teacher.
[ ]   [ ]   11. Mrs. Jensen's class had the highest scores on the test.
[ ]   [ ]   12. Jacob missed two on his spelling test.
[ ]   [ ]   13. Purple is the prettiest color.
[ ]   [ ]   14. Sacramento is the capital of California.

Categorize the words under one of the headings.

15. bed   elephant   definitions   chalkboard
    teacher   ring master   lamp   lion tamer
    words   pillow   page numbers   dresser
    tightrope walker bulletin boards parts of speech students

Things Found in a Bedroom	Things Found in a School	Things Found in a Dictionary	Things Found at a Circus

Level Orange
Bridges™

Post-Assessment 2 — Language Skills

Look at the sentence. Then follow the directions.

My mother and her sister went to the mall.

1. Draw a line between the subject and the predicate.
2. Underline the pronouns.
3. Circle the nouns.
4. Draw a box around the noun in the predicate.
5. Draw two lines under the verb.
6. Cross out the preposition.

Use a prefix or suffix to form a new word.

7. not comfortable _____
8. full of beauty _____
9. one who inspects _____
10. not usual _____
11. to state again _____
12. able to be chewed _____

Choose the correct verb to complete each sentence.

13. Our team (won   winned) the game.
14. Justin (hoped   hopped) on one foot to the finish line.
15. Erica (ran   runned) all the way home.

Choose the correct homophone to complete the sentence.

16. Please _____ your name on the _____ side of the paper.   right   write
17. I save a few _____ by using some common _____.   cents   sense
18. The nurse showed us the _____ to _____ a new baby.   weigh   way
19. Mr. Jones was _____ at the _____ meeting.   board   bored
20. They dug a _____ big enough to hold the _____ class.   hole   whole

Write S if the words are synonyms, A if the words are antonyms, or H if the words are homophones.

21. begin—end _____
22. gigantic—enormous _____
23. clothes—close _____
24. shouted—whispered _____
25. hire—fire _____
26. outstanding—exceptional _____
27. night—knight _____
28. excited—thrilled _____
29. definitely—maybe _____
30. there—their _____

© Federal Education Publishing · Level Orange

Post-Assessment 3 — Writing Skills

1. Rewrite the paragraph in cursive, adding the correct punctuation and capitalization.

my family went to the circus last saturday. can you guess what we saw there. we saw many different animals including elephants lions tigers horses dogs and monkeys. we also saw clowns with funny faces trapeze walkers high in the air and the ring master running the show. my favorite part of the circus was watching the tightrope walkers. i wonder how they balance on that thin wire. my family enjoyed the circus.

_____
_____
_____
_____
_____

2. Cross out each incomplete sentence.

I went shopping.

The mall has many stores.

Big stores and little stores.

Many things for people to buy.

3. Write the word that each abbreviation stands for.

MD _____   NY _____

Jan. _____   Tues. _____

CA _____   Aug. _____

oz. _____   tsp _____

in. _____

4. Use an apostrophe to show the correct possessive form.

Taras sister is a cheerleader.

The schools colors are red and white.

The cheerleaders uniforms all match.

That cheerleaders uniform is too big.

5. Write the contraction formed by combining the pairs of words.

we will _____   she has _____

he is _____   they are _____

what is _____   should not _____

Level Orange   Bridges™

Post-Assessment 4 — Mathematics—Page 1

Solve the problems.

1.
   - 64 + 56
   - 34 + 27
   - 91 + 79
   - 81 − 38
   - 63 − 47
   - 75 − 18

2.
   - 622 + 803
   - 703 − 178
   - 238 + 419
   - 884 − 299
   - 628 − 201
   - 506 + 36

3.
   - 7 × 8
   - 6 × 9
   - 9 × 4
   - 5 × 7
   - 8 × 8
   - 7 × 9

4.
   - 9) 72
   - 8) 48
   - 5) 220
   - 4) 328

5.
   - 405 × 8
   - 434 × 6
   - 67 × 16
   - 74 × 68
   - 32 × 58
   - 75 × 34

Write each number.

6. 3 thousands, 7 hundreds, 7 tens, and 6 ones _____
7. 2,000 + 600 + 90 + 2 _____
8. 22 thousand, 8 hundred, and 8 _____

Read and solve the problems.

9. The fifth graders were earning money for new science equipment. They wanted to buy 3 microscopes for $37.90 each. They also wanted some science books costing a total of $14. They also wanted to purchase a skeleton. The skeleton cost $247. How much money did the fifth grades need to earn? _____

10. Jonathan has 2 bills and 5 coins totaling $6.53. What bills and coins does Jonathan have? _____

11. The bus arrives at 8:15. It takes me 10 minutes to eat breakfast, 10 minutes to get dressed, and 5 minutes to feed my dog. What time do I need to wake up to make sure that I don't miss the bus? _____

12. There were 23 rows of 64 people at the concert. How many people attended the concert? _____

© Federal Education Publishing   Level Orange

Post-Assessment 4 Mathematics—Page 2

Write the fraction that tells what part is colored.

13. _____

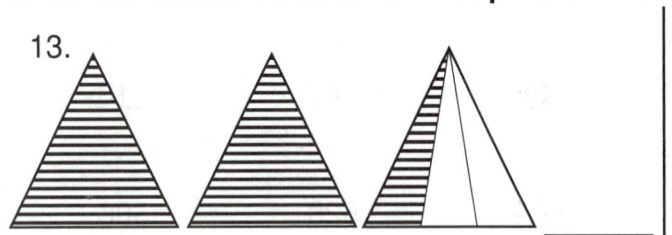

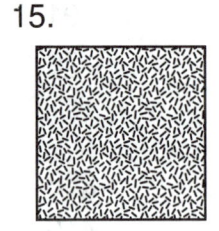

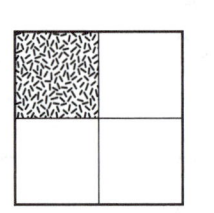

14. _____

15. _____

16. _____

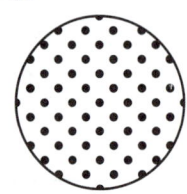

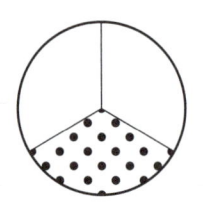

Use <, >, or = to compare the fractions.

17. 2/4 [ ] 6/12
18. 1/7 [ ] 1/5
19. 2/3 [ ] 2/4

20. 1/3 [ ] 1/8
21. 5/6 [ ] 5/8
22. 3/4 [ ] 6/10

Reduce each fraction to its simplest term. Write as a mixed number.

23. 17/3 _____
24. 9/18 _____

25. 14/2 _____
26. 5/20 _____

Rename each mixed number as an improper fraction.

27. 6 1/3 _____
28. 3 3/4 _____

29. 2 3/5 _____
30. 7 5/6 _____

Solve the problems. Write the answer in its simplest form as a mixed number.

31. 1/9 + 5/9 _____
32. 1/7 + 4/7 _____
33. 3/4 + 1/2 _____
34. 1/4 + 1/8 _____

35. 6/8 – 3/8 _____
36. 4/6 – 1/12 _____
37. 2 1/2 – 1/4 _____

Write each fraction as a decimal.

38. 5/10 _____
39. 9/10 _____

40. 7/100 _____
41. 38/100 _____

Level Orange   xxiv   Bridges™

Post-Assessment Answers

Post-Assessment 1 • Reading Skills
1. atlas
2. telephone book
3. encyclopedia
4. almanac
5. atlas
6. dictionary
7. encyclopedia
8. dictionary

9. O
10. O
11. F
12. F
13. O
14. F

15. <u>Things Found in a Bedroom:</u> bed, pillow, lamp, dresser
    <u>Things Found in a School:</u> teacher, chalkboard, bulletin boards, students
    <u>Things Found in a Dictionary:</u> words, definitions, page numbers, parts of speech
    <u>Things Found at a Circus:</u> tightrope walker, elephant, ring master, lion tamer

Post-Assessment 2 • Language Skills
1–6. My (mother) and her (sister) / went ~~to~~ the (mall).

7. uncomfortable
8. beautiful
9. inspector
10. unusual
11. restate
12. chewable

13. won
14. hopped
15. ran

16. write — right
17. cents — sense
18. way — weigh
19. bored — board
20. hole — whole

21. A
22. S
23. H
24. A
25. A
26. S
27. H
28. S
29. A
30. H

Post-Assessment 3 • Writing Skills
1. My family went to the circus last Saturday. Can you guess what we saw there? We saw many different animals including elephants, lions, tigers, horses, dogs, and monkeys. We also saw clowns with funny faces, trapeze walkers high in the air, and the ring master running the show. My favorite part of the circus was watching the tightrope walkers. I wonder how they balance on that thin wire. My family enjoyed the circus.

2. ~~Big stores and little stores.~~
   ~~Many things for people to buy.~~

3. MD — Medical Doctor   NY — New York
   Jan. — January   Tues. — Tuesday
   CA — California   Aug. — August
   oz. — ounce   tsp — teaspoon
   in. — inch

4. Tara's
   school's
   cheerleaders'
   cheerleader's

5. we'll   she's
   he's   they're
   what's   shouldn't

Post-Assessment 4 • Mathematics
1. 120   61   170   43   16   57
2. 1,425   525   657   585   427   542
3. 56   54   36   35   64   63
4. 8   6   44   82
5. 3,240   2,604   1,072   5,032   1,856   2,550
6. 3,776
7. 2,692
8. 22,808
9. $374.70
10. 1 $5 bill, 1 $1 bill, 2 quarters, and 3 pennies
11. 7:50
12. 1,472 people

13. 2 1/3
14. 1 1/4
15. 1 5/6
16. 1 1/3

17. =
18. <
19. >
20. >
21. >
22. >

23. 5 2/3
24. 1/2
25. 7
26. 1/4
27. 19/3
28. 15/4
29. 13/5
30. 47/6
31. 2/3
32. 5/7
33. 1 1/4
34. 3/8
35. 3/8
36. 7/12
37. 2 1/4

38. .5
39. .9
40. .07
41. .38

© Federal Education Publishing   xxv   Level Orange

Reading Book List

Avi
    Poppy
    Poppy and Rye

Ballard, Robert D.
    Finding the Titanic

Banks, Lynne Reid
    The Indian in the Cupboard

Blume, Judy
    Fudge-a-Mania
    Tales of a Fourth Grade Nothing

Cleary, Beverly
    Dear Mr. Henshaw
    Ellen Tebbits
    Emily's Runaway Imagination
    Henry and Ribsy
    Henry and the Paper Route
    Henry Huggins
    Muggie Maggie
    Otis Spofford

Cole, Joanna
    The Magic School Bus books
    At the Waterworks
    Hops Home
    In the Haunted Museum
    Inside the Earth
    Inside the Human Body
    Lost In the Solar System
    On the Ocean Floor

Dahl, Roald
    The BFG
    Charlie and the Chocolate Factory
    Charlie and the Great Glass Elevator
    Fantastic Mr. Fox
    George's Marvelous Medicine
    Matilda
    Witches

Danzinger, Paula
    Amber Brown Is Not a Crayon

Dicamillo, Kate
    Because of Winn-Dixie

Dixon, Franklin W.
    The Hardy Boys Mysteries

Doyle, Sir Arthur Conan
    Sherlock Holmes Mysteries
    Adventures of the Empty House
    Adventures of the Speckled Band
    Final Problem

Estes, Eleanor Ruth
    Hundred Dresses

Ferguson, Alane
    Cricket and the Crackerbox Kid

Fitzgerald, John Dennis
    The Great Brain books

Fitzhugh, Louise
    Harriet the Spy

Fleischman, Sid
    The Whipping Boy

Gardiner, John Reynolds
    Stone Fox

Grove, Vicki
    Good-Bye My Wishing Star

Hass, E. A.
    Incognito Mosquito
    Incognito Mosquito Flies Again
    Incognito Mosquito, Private Insective

Horvath, Polly
    The Trolls

Level Orange

Howe, Deborah
   Bunnicula

Keene, Carolyn
   The Nancy Drew Mysteries

Kingfisher Publications
   1,000 Facts about People
   1,000 Facts about Space
   1,000 Facts about Wild Animals
   Forest Animals
   Polar Animals
   Seashore Animals

Korman, Susan
   Alien Alert

Lowry, Lois
   All About Sam
   Anastasia Krupnik series

MacDonald, Kate
   Anne of Green Gables Cookbook

Mills, Lauren R.
   Rag Coat

Money, Walt
   Gentle Ben
   Kavik, the Wolf Dog

Mowat, Farley
   Owls in the Family

Nixon, Joan Lowery
   Search for the Shadowman

Paterson, Katherine
   The Bridge to Terabithia

Paulsen, Gary
   Dunc and Amos Hit the Big Top
   Dunc and the Flaming Ghost
   Dunc Breaks the Record
   Dunc Gets Tweaked
   Hatchet
   Escape from Fire Mountain
   Legend of Red Horse Cavern
   Rodomonte's Revenge
   Wild Culpepper Cruise

Peck, Robert Newton
   Soup

Peet, Bill
   Bill Peet: An Autobiography

Rockwell, Thomas
   How to Eat Fried Worms

Sachar, Louis
   There's a Boy in the Girls' Bathroom
   Sideways Stories From Wayside School

Schulz, Charles
   For the Love of Peanuts

Silverstein, Shel
   Where the Sidewalk Ends

Sobol, Donald J.
   Encyclopedia Brown series

Speare, Elizabeth George
   Calico Captive
   Sign of the Beaver

Stamm, Claus
   Three Strong Women

Thomas, Jane Resh
   Comeback Dog

Van Draanen, Wendelin
   Sammy Keyes and the Hotel Thief

Warner, Gertrude Chandler
   Boxcar Children books

Ready for Reading

✔ Reading has been around for thousands of years and can open your mind to new ideas by making you think in different ways than television or radio!

✔ The more you read, the smarter you get!

Books I Have Finished Reading

Title	Author	Pages	Date Finished	Great	Evaluation Okay	Bad

Level Orange

Bridges™

Incentive Contract Calendar

Month (Mes) _____

My parents and I decided that if I complete 15 days of *Bridges*™ and read _____ minutes a day, my incentive/reward will be:

(Si yo completo 15 días de *Bridges*™ y leo _____ minutos al día, mi recompensa será:)

_____

Child's Signature (Firma del Niño) _____

Parent's Signature (Firma del Padre) _____

Day 1 (Día 1)	☐	☐	____	Day 9	☐ ☐	____
Day 2	☐	☐	____	Day 10	☐ ☐	____
Day 3	☐	☐	____	Day 11	☐ ☐	____
Day 4	☐	☐	____	Day 12	☐ ☐	____
Day 5	☐	☐	____	Day 13	☐ ☐	____
Day 6	☐	☐	____	Day 14	☐ ☐	____
Day 7	☐	☐	____	Day 15	☐ ☐	____
Day 8	☐	☐	____			

bridges

Parent: Initial the ____ for daily activities and reading your child completes.
Padre: (Marque ____ para las actividades y lectura que su niño complete.)

Child: Put a ✔ in the ☐ for the daily activities 📓 completed.
Pon ✔ en ☐ para las actividades diaria que hayas completado.

Put a ✔ in the ☐ for the daily reading 📘 completed.
Pon ✔ en ☐ para las actividades diarias de lectura que hayas completado.

Try Something New
Fun Activity Ideas

1. Describe what you look like and write it down.
   Describe cómo te ves y escríbelo.

2. Make a picnic lunch for two. Invite a friend over for a picnic in your backyard.
   Prepara un picnic para el almuerzo para dos personas. Invita a un amigo al picnic en el patio.

3. Feed the birds.
   Alimenta a los pájaros.

4. Find some old socks, buttons, yarn, needle, and thread. Make puppets and name them. Then find a cardboard box and paint it. Cut a hole in the front to put the puppets through, and put on a puppet show for younger children.
   Busca medias viejas, botones, lana, aguja e hilo. Fabrica títeres y nómbralos. Luego encuentra una caja de cartén y píntala. Hazle un agujero en el frente para pasar los títeres y prepara un espectáculo de títeres para los niños menores.

5. Polish a pair of your mom's or dad's shoes and put a love note in the toe.
   Lustra un par de zapatos de tu mamá o papá y colócales una nota de amor en la punta.

6. Visit a sick neighbor, friend, or relative.
   Visita a un vecino, amigo o pariente enfermo.

7. Hold a fire drill in your home.
   Organiza un simulacro de incendio en tu hogar.

8. Start a diary.
   Comienza a escribir un diario.

9. Learn how to do something you have always wanted to do, like play the guitar, cross-stitch, rollerblade, cook pizza, train your dog, etc.
   Aprende a hacer algo que siempre hayas deseado hacer, como tocar la guitarra, bordar a punto cruz, patinar, cocinar pizza, entrenar a tu perro, etc.

10. Write a story about your friend.
    Escribe una historia sobre un amigo.

11. In the evening, look at the sky. Find the first star and make a wish.
    Por la tarde, observa el cielo, encuentra la primera estrella y pide un deseo.

12. Pick one of your favorite foods and learn how to make it.
    Elige una de tus comidas favoritas y aprende a hacerla.

13. Make a pitcher of lemonade or tropical Kool-Aid and sell it in front of your house.
    Prepara una jarra de limonada o Kool-Aid tropical y véndela en frente de tu casa.

14. Surprise a family member with breakfast in bed.
    Sorprende a un miembro de la familia llevándole el desayuno a la cama.

Level Orange — Bridges™

Day 1

Mixed Skills Practice. Watch the operation signs.
Práctica combinada.

1. 13 - 5 = _____
2. 17 - 9 = _____
3. 0 ÷ 3 = _____
4. 3 x 6 = _____
5. 6 + 4 = _____
6. 20 ÷ 4 = _____
7. 9 + 2 = _____
8. 1 x 2 = _____
9. 10 ÷ 2 = _____
10. 4 x 3 = _____
11. 13 + 5 = _____
12. 6 - 0 = _____
13. 6 x 5 = _____
14. 15 - 9 = _____
15. 30 ÷ 6 = _____
16. 6 + 9 = _____
17. 27 ÷ 3 = _____
18. 9 x 7 = _____
19. 7 + 9 = _____
20. 25 ÷ 5 = _____
21. 12 - 4 = _____
22. 8 + 5 = _____
23. 13 - 6 = _____
24. 8 x 5 = _____

Find the missing number.
Encuentra el número que falta.

25. 18 ÷ ☐ = 6
26. 5 + ☐ = 6
27. 10 - ☐ = 3
28. 24 ÷ ☐ = 3
29. ☐ ÷ 4 = 8
30. 3 x ☐ = 21
31. ☐ ÷ 6 = 4
32. ☐ + 4 = 9
33. ☐ + 6 = 12
34. 4 x ☐ = 36
35. ☐ - 6 = 7
36. ☐ x 7 = 0
37. 11 - ☐ = 2
38. ☐ x 8 = 8
39. 10 - ☐ = 8
40. 4 + ☐ = 12

Write yes before each group of words that make a sentence. Write no if the group is not a sentence. (Remember: A sentence is a group of words that express a complete thought.)
Escribe yes antes de cada grupo de palabras que forma una oración‡. Escribe no si el grupo no forma una oración.

_____ 1. Tom carried the canned food.
_____ 2. Butterflies have beautiful.
_____ 3. For his tenth birthday.
_____ 4. Turtles have hard shells.
_____ 5. Everyone enjoyed the trip.
_____ 6. Have you fastened?
_____ 7. Wash your hands before.
_____ 8. Will you feed the pets?
_____ 9. Don't forget to call me.
_____ 10. Wrapped the gift.
_____ 11. We will turn to page.
_____ 12. Ants are insects.
_____ 13. Do you have hiking boots?
_____ 14. Cats are furry.
_____ 15. Mark likes to go swimming.
_____ 16. Our green tent.

© Federal Education Publishing   Level Orange

Day 1 Food comes in various containers. Write what foods might come in the following containers (or be packaged a certain way). Then list containers of your own.

Escribe qué alimentos pueden contener estos recipientes. Luego haz una lista de algunos recipientes tuyos.

Your List

A bag of
A bucket of
A box of
A bottle of
A glass of
A pan of
A carton of
A can of
A jar of
A tube of
A cube of
A bar of

Seek and Find. The telephone book is a reference book. There is a lot of useful information in a telephone book.

Utiliza una guía telefónica para realizar estas actividades.

The **White Pages** list people's names and telephone numbers in alphabetical order by last name.

The **Yellow Pages** list businesses' telephone numbers by type of business. **Emergency** information is in the front of the book.

1. Find a friend's name and number in the telephone book and write them down. _____

2. Look up and list the phone numbers that would be helpful to you in case of an emergency. _____
_____
_____

3. Find your school's phone number. _____

4. Look up your favorite restaurant's phone number. _____

5. Look up the phone numbers of your favorite places to go. _____
_____
_____

6. Look up the phone numbers of workplaces of people you know. _____

Level Orange   Bridges™

Day 2

Add or subtract these 3- or 4-digit numbers.
Suma‡ o resta.

1. 681
   + 145

2. 569
   − 247

3. 3,744
   − 1,378

4. 8,171
   + 7,445

5. 1,355
   + 1,927

6. 248
   + 48

7. 143
   + 219

8. 2,830
   − 519

9. 9,873
   + 828

10. 5,893
    + 3,072

11. 304
    − 172

12. 4,918
    + 3,928

13. 6,219
    − 4,356

14. 2,456
    + 1,529

15. 1,375
    + 6,518

16. 428
    − 119

17. 2,709
    + 1,282

18. 7,645
    − 564

19. 1,680
    − 354

20. 6,142
    − 2,525

Add the correct word—their or there. Remember: their means "they own" or "have," and there means "in or at the place," or it can begin a sentence.
Agrega la palabra correcta: their o there.

1. _____ must be something wrong with that cow.
2. The Hills were training _____ horse to jump.
3. We are going to _____ farm tomorrow.
4. Please put the boxes over _____.
5. _____ will be sixteen people at the party.
6. Will you please sit here, not _____?
7. _____ barn burned down yesterday.
8. They will put _____ animals in Mr. Jack's barn tonight.

Write four sentences about your school. Use their in two of them and there in the other two.
Escribe cuatro oraciones sobre tu escuela. Utiliza their en dos oraciones y there en otras dos.

9. _____
10. _____
11. _____
12. _____

© Federal Education Publishing   5   Level Orange

Day 2

Suffixes. A suffix is a syllable added to the end of a base word. Add the suffix in the middle of the suffix wheel to the end of the base word. Write the new word. <u>Remember</u>: You may need to double the final consonant or change a <u>y</u> to an <u>i</u> when adding a suffix.

Agrega el sufijo del centro de la rueda de sufijos‡ al final de las palabras base. Escribe las palabras nuevas.

-ed wheel: paint, pile, shout, worry, hop (hopped), listen

-est wheel: small, crazy, fast, happy, big, fat

-ful wheel: thank, fear, wonder, cheer, beauty, success

Producers and Consumers. Write answers to the following questions or discuss them with an adult.

Escribe respuestas a estas preguntas sobre productores y consumidores.

1. Name some producers. _____

2. How are producers and consumers different? _____

3. What do profit, labor, and wages have to do with producers and consumers? _____

4. How are producers and consumers interdependent? _____

5. Must people buy what they need or want from other people? _____

6. How do you think consumers and producers of today are different from consumers and producers of years ago? _____

Level Orange

Day 3

Understanding Thousands. Write each number in standard form.
Escribe cada número en forma estándar.

1. 8 thousands, 3 tens, 9 ones
   8,039

2. 1 thousand, 7 tens, 5 ones
   _____

3. 6,000 + 300 + 10 + 2
   _____

4. 2,000 + 900 + 80 + 9
   _____

5. 3 thousands, 8 hundreds, 4 tens, 1 one
   _____

6. 6 thousands, 9 hundreds, 9 tens, 6 ones
   _____

7. 5,000 + 700 + 3
   _____

8. 1,000 + 400 + 10
   _____

9. 7 thousands, 1 hundred, 7 ones
   _____

10. 0 thousands, 4 hundreds, 7 tens
    _____

11. 9,000 + 900 + 90 + 9
    _____

12. 7,000 + 900 + 5
    _____

13. 2 thousands, 9 hundreds, 6 tens, 2 ones
    _____

14. 4 thousands, 5 tens
    _____

15. 1,000 + 8
    _____

16. 3,000 + 10 + 5
    _____

Read the following paragraph and answer the questions.
Lee el párrafo y contesta las preguntas.

    Kangaroos are furry, hopping mammals that live only in Australia. Antelope kangaroos live on the plains in the north. Gray kangaroos live mostly in the grasslands and forests of eastern and southern Australia. Red kangaroos make their home in the deserts and dry grasslands in the central part of the country, and most wallaroos live in dry, rocky hills.

1. What is the main idea of this paragraph?
   _____
   _____
   _____

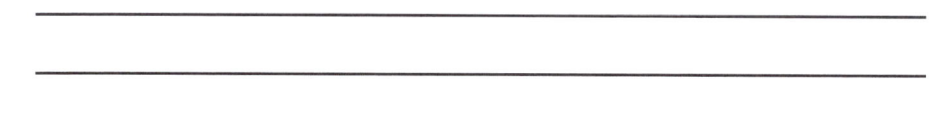

2. List some of the important details of the paragraph.
   _____
   _____
   _____
   _____

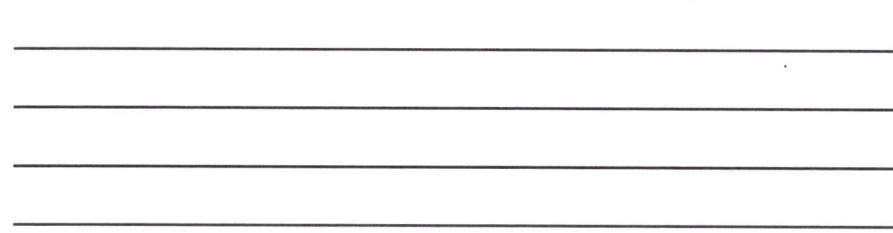

© Federal Education Publishing   Level Orange

Day 3 Products. What products might we get from the seven major regions of our country? See if you can put the correct region next to the correct products.
Coloca la región correcta al lado de los productos‡ adecuados.

- Great Lakes
- Mountain
- Southwest
- Northeast
- Plains
- Pacific
- Southeast

_____ 1. The main crops are sugarcane, oranges, soybeans, rice, peanuts, and tobacco. The main minerals are oil, iron ore, limestone, and coal. Hickory, oak, maple, and lots of other trees are used for furniture, paper, and other products.

_____ 2. Lots of different kinds of fish and shellfish are found here: cod, butterfish, clams, lobsters, squid, sea bass, flounder, sole, and swordfish. Farm products include milk, cheese, eggs, fruits, vegetables, chickens, turkeys, tomatoes, blueberries, cranberries, maple syrup, and grapes. This region also produces lots of coal.

_____ 3. Record amounts of corn, soybeans, and oats are found here. Other crops include fruits and vegetables. This area is rich in minerals, iron ore, and coal. This area is also rich in dairy products. This is called the "Corn Belt" of the United States.

_____ 4. Corn and wheat grow well here. A lot of farming, ranching, and mining is done here. This area manufactures a lot of hot dogs, flour, and breakfast cereals.

_____ 5. The largest crop in this area is cotton. Other crops are oranges, grapefruit, rice, and wheat. Ranchers raise a lot of cattle and sheep here. Silver and copper are found in this region. Fuels are also plentiful, such as coal, natural gas, uranium, and oil.

_____ 6. A wide variety of products come from here because of the two very different climate areas. Products include oil, king crab, salmon, and timber, as well as pineapple, macadamia nuts, fruits, nuts, berries, and vegetables. This area also produces petroleum and natural gas. It has the top agricultural state in the nation, as well as the top commercial fishing region.

_____ 7. Some of the major minerals found in this region are gold, lead, silver, copper, and zinc. There is also lots of natural gas, coal, and oil to be found. Wheat, peas, beans, sugar beets, and potatoes are grown here. Ranching includes beef cattle, sheep, and dairy cows.

Level Orange — Bridges™

Day 4

Estimating Sums and Differences. When estimating numbers, round them off, then add or subtract. <u>Remember</u>: Answers are not exact.
Estima las sumas‡ y las diferencias‡.

EXAMPLE: 420 + 384 = _____. 420 is close to <u>400</u>, and 384 is close to <u>400</u>, so your answer would be <u>800</u> when estimating. Try estimating these problems!

1. 88 + 19 = _____
2. 81 + 75 = _____
3. 93 - 85 = _____
4. 98 - 12 = _____
5. 93 - 39 = _____
6. 891 - 551 = _____
7. 57 - 39 = _____
8. 24 + 35 = _____
9. 209 + 179 = _____
10. 64 + 39 = _____
11. 56 - 33 = _____
12. 288 + 398 = _____
13. 78 - 18 = _____
14. 75 - 42 = _____
15. 540 + 317 = _____
16. 66 + 12 = _____
17. 30 + 71 = _____
18. 610 - 273 = _____
19. 63 + 93 = _____
20. 91 + 65 = _____
21. 247 - 210 = _____

Write the five steps to the writing or composition process. (See page 57 if you need help with the steps.) Then write a short story of your own. Use all five steps. You will need additional paper.
Escribe una historia breve. Utiliza los cinco pasos del proceso de escritura.

Story: _____

© Federal Education Publishing   Level Orange

Day 4

Prefixes. Prefixes are syllables added to the beginning of a base word. Add a prefix to these base words.

Agrega un prefijo‡ a estas palabras base.

1. Will you __un__ lock the door?
2. Can you ____call what he said?
3. The genie will ____appear if you clap your hands.
4. Janet will ____fold the napkins.
5. Do you ____agree with what I said?
6. Mother is going to ____arrange the front room.
7. The picture was the shape of a ____angle.
8. Everyone needs to come ____board now.
9. Erin and Eli will ____form in the ballet.
10. You can count on me to ____pay you.
11. Look out for the ____coming traffic!
12. The Damons have six ____phones in their house.
13. There is a big ____count on the cost of this table.
14. That was a very ____wise thing to do.

Local, State, and Federal Government Activity. Use a telephone directory to look up listings under local, state, and federal government. Record some at each level.

Busca los numeros de teléfono bajo los gobiernos locales, estaduales y federales en la guía telefónica. Anota algunos para cada nivel.

Telephone Directory

Local	Federal	State

Level Orange

Day 5

You can practice basic math facts by using "families of facts."

| 7 + 2 = 9 | 2 + 7 = 9 | 9 - 2 = 7 | 9 - 7 = 2 |
| 3 x 6 = 18 | 6 x 3 = 18 | 18 ÷ 3 = 6 | 18 ÷ 6 = 3 |

Complete the number families below.
Completa las familias de números a continuación.

1. 9, 7, 16
   9 + 7 = 16
   ___ + ___ = ___
   ___ - ___ = ___
   ___ - ___ = ___

2. 3, 9, 27
   3 x 9 = 27
   ___ x ___ = ___
   ___ ÷ ___ = ___
   ___ ÷ ___ = ___

3. 4, 8, 32
   4 x 8 = 32
   ___ x ___ = ___
   ___ ÷ ___ = ___
   ___ ÷ ___ = ___

4. 8, 5, 40
   8 x 5 = 40
   ___ x ___ = ___
   ___ ÷ ___ = ___
   ___ ÷ ___ = ___

5. 3, 8, 11
   3 + 8 = 11
   ___ + ___ = ___
   ___ - ___ = ___
   ___ - ___ = ___

6. 3, 4, 12
   3 x 4 = 12
   ___ x ___ = ___
   ___ ÷ ___ = ___
   ___ ÷ ___ = ___

7. 12, 11, 23
   12 + 11 = 23
   ___ + ___ = ___
   ___ - ___ = ___
   ___ - ___ = ___

8. 612, 208, 820
   612 + 208 = 820
   ___ + ___ = ___
   ___ - ___ = ___
   ___ - ___ = ___

Nouns are words that name people, places, or things.
Common nouns name any person, place, or thing.
Proper nouns name a particular person, place, or thing.

Draw a circle around the common nouns and underline the proper nouns in the following sentences.
Encierra en un círculo los sustantivos‡ comunes y subraya los sustantivos propios en estas oraciones.

1. Many people like to travel in England.
2. Christopher Columbus was an explorer.
3. Antarctica is a continent.
4. The ships crossed the Atlantic Ocean.
5. We paddled the canoe down the Red River.
6. Astronauts explore space for the United States.
7. San Francisco is the city by the bay.
8. Julie and Ashley visited their aunt in Boston.
9. Mt. Smart is a small mountain in Idaho.
10. Thursday is Andrew's birthday.
11. What state does Mike live in?
12. Are Hilary and her brother going to the circus?
13. Brian went to the library to get some books.

© Federal Education Publishing   Level Orange

Day 5

Draw lines between these words and their abbreviations.
Une con líneas las palabras con sus abreviaturas‡.

EXAMPLE:

Sunday	mag.	dozen	Fri.
magazine	pd.	Friday	tel.
quart	ex.	principal	univ.
November	Sun.	telephone	pt.
paid	oz.	volume	ave.
pages	ft.	pint	Oct.
ounce	Nov.	William	wk.
package	qt.	October	prin.
Doctor	pp.	street	st.
example	govt.	university	Wm.
government	Dr.	week	vol.
foot	pkg.	avenue	doz.

Our Government. There are three kinds of government: local, state, and federal (or national). Each kind handles problems of different sizes. They try to solve problems that people cannot solve alone. Put the following statements on problem solving and choices in the correct sequence (1, 2, 3, 4).
Coloca estas oraciones sobre solución de problemas y elecciones en la secuencia correcta.

_____ Write down the possible results of each choice, whether good or bad.

_____ List all the choices or possibilities there are in connection to the problem or situation.

_____ If there is more than one person involved, or if it involves <u>money</u>, people take a vote.

_____ Decide what is most important and which choice or choices will best solve the problem.

Now choose a problem or choice that you are facing and try to follow some or all of the steps above. This problem or choice may affect just you, or it might affect those around you.
Ahora escoge un problema que estés enfrentando o situación donde tengas que elegir y trata de seguir algunos o todos los pasos de arriba.

Level Orange

Day 6

Money Sense.
Resuelve estos problemas de dinero.

1. Cammie has 3 coins worth 11¢. What are the coins?
   _____
   _____

2. Janet has 6 coins worth 47¢. What are the coins?
   _____
   _____

3. Frankie has 5 coins worth 17¢. What 5 coins add up to 17¢?
   _____
   _____

4. Tenley has 7 coins. The value of the coins is 20¢. Find 7 coins with the value of 20¢.
   _____
   _____

5. Jake has 4 coins. One of them is a quarter. The value of his coins is 45¢. What coins does he have?
   _____
   _____

6. Gary has 6 coins worth 40¢. Find the 6 coins that Gary has with the value of 40¢.
   _____
   _____

Singular (One) and Plural (More Than One) Nouns. Write the singular or plural form of the following nouns.
Escribe el singular‡ o plural‡ de los siguientes sustantivos‡.

EXAMPLE:
bee — *bees*

1. bunny _____
2. cities _____
3. toe _____
4. buses _____
5. branch _____
6. foot _____
7. sheep _____
8. men _____
9. face _____
10. berries _____
11. donkey _____
12. stitch _____
13. oxen _____

EXAMPLE:
boys — *boy*

14. windows _____
15. child _____
16. libraries _____
17. movie _____
18. goose _____
19. deer _____
20. boxes _____
21. class _____
22. woman _____
23. tax _____
24. circuses _____
25. turkeys _____
26. book _____

© Federal Education Publishing   13   Level Orange

Day 6

Which word referent should be used in place of the word or words in parentheses? Write it in the blank. <u>He</u>, <u>she</u>, <u>you</u>, <u>it</u>, <u>they</u>, <u>him</u>, <u>her</u>, <u>them</u>, <u>then</u>, <u>here</u>, <u>us</u>, and <u>there</u> are all word referents.

Usa <u>he</u>, <u>she</u>, <u>you</u>, <u>it</u>, <u>they</u>, <u>him</u>, <u>her</u>, <u>them</u>, <u>then</u>, <u>here</u>, <u>us</u>, o <u>there</u> para reemplazar las palabras entre paréntesis.

Barbara and Ashley were best friends. (Barbara and Ashley) _____ had decided to go on a trip together this summer. With maps and brochures scattered all over Barbara's floor, (Barbara and Ashley) _____ started looking for a place to go. One brochure described an interesting place. (The brochure) _____ was about Yellowstone Park. "Let's go (Yellowstone) _____!" cried Ashley. "(Yellowstone) _____ would be a fun place to go. I think we should ask my brother to go with us," said Barbara. " (My brother) _____ could do a lot of the driving for (Barbara and Ashley) _____."

Tom's car was packed and ready to go the next morning. (The car) _____ was a new 4x4 Ranger. (Barbara, Ashley, and Tom) _____ would have taken Barbara's car, but (Barbara's) _____ car had a flat tire.

After driving for two days the travelers got to Yellowstone Park. Tom shouted, "At last we are (at Yellowstone) _____!" (Tom) _____ was tired of driving. (The trip) _____ turned out to be a fun trip for (Ashley, Barbara, and Tom) _____.

Points of Interest.
What makes the state, town, or country that you live in an interesting place? Write an advertisement to get people to visit or even live in your state, town, or country. What are the points of interest? What makes it special and different from other places?

Escribe lo que hace que tu estado, pueblo o país sea un lugar interesante.

_____
_____
_____
_____
_____
_____

Day 7

Write the number that is 10 more than the number shown below, and then write the number that is 10 less than the number.

Escribe el número que sea 10 más que el número dado y luego escribe el número que sea 10 menos.

1. 59	2. 496	3. 951	4. 392
EX. **69** , **49**	____ , ____	____ , ____	____ , ____
5. 164	6. 703	7. 73	8. 1,946
____ , ____	____ , ____	____ , ____	____ , ____

Do the same thing as above, except use 100 more than the number and 100 less than the number.

Realiza lo mismo que antes pero utilizando 100 más y 100 menos.

9. 150	11. 555	13. 871	15. 3,102
____ , ____	____ , ____	____ , ____	____ , ____
10. 703	12. 493	14. 1,956	16. 5,691
____ , ____	____ , ____	____ , ____	____ , ____

Write a proper noun for each of the common nouns listed below.
Remember: Proper nouns start with capital letters.

Escribe un sustantivo‡ propio para cada uno de los sustantivos comunes escritos a continuación.

EXAMPLE:

building *White House*

1. national park _____
2. holiday _____
3. dam _____
4. state _____
5. river _____
6. person _____
7. desert _____
8. day _____
9. island _____
10. street _____

Now write a common noun for the following proper nouns.
Escribe un sustantivo común‡ para los sustantivos propios.

1. Golden Gate _____
2. San Francisco _____
3. Pacific _____
4. November _____
5. Canada _____
6. Joseph _____
7. Liberty Bell _____
8. Pete's Dragon _____
9. Jupiter _____
10. Indians _____

© Federal Education Publishing — Level Orange

Day 7

Write about fathers; then draw a picture. Fathers should always... Father should never... If I were a father I would want to always...

Escribe sobre tu padre y luego haz un dibujo.

Draw your picture here!

Level Orange

Bridges™

Day 8

Adding Thousands. If you have a calculator, check your answers.
Suma.

1.	2,456	2.	9,873	3.	7,125	4.	4,678
	+ 1,527		+ 1,828		+ 2,008		+ 3,321

5.	18,086	6.	8,377	7.	10,308	8.	19,873
	+ 12,302		+ 13,674		+ 23,548		+ 1,828

9.	626	10.	3,481	11.	1,465	12.	430
	8,024		309		388		2,824
	+ 3,643		+ 4,877		+ 3,035		+ 4,099

A singular (one) possessive noun is usually formed by adding 's—animal's. A plural (two or more) possessive noun is usually formed by adding s'—animals'. Choose a singular or plural possessive noun from the Word Box to fill in the blanks. <u>Hint</u>: Look at the word after the blank to help you decide if you need a singular or plural.

Elige un sustantivo posesivo singular o plural para completar los espacios en blanco.

Word Box
- birds'
- woman's
- child's
- dog's
- children's
- Rabbits'
- cows'
- lady's
- plumbers'
- Ann's

1. The _____ toy is broken.
2. _____ tails are fluffy.
3. My _____ leash is black.
4. After the accident, the _____ tools were all over the road.
5. The _____ pets are in a pet show.
6. The _____ coat is made of fur.
7. We hope that _____ picture will win the prize.
8. The _____ mooing was loud and noisy.
9. That _____ hat blew away in the windstorm.
10. The _____ nests were high up in the trees.

© Federal Education Publishing   Level Orange

Day 8

Write the contractions to fill in the circles of the puzzle.
Escribe las contracciones en los círculos.

1. I would
2. is not
3. they will
4. should have
5. who are
6. these will
7. must not
8. there have
9. need not
10. it had
11. will not
12. what has
13. might have
14. one is

Regions of Our Country. Our country is divided into seven regions. <u>Great Lakes</u>, <u>Plains</u>, <u>Mountain</u>, and <u>Pacific</u> are all regions named after bodies of water or important landforms. The other three major regions, <u>Southwest</u>, <u>Southeast</u>, and <u>Northeast</u>, are named for intermediate directions. Label the seven major regions of our United States.

Coloca el nombre de las siete regiones más grandes de los Estados Unidos.

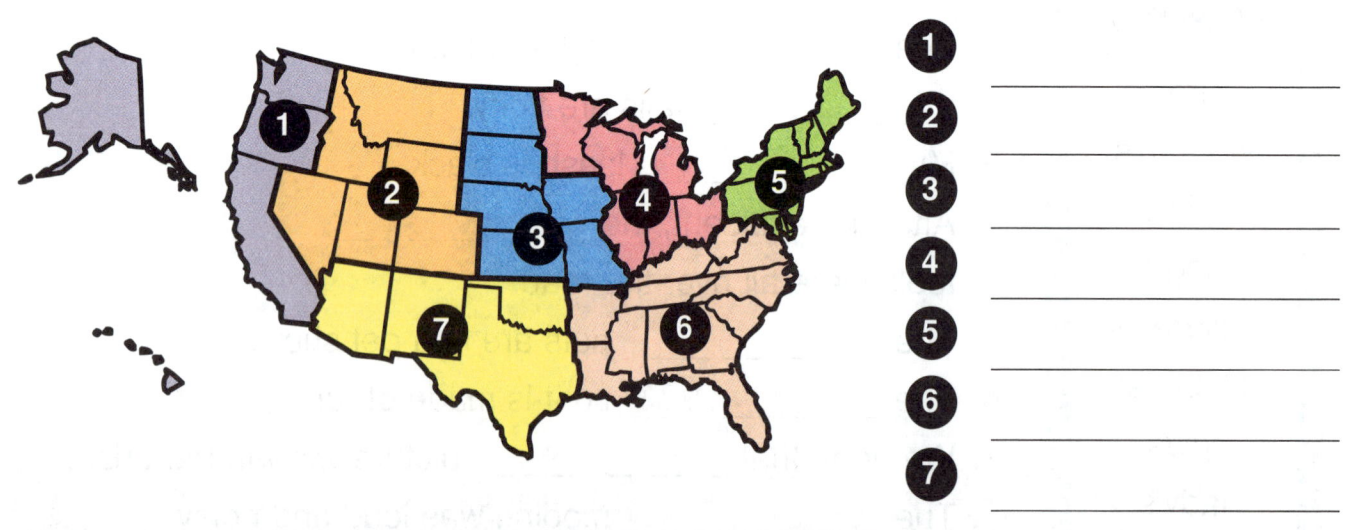

1. _____
2. _____
3. _____
4. _____
5. _____
6. _____
7. _____

*Something to think about. What about Hawaii and Alaska? What region or direction would they belong to?

Hawaii _____   Alaska _____

Level Orange

Subtracting Thousands. Check your answers with a calculator if you have one.
Resta.

1. 8,425
   − 3,519

2. 4,888
   − 1,777

3. 4,314
   − 2,532

4. 3,826
   − 49

5. 9,453
   − 3,168

6. 5,835
   − 1,290

7. 2,182
   − 396

8. 6,922
   − 5,833

9. 8,000
   − 5,603

10. 2,493
    − 1,617

11. 22,318
    − 17,725

12. 57,260
    − 23,458

Write the singular and plural possessive forms of the following nouns.
Escribe las formas posesivas singulares y plurales de estos sustantivos‡.

Singular	Possessive	Plural	Possessive
boy	*boy's*	boys	*boys'*
key		keys	
bird		birds	
mouse		mice	
puppy		puppies	
woman		women	
class		classes	
rollerblade		rollerblades	
flag		flags	
computer		computers	

Day 9

Level Orange

Day 9

Cross out the word that does not belong in the sentence.
Tacha la palabra que no pertenezca a la oración.

EXAMPLE: It's great that we ~~us~~ often agree on things.

1. All butterflies will be gone went by October.
2. Idaho are is known as the "Potato State."
3. She will hid hide behind that large old tree.
4. I have ridden rode my horse regularly this summer.
5. Our dog consistently goes to that corner to dig digging.
6. My baby sister always drinks dranks her milk.
7. Lee Ann had to swept sweep out the garage.
8. I were was very irritated with my friend.
9. How long have you known know Susan Green?
10. We have has been forbidden to go into the cave.
11. Have you done did your chores?
12. The scared boy ran run all the way home.
13. He has done did well in all sports.
14. The wind has blew blown for five days.

Time Zones. Unscramble the answers.
Ordena las respuestas.

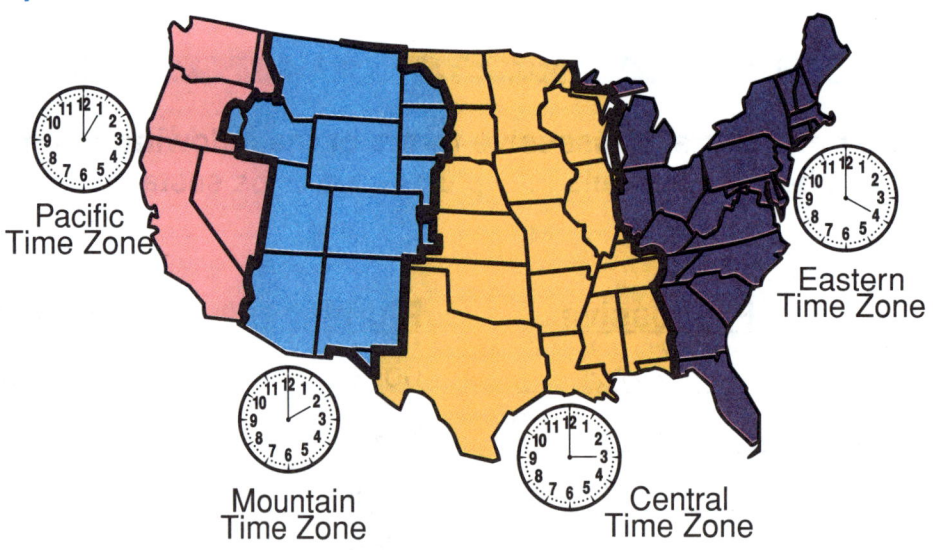

1. Time zones are different because of the usn. _____
2. As we go east the time is treal. _____
3. As we go west the time is rrilaee. _____
4. You can find time zone maps in a lwdro manaacl. _____
5. If you want to find the time in a certain zone to the east you might want to dad suohr _____, not trtbuacs suohr. _____
6. Remember, different parts of the world receive sunlight at different times. That is why we have different meit sonze. _____

Level Orange   20   Bridges™

Day 10

Multiplication. Find each product.
Multiplica.

EXAMPLE:
1. 9 x 2 = 18
2. 8 x 4 = _____
3. 5 x 6 = _____
4. 7 x 3 = _____
5. 4 x 6 = _____
6. 9 x 5 = _____
7. 8 x 6 = _____
8. 5 x 7 = _____
9. 3 x 9 = _____
10. 7 x 6 = _____
11. 1 x 9 = _____
12. 4 x 7 = _____
13. 8 x 3 = _____
14. 3 x 3 = _____
15. 6 x 3 = _____
16. 6 x 9 = _____
17. 6 x 6 = _____
18. 9 x 4 = _____
19. 7 x 7 = _____
20. 7 x 8 = _____
21. 7 x 9 = _____
22. 9 x 9 = _____
23. 8 x 5 = _____
24. 3 x 4 = _____
25. 5 x 5 = _____
26. 8 x 7 = _____
27. 7 x 3 = _____
28. 8 x 8 = _____
29. 9 x 11 = _____
30. 9 x 10 = _____
31. 9 x 7 = _____
32. 8 x 9 = _____

Main Verbs and Helping Verbs. Helping verbs help the main verb. The main verb shows action. Underline the main verbs. Circle the helping verbs.
Subraya los verbos[‡] principales. Encierra en un círculo los verbos auxiliares[‡].

EXAMPLE:
1. It (has been) raining for five days.
2. Jack had finished his lessons before 10:00.
3. I have enjoyed the children this month.
4. We were cleaning the house for our friend.
5. The babies have been sleeping for two hours.
6. Two rafts were floating down the river.

Fill in the blank with a helping verb.
Completa los espacios en blanco con verbos auxiliares.

7. David _____ diving into the pond.
8. The pool _____ _____ used all summer.
9. I _____ waiting for them to fix it.
10. They _____ _____ working on it for three weeks.
11. It _____ _____ fun without the pool.
12. Seven sheep _____ running loose in the street.

© Federal Education Publishing 21 Level Orange

Day 10

The months of the year and the days of the week are written below in order. On the lines below write the months and days in alphabetical order.

Escribe los meses y días en orden alfabético. Lee la información dada y luego completa los espacios en blanco.

January   February   March   April   May   June   July   August   September October   November   December   Sunday   Monday   Tuesday Wednesday   Thursday   Friday   Saturday

1. _____
2. _____
3. _____
4. _____
5. _____
6. _____
7. _____
8. _____
9. _____
10. _____
11. _____
12. _____
13. _____
14. _____
15. _____
16. _____
17. _____
18. _____
19. _____

World Globe. Read the information given; then label the following.

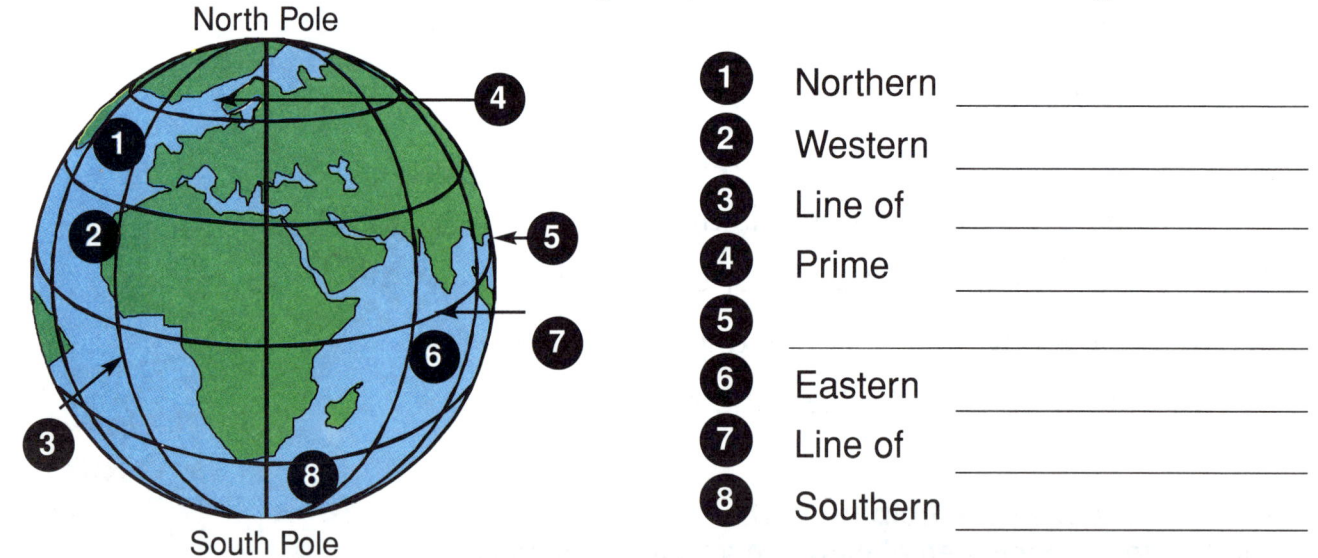

North Pole

South Pole

1. Northern _____
2. Western _____
3. Line of _____
4. Prime _____
5. _____
6. Eastern _____
7. Line of _____
8. Southern _____

We use different terms to locate places on maps and globes. We use lines of <u>latitude</u> to go around the globe from east to west. These lines run parallel to each other, never touching each other. Lines of <u>longitude</u> run north and south on a map or globe and are sometimes called <u>meridians</u>.

The <u>equator</u> is a line of <u>latitude</u> running west to east that divides the earth in half. The top half is called the <u>Northern Hemisphere</u>; the bottom half is called the <u>Southern Hemisphere</u>. The Prime Meridian is a line of <u>longitude</u>. It runs from north to south. All longitudes are determined based on the <u>prime meridian</u>.

Level Orange   22   Bridges™

Day 11

Adding or Subtracting Thousands. Check your answers using a calculator if you have one.
Suma‡ o resta.

1. 7,458
  − 3,762
	2. 8,562
	  + 2,163
		3. 5,585
		  − 2,609
			4. 6,052
			  − 5,381
				5. 7,871
				  + 1,695

6. 36,814
  − 7,523
	7. 53,397
	  + 39,288
		8. 19,506
		  + 34,947
			9. 18,103
			  − 9,079
				10. 43,470
				  − 3,746

11. 3,245
  5,029
  + 6,981
	12. 9,421
	  8,389
	  + 4,506
		13. 3,340
		  7,189
		  + 4,482
			14. 46,306
			  18,782
			  + 3,115
				15. 36,814
				  17,288
				  + 29,397

Present tense verbs happen now. Past tense verbs have already happened. Write the past or present tense for these verbs.
Escribe el tiempo pasado o presente de estos verbos‡.

EXAMPLE: stay—present tense; stayed—past tense.

Present	Past		Present	Past
1. hop	_____	6.	_____	thanked
2. skate	_____	7.	_____	called
3. love	_____	8.	_____	sprained
4. play	_____	9.	_____	wrapped
5. work	_____	10.	_____	hugged

Past Tense with a Helper. Write the past tense.
Escribe el tiempo pasado.

Present Tense	Past Tense with Helping Verb
EXAMPLE:	
1. walk	has, have, had *walked*
2. jog	has, have, had _____
3. hurry	has, have, had _____
4. empty	has, have, had _____
5. chase	has, thave, had _____

© Federal Education Publishing

Level Orange

Day 11

The Continental Congress adopted the first official American flag in Philadelphia, Pennsylvania, on June 14, 1777. History tells us that at that particular time the thirteen colonies were fighting for their liberty. The flag was a symbol of unity. Choose one or more of the following activities.

Elige y escribe sobre uno o más de los siguientes temas.

1. Compare our flag today with the first American flag. Write a short paragraph about it.
2. Write what your life may have been like during that time, compared to what it is now.
3. Find out what the stars, stripes, and colors of the flag stand for and write a paragraph.

Your Choice of Rooms. Choose a room in your house and measure the floor space. Measure it in either feet or meters. Draw and label it.

Mide una habitación de tu casa en pies o en metros. Dibújala y coloca los datos.

Level Orange

Bridges™

Day 12

Division. Find each quotient.
Divide.

1. 20 ÷ 4 = _____
2. 28 ÷ 4 = _____
3. 14 ÷ 7 = _____
4. 0 ÷ 2 = _____
5. 42 ÷ 6 = _____
6. 30 ÷ 5 = _____
7. 32 ÷ 4 = _____
8. 25 ÷ 5 = _____
9. 81 ÷ 9 = _____
10. 49 ÷ 7 = _____
11. 18 ÷ 6 = _____
12. 63 ÷ 7 = _____
13. 40 ÷ 5 = _____
14. 36 ÷ 9 = _____
15. 72 ÷ 9 = _____
16. 54 ÷ 6 = _____
17. 48 ÷ 6 = _____
18. 32 ÷ 8 = _____
19. 45 ÷ 9 = _____
20. 36 ÷ 6 = _____
21. 54 ÷ 9 = _____
22. 48 ÷ 8 = _____
23. 63 ÷ 9 = _____
24. 99 ÷ 9 = _____

Fill in the blanks with the past tense verb.
Hint: You will have to change the spelling.
Completa los espacios en blanco con los verbos‡ en tiempo pasado.

Past Tense

1. Bells ring.   Bells ___rang___.
2. We eat.   We _____.
3. I wear it.   I _____ it.
4. You make some.   You _____ some.
5. They sing.   They _____.
6. I throw.   I _____.
7. I say.   I _____.
8. They take.   They _____.

Fill in the blank with the past tense of the verb.
Completa los espacios en blanco con los verbos en tiempo pasado‡.

9. Sam _____ he wanted to stay in touch with Kit.   (know)
10. Katie _____ a letter to Ron.   (write)
11. He _____ his friend with him.   (bring)
12. The men _____ to dig the ditch.   (begin)
13. That little girl _____ her doll again.   (break)
14. I _____ her new car to the play.   (drive)

© Federal Education Publishing   25   Level Orange

Day 12

Replace the word <u>said</u> in these sentences with another word that fits the meaning.

Reemplaza la palabra <u>said</u> en estas oraciones por otra palabra que coincida con el significado.

EXAMPLE:
1. The man (said) ___*yelled*___, "Get that cat out of here!"
2. Margaret (said) _____, "Please, don't do that."
3. Mother always (said) _____, "A stitch in time saves nine."
4. "This is my country," (said) _____ the man with a tall hat.
5. "Is it time to go home so soon?" (said) _____ Mike.
6. "I don't like vegetables in soups," (said) _____ Dad.
7. "My sore throat still hurts," (said) _____ Nicholas.
8. The weatherman (said) _____ that it will be windy today.
9. The boy with a mouth full of candy (said) _____ he wanted more.
10. I called Megan on the phone, and she (said) _____, "There's no school today."
11. The shopkeeper (said) _____, "Do you want red or orange socks?"
12. Kristine Jones (said) _____ her mother makes the best cookies.

According to the encyclopedia, the sun was born about 4,600,000,000 years ago. What else do you know about the sun? Read and then write some interesting facts about the sun. You may want to write about the things you like to do during hot weather when the sun shines.

Lee y luego escribe sobre hechos interesantes acerca del sol.

_____
_____
_____
_____
_____
_____
_____
_____

Level Orange

Bridges™

Day 13

Multiplication with Three Factors. Find the product of the three factors.
Encuentra el producto⁺ de estos tres factores.

EXAMPLE: 6 x 1 x 3 = __18__ — 6 x 1 x 3 = 6 x 1 = 6 x 3 = 18

1. 2 x 4 x 2 = ___
2. 3 x 3 x 5 = ___
3. 4 x 2 x 2 = ___
4. 2 x 5 x 1 = ___

5. 4 x 2 x 4 = ___
6. 2 x 3 x 7 = ___
7. 0 x 9 x 9 = ___
8. 3 x 2 x 3 = ___

9. 3 x 3 x 3 = ___
10. 5 x 2 x 2 = ___
11. 4 x 2 x 5 = ___
12. 2 x 3 x 6 = ___

13. 1 x 2 x 3 = ___
14. 3 x 3 x 0 = ___
15. 3 x 5 x 0 = ___
16. 1 x 3 x 5 = ___

17. 2 x 3 x 4 = ___
18. 2 x 2 x 3 = ___
19. 4 x 3 x 2 = ___
20. 8 x 1 x 8 = ___

21. 3 x 3 x 8 = ___
22. 3 x 5 x 1 = ___
23. 6 x 3 x 1 = ___
24. 4 x 1 x 3 = ___

Write four sentences using the word are. Write four sentences using the word our.
Escribe cuatro oraciones usando la palabra are y cuatro usando la palabra our.

1. Our house is almost finished.
2. When are you going to live in it?
3. _____
4. _____
5. _____
6. _____
7. _____
8. _____

Now write two sentences using it's and its.
Remember: It's is a contraction of it is, and its is a possessive pronoun.
Escribe dos oraciones usando it's e its.

1. _____
2. _____
3. _____
4. _____

© Federal Education Publishing   Level Orange

Day 13

A Trip to Outer Space. We're planning a big trip into outer space! You are invited to come along, too. You can even invite a few friends. What will you pack? Why? Where shall we go? What needs to be done? What do you think will happen? What will it be like? Think, then write!
¡Lee, piensa y luego escribe!

Day 14

Problem Solving.
Solución de problemas.

1. Jennifer bought a package of candy for $2.50. The tax was 19¢. She used a coupon for 42¢ off the price of the candy. How much did she pay? _____

2. Elsie worked at a grocery store keeping the shelves full. She worked 4 hours on Wednesday and 5 hours on Friday. She earned $5 an hour. How much did she earn that week? _____

3. Randy bought a box of cookies for $1.98. He used a 20¢ coupon on "Double Coupon Day." On this particular day, the store took off double the coupon's value. How much did Randy pay for that box of cookies? _____

4. Bradley bought a shirt for $5 off the original price of $24. The tax was $1.40. How much did Bradley pay? _____

5. Gayle bought a 6-pack of canned orange juice for $2.89. The store had a special for 74¢ off the original price. The tax was 60¢. How much did Gayle spend? _____

Match the word to the meaning.
Une la palabra con su significado.

EXAMPLE:

1. honorable
2. current
3. knowledge
4. suspicion
5. exact
6. lantern
7. profession
8. universal
9. agriculture
10. declare
11. wilderness
12. ordinary
13. comical
14. tremendous
15. generation

a kind of light
occupation, source of livelihood
to make clearly known
good reputation
usual, familiar, common
very large, great
leaving no room for error
now in progress
uninhabited region
all the people born about the same time
information, awareness, understanding
humorous, funny
understood by all
the science and art of farming
suspecting or being suspected

© Federal Education Publishing   29   Level Orange

Day 14

Here are some words you should know how to spell. Read the meanings below and write the word by its meaning.

Escribe la palabra en el espacio en blanco al lado del significado correcto.

| gnaw | doubt | knit | gnat | glisten | plain |
| pause | pedal | scene | tow | comfort | admire |

1. make something with long needles out of yarn _____
2. to have high regard for, with wonder and delight _____
3. a lever worked with the foot _____
4. shine or sparkle _____
5. to not believe; to feel unsure _____
6. a short stop or wait _____
7. to pull by a rope or chain _____
8. freedom from hardship; to ease _____
9. flatland; not fancy _____
10. part of a play; show strong feelings in front of others _____
11. to bite at something or wear away _____
12. small fly or insect _____

Continents. Have you ever really looked at the shapes of the continents on a world map? It almost seems as if the continents are part of a big puzzle. Trace the world map below. Then cut out the following major continents and islands: North and South America, Australia, Europe-Asia, Greenland, and Africa. Try to fit all of the continents together so that no (or very little) space exists between them.

Encuentra un mapa del mundo y luego traza y corta los continentes más grandes y las islas. Intenta armar el mapa.

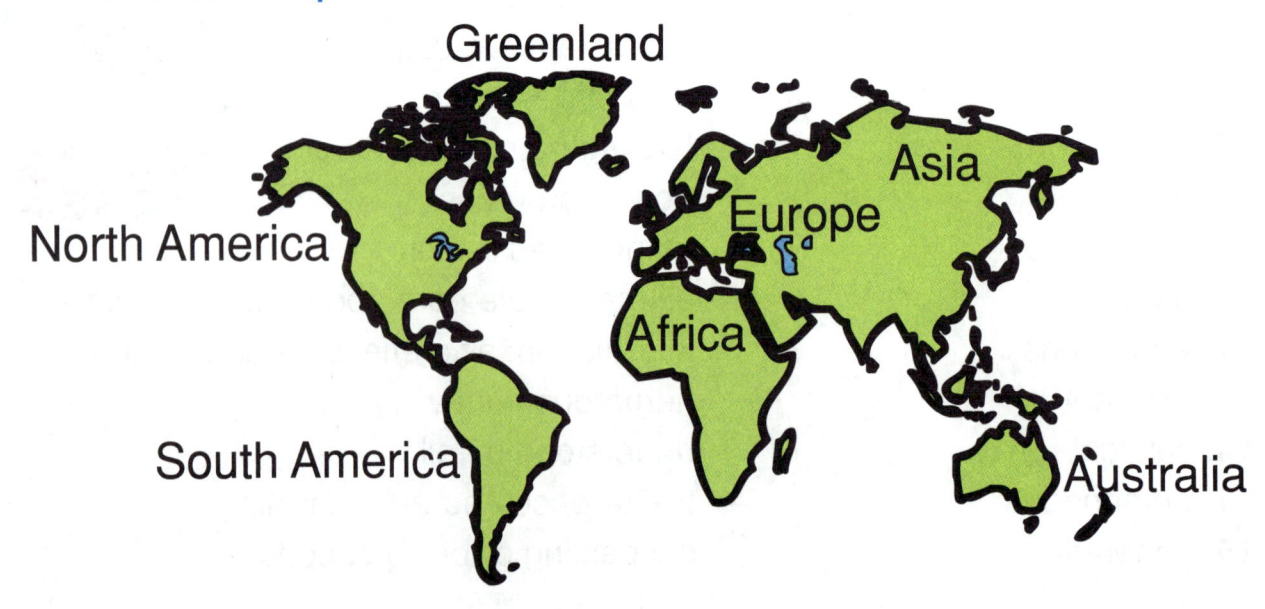

Level Orange 30 Bridges™

Day 15

Divide to find the quotient.
Divide para encotrar el cociente.

1. 4)28
2. 5)40
3. 7)49
4. 6)30

5. 8)72
6. 9)45
7. 8)32
8. 3)15

9. 7)56
10. 6)24
11. 7)14
12. 6)54

13. 9)9
14. 7)28
15. 6)42
16. 8)56

17. 7)35
18. 6)48
19. 9)81
20. 8)24

21. 8)40
22. 9)72
23. 7)63
24. 7)42

You have been out of school for a few weeks now. Write a story telling what you have been doing for the past few weeks. Be sure to follow the five steps of the writing process.
Escribe una historia sobre lo que has hecho las últimas semanas.

Level Orange

Day 15

Below are the days of the week and the months of the year spelled with dictionary symbols. Write the words to the side. Don't forget capital letters.

A continuación se encuentran los días y meses escritos en símbolos de diccionario. Escribe las palabras al lado.

1. /ā´prəl/ _April_
2. /jan´ūre´ē/ _____
3. /mun´dā/ _____
4. /sep tem´bər/ _____
5. /dē sem´bər/ _____
6. /sat´ər dā/ _____
7. /mā/ _____
8. /feb´rüer´ē/ _____
9. /tūz´dā/ _____
10. /frī´dā/ _____
11. /märch/ _____
12. /wenz´dā/ _____
13. /jün/ _____
14. /sun´dā/ _____
15. /nō vem´bər/ _____
16. /o´gest/ _____
17. /thərz´dā/ _____
18. /ok tō bər/ _____
19. /jülī´/ _____

Rocks. Rocks are found almost everywhere. There is much to see and learn about rocks. Geologists are scientists who study rocks. All rocks are made up of one or more minerals. Scientists have discovered over 2,000 minerals. Rocks are changed by water, plants, and other forces of nature. Below are words you need to know when talking about rocks. Look up each word in the dictionary and write down a short definition for it.

Busca en el diccionario estas palabras sobre rocas y escribe una definición breve para cada una.

1. igneous _____
2. sedimentary _____
3. metamorphic _____
4. mineral _____
5. crystal _____
6. lava _____
7. magma _____
8. anthracite _____
9. bituminous _____
10. coal _____

Level Orange
Bridges™

Incentive Contract Calendar

Month (Mes) _____

My parents and I decided that if I complete 15 days of *Bridges*™ and read _____ minutes a day, my incentive/reward will be:

(Si yo completo 15 días de *Bridges*™ y leo _____ minutos al día, mi recompensa será:)

_____

Child's Signature (Firma del Niño) _____

Parent's Signature (Firma del Padre) _____

Day 1 (Día 1)	☐	☐	_____	Day 9	☐ ☐	_____
Day 2	☐	☐	_____	Day 10	☐ ☐	_____
Day 3	☐	☐	_____	Day 11	☐ ☐	_____
Day 4	☐	☐	_____	Day 12	☐ ☐	_____
Day 5	☐	☐	_____	Day 13	☐ ☐	_____
Day 6	☐	☐	_____	Day 14	☐ ☐	_____
Day 7	☐	☐	_____	Day 15	☐ ☐	
Day 8	☐	☐	_____			

bridges

Parent: Initial the ____ for daily activities and reading your child completes.

Padre: (Marque ____ para las actividades y lectura que su niño complete.)

Child: Put a ✔ in the ☐ for the daily activities ▱ completed.

Pon ✔ en ☐ para las actividades diaria que hayas completado.

Put a ✔ in the ☐ for the daily reading 📘 completed.

Pon ✔ en ☐ para las actividades diarias de lectura que hayas completado.

Try Something New
Fun Activity Ideas

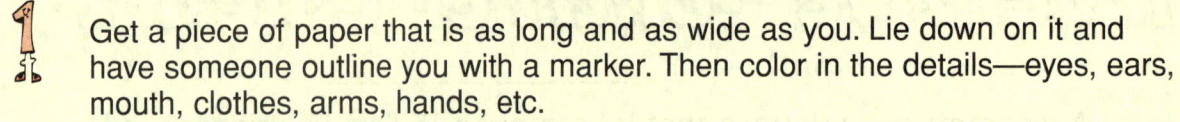

1. Get a piece of paper that is as long and as wide as you. Lie down on it and have someone outline you with a marker. Then color in the details—eyes, ears, mouth, clothes, arms, hands, etc.
   Consigue un pedazo de papel que sea tan largo y ancho como tú. Acuéstate sobre él y pídele a alguien que trace tu contorno con un marcador. Luego colorea los detalles: ojos, oídos, boca, vestimenta, brazos, manos, etc.

2. Invite your friends over for popcorn and vote on your favorite movie. Watch the winning movie; then choose parts and act out the movie in your own way.
   Invita a tus amigos a comer palomitas y voten por su película favorita. Miren la película ganadora y luego elijan partes y actúen la película a su manera.

3. Visit the library and attend story time.
   Visita la biblioteca y asiste a los relatos de cuentos.

4. With bright colored markers, draw a picture of your favorite place to go. Paste it to a piece of posterboard and cut it into pieces for a jigsaw puzzle.
   Haz un dibujo con marcadores de colores brillantes del lugar al que más te gustaría ir. Pégalo a un pedazo de cartón y córtalo en pedacitos para hacer un rompecabezas.

5. Give your dog a bath, or ask your neighbor or friend if you can give their dog a bath.
   Baña a tu perro o pregúntale a un vecino o amigo si puedes bañar el suyo.

6. Pack a lunch and go to the park.
   Prepara un almuerzo y vé al parque.

7. Roast marshmallows over a fire or barbecue.
   Tuesta malvaviscos en el fuego o en un asador.

8. Draw the shape of your state and put a star where you live. Draw your state flower, motto, and bird.
   Dibuja la forma de tu estado y coloca una estrella donde vives. Dibuja la flor, el lema y el pájaro de tu estado.

9. Make a batch of cookies and take them to a sick friend, neighbor, or relative.
   Cocina galletas y llévaselas a un amigo, vecino o pariente enfermo.

10. Plant some flower or vegetable seeds in a pot and watch them grow.
    Planta semillas de flores o verduras en una maceta y observa cómo crecen.

11. Organize an earthquake drill for your family.
    Organiza un simulacro de terremoto para tu familia.

12. Pick one of your favorite foods and learn how to make it.
    Elige una de tus comidas favoritas y aprende a hacerla.

13. Invent a new game and play it with your friends.
    Inventa un juego y juégalo con tus amigos.

Level Orange   Bridges™

Day 1

Write the rest of the number families.
Termina de escribir las familias de números.

1. 6 x 9 = 54 9 x 6 = 54 54 ÷ 6 = 9 54 ÷ 9 = 6	2. 7 x 8 = 56	3. 6 x 7 = 42	4. 63 ÷ 9 = 7
5. 48 ÷ 6 = 8	6. 72 ÷ 8 = 9	7. 6 x 9 = 54	8. 32 ÷ 8 = 4
9. 36 ÷ 4 = 9	10. 9 x 7 = 63	11. 5 x 9 = 45	12. 90 ÷ 9 = 10

Prefixes and suffixes. Remember: Prefixes are added to the beginning of a base word. Suffixes are added to the end of a base word. Add a prefix to these words. Use mis-, un-, and re-. Write the whole word.
Agrega un prefijo a estas palabras. Usa mis-, un- y re-

mis-   un-   re-

1. lucky _____
2. spell _____
3. build _____
4. judge _____
5. fill _____
6. able _____

Add a suffix to these words. Use -er, -less, -ful, and -ed. Write the whole word.
Agrega un sufijo a estas palabras. Utiliza –er, -less y –ed.

7. use _____
8. care _____
9. sing _____
10. spell _____
11. hope _____
12. teach _____
13. paint _____
14. report _____

Now write two sentences using words of your choice from each of the two word lists above.
Escribe dos oraciones usando palabras de la lista de arriba.

1. _____
2. _____

© Federal Education Publishing   35   Level Orange

Day 1

Opinions. Everyone has an opinion on most things that happen around them. People will listen to your opinion more often if you state clearly and plainly why you feel as you do.

Write your opinion on one of the following topics or choose one of your own to write about.

Escribe tu opinión sobre uno de estos temas o sobre uno que elijas.

1. People should always wear seatbelts.
2. Children should be able to eat anything they want.
3. Schoolchildren should never have homework to do.
4. We should always help other people, whether they are in our country or not.

Find the product by multiplying.
Multiplica.

EXAMPLE:
$$\begin{array}{r} \overset{1}{12} \\ \times 6 \\ \hline 72 \end{array}$$

1. 12 × 4
2. 22 × 6
3. 18 × 2
4. 23 × 4
5. 42 × 5

6. 23 × 7
7. 34 × 6
8. 16 × 5
9. 78 × 5
10. 93 × 6

11. 86 × 7
12. 69 × 9
13. 57 × 4
14. 62 × 6
15. 97 × 7
16. 75 × 8

17. 33 × 3
18. 21 × 5
19. 85 × 8
20. 68 × 9
21. 45 × 3
22. 99 × 9

Think of your five senses to help you describe the words below. Try to come up with a word for each sense.
Utiliza tus cinco sentidos para describir las palabras a continuación. Trata de pensar en una palabra para cada sentido.

EXAMPLE:	taste	touch	smell	sight	sound
fire	smoky	hot	smoky	bright	crackle
candy bar	sweet	smooth	chocolate	brown	crunchy

1. a red rose _____
2. a rainbow _____
3. a barnyard _____
4. a snake's skin _____
5. rollerblades _____
6. a snowflake _____

Choose one of the above and write a paragraph about it. Be very descriptive and put in a lot of details.
Escribe un párrafo sobre una de las cosas que has descrito. Utiliza muchos detalles.

_____
_____
_____
_____

© Federal Education Publishing — 37 — Level Orange

Day 2

Prefixes and suffixes can be added to word parts as well as base or root words. Add a prefix or suffix to these word parts, then find and fill in the word shapes below.

Agrega un prefijo‡ o sufijo a estas partes de palabras y luego completa las formas.

1. _du_ plex
2. ___ mit
3. don ___
4. sel ___
5. pott ___
6. ___ gress
7. ___ tant
8. syll ___
9. ___ dora
10. gran ___
11. ___ plicate
12. ___ sent
13. ___ most
14. fur ___
15. ___ do
16. sta ___

Mystery Word. Read the following clues to discover the mystery word.
Lee las pistas para descubrir la palabra misteriosa.

1. The top layer of the earth's surface.
2. It's composed of mineral particles mixed with animal and plant matter.
3. A well-organized, complicated layer of debris covering most of the earth's land surface.
4. It is shallow in some places and deep in other places.
5. It can be very red or very black, as well as other shades and colors.
6. It is one of the most important natural resources of any country.
7. It is so important that we need to make great efforts to conserve it.
8. It takes a long time for it to form.
9. There are different kinds or types.
10. A geologist thinks of it as material that covers the solid rock below the earth's surface.
11. The engineer thinks of it as material on which to build buildings, roads, earth dams, and landing strips.
12. To the farmer and most other people, it is a thin layer of the earth's surface that supports the growth of all kinds of plants.

Mystery Word

Level Orange 38 Bridges™

Day 3

Complete the tables.
Completa las tablas.

1. There are 5 pennies in a nickel.

pennies	5	10	15	20	25	30
nickels	1					

2. There are 10 dimes in a dollar.

dimes	10	20	30			
dollars	1	2				

3. There are 6 cans of pop in each carton.

cans	6	12		24		36
cartons	1		3		5	

4. You can get 6 swimming lessons for $20.

lessons	6	12	18			36
money	$20			$80	$100	

When you write something, your reader should be able to understand clearly what you are trying to say. Read the sentences below and change the underlined word to a more descriptive or exact word.
Cambia la palabra subrayada por una palabra más descriptiva o exacta.

EXAMPLE: This is a good book.
This is an awesome book.

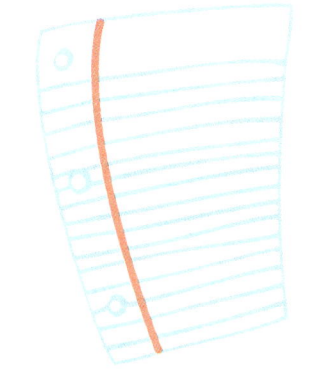

1. My teacher is nice. _____
2. Your things will be safe here. _____
3. That is a big building. _____
4. A car went by our house. _____
5. Our pictures of the trip turned out bad. _____
6. This is a good sandwich. _____
7. The little boy saw a pretty butterfly. _____
8. Many big worms were crawling on the ground. _____
9. We had a bad winter. _____
10. These grapes are awful. _____

Day 3

Most words spelled backwards don't mean anything, but some do. Here are clues for some words that become different words when they are written backwards.

Lee estas pistas de palabras que se convierten en palabras diferentes si se escriben al revés.

1. Spell a word backwards for something you cook in, and you will have a word that means siesta. _pan_ & _nap_

2. Spell a word backwards for a name, and you will have something you turn on to get water. _____ & _____

3. Spell a word backwards for something you catch a fish in, and you will have a number. _____ & _____

4. Spell a word backwards for something to carry things in, and you will get a word that tells what you like to do with your friends. _____ & _____

5. Spell a word backwards for something a train needs, and you will get a word for someone who is not honest. _____ & _____

6. Spell a word for "victory" backwards, and you will have a word that means "at once." _____ & _____

7. Spell a word backwards for something to catch a mouse in, and you will get a word that means something less than whole. _____ & _____

8. Spell a word backwards for a tool that cuts wood, and you will get a word that is a verb. _____ & _____

9. Spell a word backwards for a flying mammal, and you will get a word that means "a bill or check." _____ & _____

10. Spell a word backwards for the end of your pen, and you will have a word that means a hole in the ground. _____ & _____

11. Spell a word backwards that means something you bathe in, and you will have a word that means "other than." _____ & _____

12. Spell a word backwards for "an instrument used in doing work," and you will get a word that means "things taken in a robbery." _____ & _____

13. Spell a word backwards for something that means "to have life," and you will get a word that means "wicked." _____ & _____

14. Spell a word backwards for a word that means "a girl," and you will have a word that means "to fall behind." _____ & _____

Level Orange

Day 4

Measuring in Centimeters. Your little finger is about 1 centimeter wide. If you don't have a centimeter tape, use a string and this centimeter ruler to measure for the following activities.

Encuentra estas medidas en centímetros.

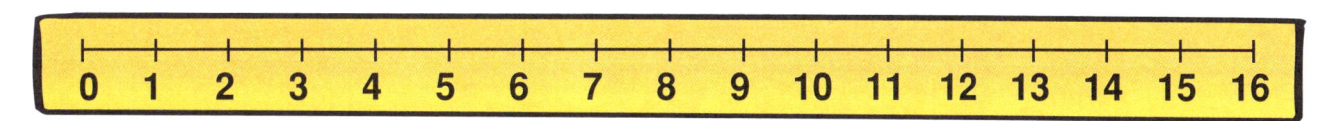

1. The length of your shoes _____
2. The length and width of this book _____, _____
3. Your neck measurement _____
4. Your waist measurement _____
5. Your kitchen table length and width _____, _____
6. The width of a chair in your home _____
7. Your height in centimeters _____
8. The length of the pencil or pen that you use _____

How many other things can you measure? Try estimating, then check to see how close you come to the exact measurement.

Intenta estimar[‡] otras cosas que puedas medir. Luego revisa cuán cerca estabas de la medida real.

_____
_____
_____
_____

Underline the pronouns in the following sentences.
Remember: A pronoun takes the place of a noun.

Subraya los pronombres[‡] en estas oraciones.

1. Will you go with us?
2. He did a good job.
3. She went with me.
4. We ate all of them.
5. It is time for her to go.
6. They will help us today.
7. I thanked him for it.
8. You and I need to hurry.
9. Tomorrow we will go home.
10. This book came for him.
11. A package came for us.
12. You are a good sport.
13. He and I ate the apples.
14. Animals like them also.
15. It was very good.
16. How did she do?

© Federal Education Publishing   41   Level Orange

Day 4

The Fourth of July is our nation's birthday. Another name for it is spelled out in the boxes of the puzzle. Finish the puzzle by writing the appropriate words from the firecrackers. You will not use all of the words.

Termina el crucigrama escribiendo las palabras apropiadas de los cohetes en los espacios en blanco.

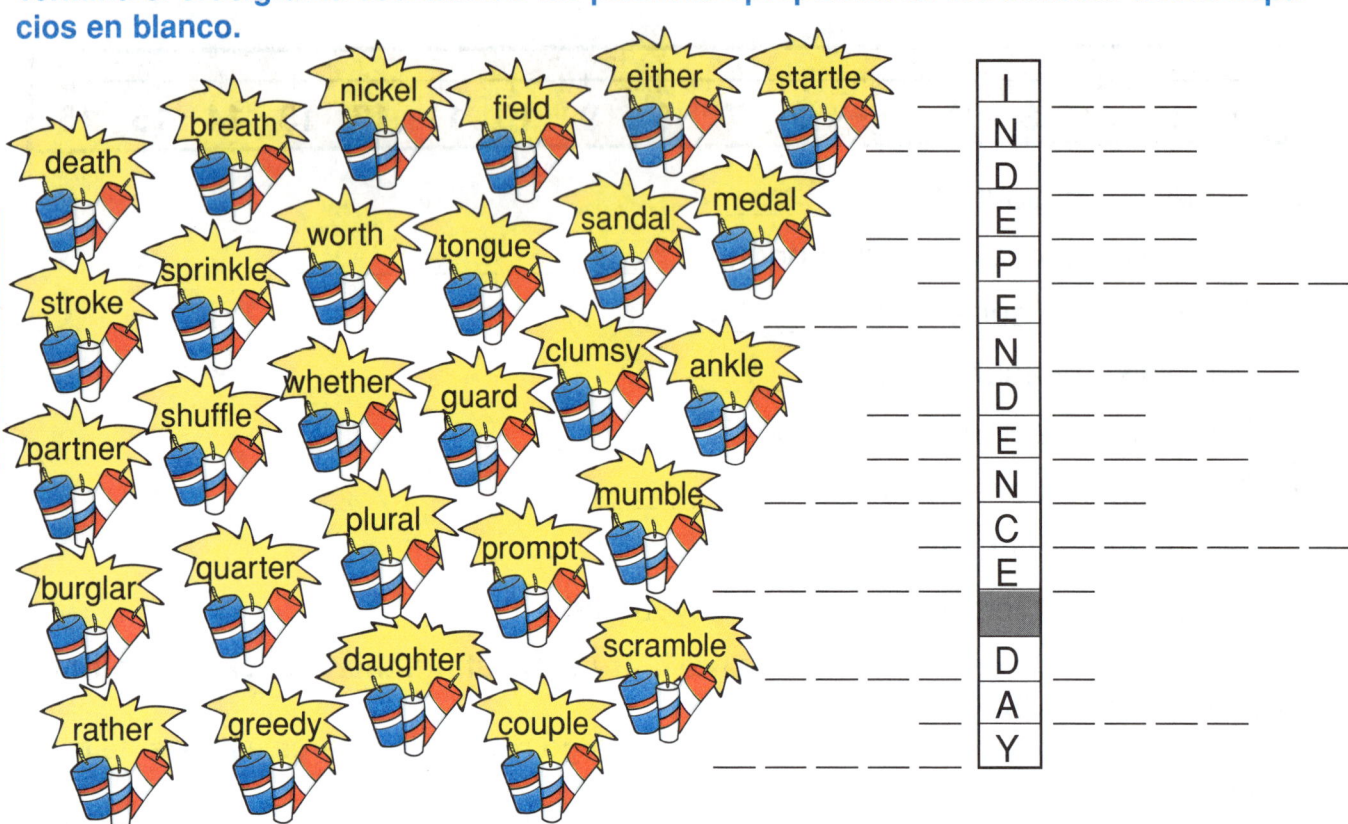

Firecracker words: death, breath, nickel, field, either, startle, worth, sprinkle, tongue, sandal, medal, stroke, whether, clumsy, ankle, partner, shuffle, guard, mumble, plural, prompt, burglar, quarter, daughter, scramble, rather, greedy, couple

Puzzle letters (vertical): I N D E P E N D E N C E ▪ D A Y

Bugs, Bugs, and More Bugs. The world has so many different kinds of bugs, but there's always room for one more. Create a brand new type of bug. Describe it. Where does it live? What does it do? What does it eat? How does it survive? Who are its friends or enemies?

Crea un nuevo tipo de insecto. Describelo.

_____
_____
_____
_____
_____
_____
_____
_____
_____
_____
_____

Level Orange   Bridges™

Day 5

Multiplying with tens and hundreds is fast and fun.
Multiplicación con decenas y centenas.

1. 4 x 10 = _____
2. 600 x 6 = _____
3. 7 x 800 = _____
4. 30 x 8 = _____
5. 5 x 20 = _____
6. 800 x 5 = _____
7. 8 x 90 = _____
8. 50 x 6 = _____
9. 600 x 5 = _____
10. 4 x 100 = _____
11. 7 x 80 = _____
12. 7 x 500 = _____
13. 900 x 7 = _____
14. 600 x 4 = _____
15. 900 x 4 = _____
16. 8 x 900 = _____
17. 800 x 2 = _____
18. 7 x 900 = _____
19. 3 x 10 = _____
20. 700 x 6 = _____
21. 3 x 800 = _____
22. 7 x 40 = _____
23. 9 x 10 = _____
24. 10 x 100 = _____
25. 4 x 60 = _____
26. 80 x 2 = _____
27. 500 x 4 = _____
28. 7 x 700 = _____
29. 30 x 8 = _____
30. 800 x 6 = _____
31. 9 x 500 = _____
30. 9 x 300 = _____
33. 300 x 5 = _____

Pronouns such as I, you, he, she, it, we, and they can be the subject of a sentence. Read these sentences. The subject is underlined. Rewrite the sentences and use a subject pronoun in place of the underlined subject. Write in cursive.
Vuelve a escribir estas oraciones. Utiliza un pronombre‡ subjetivo en el lugar del sujeto‡ subrayado.

1. Jim and I went fishing with our dad.
   _____

2. The weather was sunny and warm.
   _____

3. Ann and Sue can help us with the bait.
   _____

4. Mr. Jack broke his leg.
   _____

5. Kathy is going to New York on a vacation.
   _____

6. Ryan will paint the scenery.
   _____

© Federal Education Publishing   Level Orange

Day 5

Categorize these words under one of the headings.

Hint: There can be eight words under each heading.

Remember: Categorizing words means to put them in groups that have something in common. One row of examples is given.

Categoriza estas palabras bajo uno de los encabezados.

interstate	add	region	colony	oxygen	solid
bacteria	city	hemisphere	stop	column	inch
debate	larva	yield	basin	hexagon	canal
environment	speed	equal	fossil	candidate	intersection
measure	insect	bay	caution	map	estimate
numerator	freedom	society	elevation	freeway	railroad
patriot	habitat	civilization	mineral	detour	quotient

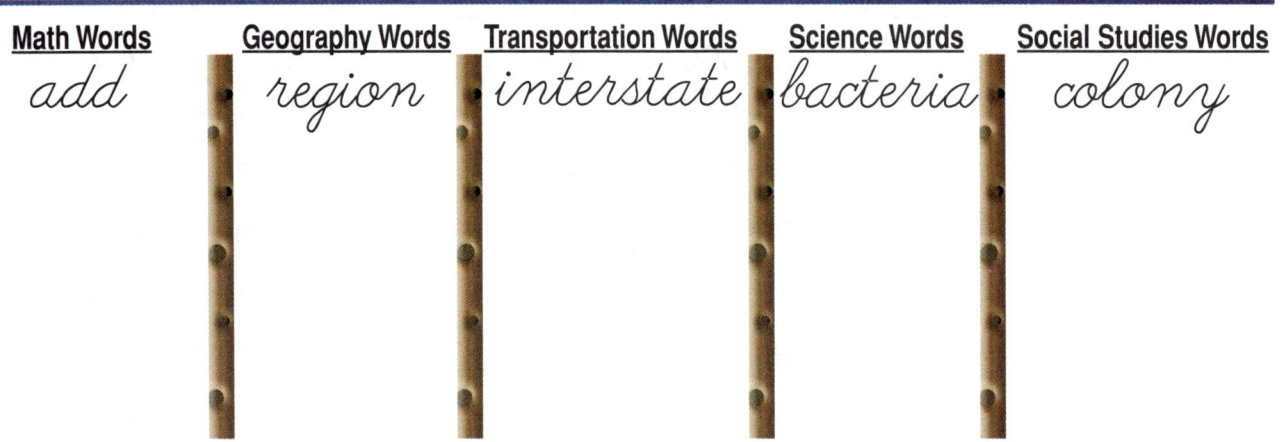

Math Words	Geography Words	Transportation Words	Science Words	Social Studies Words
add	region	interstate	bacteria	colony

What about These Animals in Our Country? Buffalo, condors, and grizzly bears have all but disappeared from our country. The symbol of our country, the bald eagle, is very rare in most states. Bald eagles and bears live in mountainous regions. Prairie dogs and antelope live on the plains. Alligators live in marshy areas. Rattlesnakes live in the desert. Wild turkeys can be found in wilderness areas. These are all animals found in our country. There are also many others. Choose one of the following to do on a separate piece of paper.

Elige una de estas actividades para hacer en papel aparte.

1. Choose and draw a picture of an animal from our country. Place it in the correct habitat. Color it accurately. What other interesting animals do you think might belong in this area? Draw them. What other important information does your picture show?

2. If you choose not to draw a picture about an animal, write a paragraph about one. Use the same type of information that the picture would portray.

What animal(s) did you choose? _____

Level Orange   44   Bridges™

Day 6

Addition and multiplication are related. Answer the addition problems and then write the related multiplication problem.
Resuelve los problemas de adición y luego escribe problemas de multiplicación relacionados.

EXAMPLE: 10 + 10 + 10 + 10 + 10 = 50 or 5 x 10 = 50

1. 20 + 20 + 20 = _____   _____ x _____ = _____

2. 9 + 9 + 9 + 9 + 9 + 9 = _____   _____ x _____ = _____

3. 100 + 100 + 100 + 100 = _____   _____ x _____ = _____

4. 8 + 8 + 8 + 8 + 8 + 8 + 8 + 8 = _____   _____ x _____ = _____

5. 12 + 12 + 12 + 12 = _____   _____ x _____ = _____

6. 75 + 75 + 75 = _____   _____ x _____ = _____

7. 35 + 35 + 35 + 35 + 35 + 35 = _____   _____ x _____ = _____

8. 51 + 51 + 51 + 51 + 51 = _____   _____ x _____ = _____

Use the pronouns me, her, him, it, us, you, and them after action verbs. Use I and me after the other nouns or pronouns. Circle the correct pronoun in each sentence.
Encierra en un círculo el pronombre‡ correcto para cada oración‡.

1. Lily and (I, me) like to visit museums.
2. (They, Them) were very juicy oranges.
3. He helped her and (I, me).
4. (We, Us) tried not to fall as much this time.
5. Miss Green gave a shovel and bucket to (he, him).
6. (I, Me) wanted a new horse for Christmas.
7. Rick asked (she, her) to come with us.
8. Jason went with (they, them) to the mountain.
9. Mother asked (I, me) to fix the dinner.
10. Carla got some forks for (we, us).
11. Please, teach that trick to Lisa and (I, me).
12. She and (I, me) swam all day.

© Federal Education Publishing   45   Level Orange

Day 6

Study this table about trees, and use it to answer the questions below. Can you identify the trees around you?

Utiliza esta tabla sobre árboles para contestar las preguntas a continuación.

Tree	Bark	Wood	Leaves
Elm	brown and rough	strong	oval-shaped, saw-toothed edges, sharp points
Birch	creamy white, peels off in layers	elastic, won't break easily	heart-shaped or triangular with pointed tips
Oak	dark gray, thick, rough, deeply furrowed	hard, fine-grained	round, finger-shaped lobes
Willow	rough and broken	brown, soft, light	long, narrow, curved at tips
Maple	rough gray	strong	grow in pairs and are shaped like your open hand
Hickory	loose, peels off	white, hard	shaped like spearheads
Christmas Holly	ash colored	hard and fine-grained	glossy, sharp-pointed

1. Which tree has heart-shaped leaves? _____
   Hand-shaped? _____
2. How many trees have hard wood? _____
3. Which trees have sharp-pointed leaves? _____
4. Which tree has wood like a rubber band? _____
5. How many different colors of bark does the table show? _____
   Name them _____
6. Which tree do you think we get syrup from? _____
7. Which tree bark do you think Indians used to cover their canoes? _____
8. Which wood do you think is best for making furniture? _____, _____, and _____
9. Why do you think the holly tree is called Christmas Holly? _____
10. Look around your yard and neighborhood. Can you identify any of the trees from the table? If so, which ones? _____

Level Orange

Bridges™

Day 7

Complete this multiplication table.
Completa esta tabla de multiplicación.

x	10	20	30	40	50	60	70	80	90
1	10	20					70		
2						120			
3		60							270
4				160					
5						350			
6									
7			210						
8						480			
9				360					

How does multiplying by hundreds differ from multiplying by tens?
_____

Could you change this table to show multiplying by hundreds? _____
How? _____

Using Its, It's, Your, and You're. It's and you're are contractions. Its and your are possessive pronouns. Fill in the blanks with it's, its, your, or you're.
Completa los espacios en blanco con it's, its, your, o you're.

1. I hope _____ coming to my barn dance.
2. The dance will be for _____ friends also.
3. Do you think _____ too cold for a barn dance?
4. _____ starting time is eight o'clock.
5. Will _____ family come to the dance with you?
6. _____ floor is long and wide.
7. _____ coming early, aren't you?
8. I think I will need _____ help.
9. _____ going to last about four hours.
10. _____ bound to be a lot of fun.

Write a sentence of your own for each word.
Escribe una oración‡ con cada palabra.

11. It's _____
12. its _____
13. you're _____
14. your _____

© Federal Education Publishing — Level Orange

Day 7

Read this crazy story. Every time you come to an underlined word, write the abbreviation for it.

Cuando te encuentres con una palabra subrayada, escribe la abreviatura.

Last January _Jan._ we moved from Georgia _____ to New York _____. It was a very long trip. We had to walk most of the way because the car broke down. We left on Monday _____, March _____ 10 and didn't get there until five years _____ later.

On the trip I had to learn how to measure. One day I measured gallons _____, inches, _____, yards _____, and grams _____. I also learned about science _____, adverbs _____, and adjectives _____. It was a boring trip!

We only traveled about two miles per hour _____. That's why it took us so long. Also, we stopped at a number _____ of relatives' places and stayed for months _____ on end.

Next time let's fly!

Name an animal or insect that begins with the letters given. If there is not one that begins with that letter, leave it blank or put an X in the box.

Nombra un animal o insecto que comience con las letras dadas. Si no encuentras uno, coloca una X en el recuadro.

	s	d	r	t
insects				
birds				
reptiles				
rodents				
spiders				
zoo animals				
wild animals				
farm animals				
ocean animals				
dinosaurs				

Level Orange

Day 8

What about Time? You know that 60 seconds = 1 minute, 60 minutes = 1 hour, 24 hours = 1 day, 7 days = 1 week, 52 weeks = 1 year, 12 months = 1 year, and 365 days = 1 year (except leap year, which has 366 days).

Use what you know to complete the following.
Aplica lo que sabes sobre el tiempo para completar los espacios en blanco.

1. Phillip is in the fourth grade. He is 10 _____ old.
2. There are 30 _____ in June.
3. Nancy's baby brother started to walk at the age of 11 _____.
4. We have 48 _____ in 2 days.
5. Nick's swimming lesson is 25 _____ long.
6. It took Leslie 10 _____ to comb her hair.
7. Mother's Day is celebrated once a _____.
8. Many children get about 3 _____ summer vacation.
9. It takes about 1 _____ to blink your eyes.
10. Most children go to school 5 _____ a week.
11. There are 30 _____ in half a minute.
12. It took Monica 2 and a half _____ to do all her chores.

Write these words in alphabetical order. Be sure to look at the third or fourth letters.
Ordena estas palabras en orden alfabético.

1. events, evening, every, eventually

   _____ _____ _____ _____

2. tremendous, treatment, tree, treasure

   _____ _____ _____ _____

3. coast, coconut, coal, collect, color

   _____ _____ _____ _____ _____

4. entrance, entry, end, enthusiasm, enough

   _____ _____ _____ _____ _____

5. grandfather, graph, grain, grateful, grab, graduated

   _____ _____ _____ _____ _____ _____

© Federal Education Publishing — 49 — Level Orange

Day 8

What Does It Really Mean? Write what you think these idiomatic expressions mean.

Escribe lo que crees que significan estas frases idiomáticas.

1. She was really <u>pulling my leg</u>. _____
2. Do you think we'll <u>be in hot water</u>? _____
3. If you don't <u>button your lip</u>, I'll scream! _____
4. Sonny, please <u>get off my back</u>! _____
5. When you are having fun, <u>time flies</u>. _____
6. You've <u>hit it on the head</u>, Andrew. _____
7. Ryan will <u>lend a hand</u> tomorrow. _____
8. In the winter, my bedroom is <u>like an icebox</u>. _____
9. Mrs. Tune always has beautiful flowers; she <u>must have a green thumb</u>.
   _____
10. My brother's stomach is <u>a bottomless pit</u>. _____

A Litter Graph. Go on a "litter" walk. In a plastic bag, gather up litter as you go. Only pick up safe litter. Do not pick up anything marked hazardous waste, needles, or litter you are unsure of. When you are finished, bring it home. Categorize what you have found and display it in a bar graph.

Recoje basura cuando hagas una caminata. Solamente recoje basura segura. No recojas nada peligroso. Categoriza lo que encuentres y ponlo en una gráfica de barras.

Type of Litter	1	2	3	4	5	6	7	8	9	10	more than 10

Level Orange

Day 9

Place Value Division Patterns. We know that 8 ÷ 2 = 4, so 80 ÷ 2 = 40, and 800 ÷ 2 = 400. Do the following division patterns.
Resuelve los siguientes patrones de división.

1. 9 ÷ 3 = _____ 90 ÷ 3 = _____ 900 ÷ 3 = _____
2. 8 ÷ 2 = _____ 80 ÷ 2 = _____ 800 ÷ 2 = _____
3. 12 ÷ 4 = _____ 120 ÷ 4 = _____ 1,200 ÷ 4 = _____
4. 6 ÷ 3 = _____ 60 ÷ 3 = _____ 600 ÷ 3 = _____
5. 30 ÷ 6 = _____ 300 ÷ 6 = _____ 3,000 ÷ 6 = _____
6. 72 ÷ 8 = _____ 720 ÷ 8 = _____ 7,200 ÷ 8 = _____
7. 32 ÷ 8 = _____ 320 ÷ 8 = _____ 3,200 ÷ 8 = _____
8. 49 ÷ 7 = _____ 490 ÷ 7 = _____ 4,900 ÷ 7 = _____
9. 56 ÷ 8 = _____ 560 ÷ 8 = _____ 5,600 ÷ 8 = _____
10. 25 ÷ 5 = _____ 250 ÷ 5 = _____ 2,500 ÷ 5 = _____
11. 40 ÷ 8 = _____ 400 ÷ 8 = _____ 4,000 ÷ 8 = _____
12. 63 ÷ 9 = _____ 630 ÷ 9 = _____ 6,300 ÷ 9 = _____

Use your Dictionary

Look up the word <u>meet</u> in a dictionary. At the end of each sentence, write what part of speech (noun or verb) <u>meet</u> is. Then write the number for the meaning of the word <u>meet</u>.
Busca la palabra <u>meet</u> en un diccionario. Al final de cada oración‡ escribe si <u>meet</u> es un sustantivo‡ o un verbo‡. Luego escribe el número del significado que aparece en el diccionario.

EXAMPLE: I will <u>meet</u> you at three.   *Verb – 2*

1. Tomorrow we are going to have a track <u>meet</u>. _____
2. I hope he doesn't <u>meet</u> with disaster. _____
3. We need to <u>meet</u> the plane at seven P.M. _____
4. He will have to <u>meet</u> the payments every month. _____
5. It was nice to <u>meet</u> and talk with you yesterday. _____
6. Are you going to <u>meet</u> your friends later? _____

Level Orange

Day 9

Someone or Something with Power. What is power? Choose something or someone with power. How do they have power? How did they get it? Could they lose it? Do they use it? How? Why? Do you have power? Yes you do! What are some of the powers that you have? What are some that you don't have that you would like to have?

Elige algo o alguien con poder y escribe sobre él.

Day 10

Find the quotients and the remainders. Use a separate piece of paper to show your work.
Encuentra los cocientes‡ y los restos.

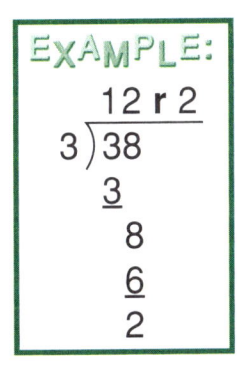

EXAMPLE:
```
     12 r 2
3 ) 38
     3
     8
     6
     2
```

1. 2) 65
2. 5) 57
3. 3) 95
4. 4) 85
5. 9) 100
6. 3) 37
7. 4) 47
8. 5) 58
9. 7) 79
10. 4) 87
11. 3) 68
12. 4) 35

Draw a line between the syllables. First, try to remember what you have learned about where to divide them. Then use a dictionary if you need more help.
Separa las sílabas‡ con una línea. Utiliza el diccionario si necesitas ayuda.

EXAMPLE: col/or

1. column
2. inflate
3. slashing
4. pigeon
5. afraid
6. frozen
7. tennis
8. harness
9. gable
10. alphabet
11. soviet
12. bicycle
13. difficult
14. kerosene
15. liveliness
16. glorious
17. understood
18. jewelry
19. generation
20. vegetable
21. evidence
22. memory
23. quality
24. splendid
25. museum
26. hospital
27. ordinary

© Federal Education Publishing   53   Level Orange

Day 10

The next time you watch TV or read a magazine, look at the commercials or ads. In the boxes below, write down what you think is true about the commercials or ads and what you think is false.

Elige algunos comerciales. Escribe lo que crees que es verdadero y falso sobre ellos.

What is the commercial or ad about?	TRUE	FALSE
	1.	1.
	2.	2.
	3.	3.
	4.	4.
	5.	5.

Conserving Energy. Recycling saves energy and natural resources. Besides recycling, how can we conserve energy? Write down ways to conserve energy with the following:

Escribe formas de conservar energía en las siguientes áreas[‡]:

water _____

lights _____

heat _____

electricity _____

transportation _____

cold weather _____

refrigerator _____

buying things _____

bathroom _____

Level Orange   Bridges™

Day 11

Write the fraction that describes the shaded section.
Escribe la fracción‡ que describe la porción sombreada.

EXAMPLE:

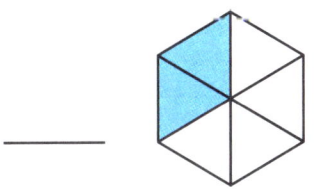

1. $\dfrac{1}{2}$ 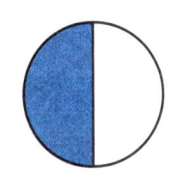
2. ___ 
3. ___
4. ___ 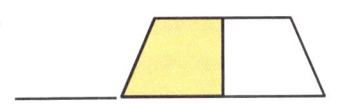
5. ___ 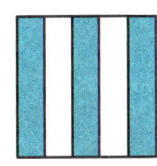
6. ___ 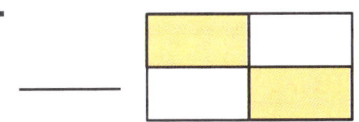
7. ___ 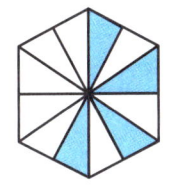
8. ___ 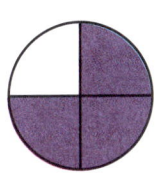
9. ___ 
10. ___ 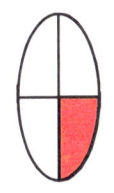
11. ___ 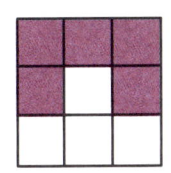
12. ___

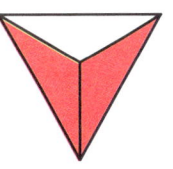

A dictionary gives us a lot of information about words. Look up the following words in a dictionary and write down the special spelling of each. Also write down a short definition for each word.
Busca estas palabras en un diccionario. Escribe la ortografía especial y una pequeña definición de cada una.

	Special Spelling	**Definition**
1. blue•bon•net	blü´bon´net	the cornflower
2. mas•sive		
3. suit•case		
4. cir•cus		
5. glox•in•i•a		
6. rig•ging		
7. di•lem•ma		
8. meas•ure		
9. stu•dent		
10. un•or•gan•ized		
11. def•i•ni•tion		
12. yaws		
13. re•spect		
14. blun•der•buss		

© Federal Education Publishing   55   Level Orange

Day 11

Practice writing and spelling these homonyms. Write in cursive. After you know how to spell them, have someone give you a test to see if you can spell them without looking. Write each word twice.

Practica escribir y deletrear estos homónimos[‡].

way	_____	_____	sight	_____	_____
weigh	_____	_____	site	_____	_____
base	_____	_____	arc	_____	_____
bass	_____	_____	ark	_____	_____
threw	_____	_____	tide	_____	_____
through	_____	_____	tied	_____	_____
scene	_____	_____	waist	_____	_____
seen	_____	_____	waste	_____	_____
			sore	_____	_____
			soar	_____	_____
			pare	_____	_____
			pair	_____	_____
			pear	_____	_____

Water in the Air. There is water in the air. How does it get there? Clouds and rain are made from water vapor in the air.

Try this to help explain how water gets into the air. Take 3 or more drinking glasses that are all about the same size. Fill the glasses almost full of water. Place them in different areas such as warm places, cool places, dark places, windy places, outside places, inside places, and other places of your choice. Watch them for 4 or 5 days or longer. Check the water levels. What happened to the water in the glasses? Where did it go? Explain in your own words where you think the water vapor in the atmosphere comes from and where it goes?

Trata de hacer este experimento. Escribe sobre los resultados.

_____
_____
_____
_____
_____
_____

Level Orange   Bridges™

Comparing Fractions. Use the fraction table to help find out which fraction is greater and which fraction is less. Use >, <, or =.

Utiliza esta tabla de fracciones para decidir qué fracción es mayor. Utiliza >, < ó =.

Day 12

1. $\frac{1}{2}$ ○ $\frac{1}{4}$ 2. $\frac{2}{3}$ ○ $\frac{1}{3}$

3. $\frac{1}{4}$ ○ $\frac{1}{6}$ 4. $\frac{2}{6}$ ○ $\frac{1}{3}$

5. $\frac{4}{8}$ ○ $\frac{2}{10}$ 6. $\frac{1}{12}$ ○ $\frac{1}{10}$

7. $\frac{3}{4}$ ○ $\frac{2}{8}$ 8. $\frac{2}{5}$ ○ $\frac{1}{3}$

9. $\frac{3}{8}$ ○ $\frac{10}{12}$ 10. $\frac{2}{8}$ ○ $\frac{1}{4}$

11. $\frac{1}{5}$ ○ $\frac{2}{10}$ 12. $\frac{1}{3}$ ○ $\frac{2}{4}$

13. $\frac{1}{6}$ ○ $\frac{1}{3}$ 14. $\frac{3}{12}$ ○ $\frac{1}{3}$

15. $\frac{5}{10}$ ○ $\frac{3}{6}$ 16. $\frac{1}{2}$ ○ $\frac{6}{10}$

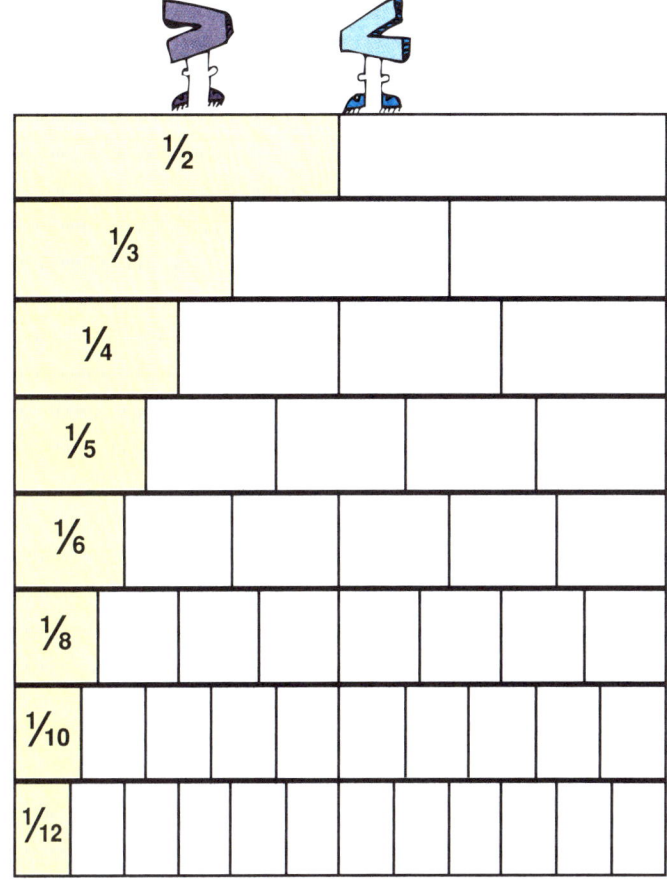

Write a short report. **Remember:** A report is only facts about a topic. Look in an encyclopedia for help. Follow these steps: Choose a topic and plan your report, write, revise, proofread, and make a final copy.

Escribe un informe breve. Sigue estos pasos: Elige un tema, planea, escribe, revisa, edita y haz una copia final.

Day 12

These letters are in alphabetical order. See if you can make a word from them. The first letter is underlined.

Estas letras están escritas en orden alfabético. Trata de ver si puedes formar una palabra con ellas. La primera letra está subrayada.

EXAMPLE:
1. abbelo<u>p</u>r   probable
2. ae<u>j</u>losu   _____
3. eeen<u>p</u>rrst   _____
4. beeemm<u>r</u>r   _____
5. beknno<u>u</u>   _____
6. c<u>d</u>ffiilut   _____
7. <u>a</u>ccdginor   _____
8. ee<u>g</u>mnnortv   _____
9. aaegi<u>m</u>nz   _____
10. eior<u>s</u>su   _____
11. ghho<u>t</u>tu   _____
12. irst<u>w</u>   _____
13. aeginr<u>v</u>   _____
14. d<u>i</u>nrstuy   _____
15. <u>c</u>eenrt   _____
16. ehils<u>t</u>w   _____
17. <u>a</u>inosux   _____
18. deilor<u>s</u>   _____
19. aa<u>b</u>eggg   _____
20. elrtuu<u>v</u>   _____

Put the letters in these words in alphabetical order.
Ordena alfabéticamente las letras de estas palabras.

21. creature _____
22. fountain _____
23. basement _____
24. factory _____
25. hospital _____
26. committee _____
27. paragraph _____
28. kingdom _____

Blow Up a Balloon. Here is an experiment that you can do in your home with an adult's permission. Get a balloon and blow it up several times until the balloon becomes easy to enlarge. Put one tablespoon of baking soda in the balloon, then put 3 tablespoons of white vinegar into a soda pop bottle. Now put the balloon opening around the mouth of the soda pop bottle. Move the balloon so the baking soda falls down and mixes with the vinegar. Draw a picture of what happens and write a couple of sentences to go with your picture.

Intenta este experimento con la ayuda de un adulto. Escribe sobre los resultados.

Draw what happens!

Level Orange   58   Bridges™

Day 13

Multiplying 3-digit Numbers by 1-digit Numbers
Multiplica estos números de 3 dígitos por números de 1 dígito.

EXAMPLE: 6 x 3 = 18   3 x 80 = 240   3 x 100 = 300   or
 18 + 240 + 300 = 558

 21
 186
 x 3
 558

1. 162
   x 5

2. 398
   x 2

3. 904
   x 8

4. 329
   x 5

5. 240
   x 7

6. 432
   x 6

7. 412
   x 8

8. 542
   x 9

9. 506
   x 5

10. 554
    x 6

11. 473
    x 9

12. 257
    x 8

Put commas in the following sentences to separate words in a series.
Coloca las comas en estas oraciones para separar las palabras de las series.

1. Nan Tom Julie and James are going to a movie.
2. Anne took her spelling reading and math books to school.
3. The snack bar is only open on Monday Tuesday Friday and Saturday.
4. Our new school flag is blue green yellow black and orange.
5. Women men children and pets enjoy sledding.
6. Have you ever seen baby kittens piglets or goslings?
7. Carla and Mark bought postcards film candy and souvenirs.

Now write four sentences of your own. Name at least three people, sports, or foods in a series. Be sure to put in the commas.
Escribe cuatro oraciones propias. Nombra por los menos personas, deportes o comidas en una serie. Asegúrate de agregar las comas.

8. _____
9. _____
10. _____
11. _____

© Federal Education Publishing   Level Orange

Day 13

Parents and Family. What do you think your parents and family have in mind for your life? What do they want you to accomplish? What would they like to see you do? How do you feel about it? Think and write about it.

Piensa y escribe sobre lo que tus padres desean que logres.

Day 14

How Many Times In a Minute? Use a watch with a minute hand or a stopwatch to time yourself as you do the following activities. Then use that information to calculate how many times you could do those things in 5 minutes, 8 minutes, 10 minutes, and 15 minutes.

Utiliza un reloj para contestar las preguntas 1 a 8. Utiliza tus respuestas para calcular cuántas veces harías estas cosas en 5, 8, 10 y 15 minutos.

1. How far can you hop in a minute? _____

2. How far can you walk in a minute? _____

3. How many jumping jacks can you do in a minute? _____

4. How many times can you toss a ball and catch it in a minute? _____

5. How many times can you bounce a ball in a minute? _____

6. How many times do you breathe in a minute? _____

7. How many times does your heart beat in a minute? _____

8. How many times can you write your name in a minute? _____

Activity	Minutes				
	1	5	8	10	15
hop					
walk					
jumping jacks					
toss and catch ball					
bounce ball					
breathe					
heart beats					
write name					

Put commas after <u>yes</u> or <u>no</u> when they begin a sentence and before and/or after names when that person is being spoken to. Put the commas in these sentences.
Coloca las comas donde corresponda en estas oraciones.

1. Yes I will go with you John.
2. Kirk do you want to go?
3. No I need to finish this.
4. John I am glad Sam will come.
5. Nicky what happened?
6. Don I fell on the sidewalk.
7. Aaron do you play tennis?
8. No Eli I never learned how.

9. Come on T. J. let's go to the game.
10. Yes I was x-rayed at the doctor's.
11. Mom thanks for the help.
12. Tell me Joe did you do this?
13. Yes but I'm sorry I did.
14. Well Joe try to be more careful next time.
15. Okay Dad I'll never do it again.
16. George do you like basketball?

© Federal Education Publishing — Level Orange

Day 14

Do you know when the holidays come? Fill in the blanks with the date or name of the correct holiday. Use a calendar if you need help.

Escribe la fecha o el nombre de las fiestas en los espacios en blanco.

1. Many children look forward to _____ or _____ in December.
2. On January 1 we celebrate _____.
3. In May we have _____.
4. Be sure to wear green in March. It's _____ _____ _____.
5. In October 1492 he sailed the ocean blue. _____.
6. On February 14 be sure to send your sweetheart a _____.
7. On July 4 we celebrate _____.
8. October 31 can be really scary. _____.
9. Sometimes it comes in March; sometimes it comes in April: _____.
10. Do you work on _____ in September?
11. _____ and _____ also have birthdays in February.
12. In June we also have _____.
13. Martin Luther King Jr.'s birthday is in _____.
14. Because the Pilgrims came, we have _____.
15. _____ is in June.
16. On November 11 we honor our _____.

Word Search. Find and circle words that harm our environment.

Encuentra y encierra en un círculo las cosas que dañan nuestro medioambiente.

c	a	r	s	i	p	o	c	a	l	o	c	t	w
j	l	o	p	p	o	s	f	i	d	h	s	r	
f	a	c	t	o	r	i	e	s	g	t	a	d	n	a
p	k	n	s	l	a	s	w	a	s	t	e	s	p
l	c	g	l	g	o	a	e	b	e	i	e	h	p
r	a	q	s	u	u	n	g	d	w	r	l	m	l	e
b	r	n	b	t	m	k	e	s	i	t	t	e	a	r
b	a	t	j	i	l	l	k	m	t	b	k	m	n	s
c	a	r	b	o	n	m	o	n	o	x	i	d	e
v	u	a	f	n	j	c	b	g	m	e	s	f	a
p	t	s	f	l	o	o	d	s	i	d	l	g	i	z
s	o	h	s	t	r	i	n	g	r	a	g	s	l	r
t	s	p	e	o	p	l	e	c	s	t	y	l	t
u	e	t	r	p	e	s	t	i	c	i	d	e	s	s
g	x	v	e	c	k	m	a	n	c	f	o	e	n
n	h	x	o	n	a	e	h	g	l	a	s	s	e	o
o	a	c	u	b	h	g	a	r	b	a	g	e	u	t
w	u	j	a	c	f	a	c	t	p	a	p	e	r
s	t	y	r	o	f	o	a	m	v	a	r	m	a
s	t	u	f	f	g	n	p	l	a	s	t	i	c

litter, bottles, garbage, trash, cars, people, rags, smoke, waste, pollution, cans, landfills, stuff, junk, auto exhaust, carbon monoxide, factories

gum, cartons, poison, chemicals, paper, styrofoam, pesticides, sewage, bags, smog, weeds, floods, wrappers, plastic, string, glass

Level Orange 62 Bridges™

Day 15

Find the quotient and the remainder by division.
Encuentra el cociente† y el resto.

1. 8)963
2. 2)741
3. 8)960
4. 4)561

5. 7)915
6. 8)887
7. 5)753
8. 4)882

9. 9)918
10. 7)716
11. 3)919
12. 9)908

13. 4)835
14. 9)967
15. 8)842
16. 3)667

17. 5)182
18. 6)424
19. 4)392
20. 6)438

21. 7)948
22. 6)787
23. 4)721
24. 8)736

Using Punctuation Marks. Put periods and question, exclamation, and quotation marks in the following sentences.
Coloca los puntos, las comillas‡ y los signos de interrogación y exclamación en estas oraciones.

1. Nate, do you have the map of our town asked Kit
2. What an exciting day I had cried Mary
3. I said the puppy fell into the well
4. Did you learn that birds' bones are hollow asked Mrs. Tippy
5. She answered No, I did not learn that
6. Wayne exclaimed I won first prize for the pie eating contest
7. I'm tired of all work and no play said Sadie
8. I agree with you replied Sarah
9. Mr. Harris said this assignment is due tomorrow
10. It will be part of your final grade he added

© Federal Education Publishing   63   Level Orange

Day 15

Circle the two words in each group that are spelled correctly.
Encierra en un círculo dos palabras de cada grupo que estén escritas correctamente.

A
gabel
genuine
gracefull
graine
great

B
suger
surpize
terrible
straight
sonday

C
allready
among
aunte
awhile
addvise

D
where
weather
wite
weare
rotee

E
jackit
junior
jujment
justece
journey

F
rimind
remain
fouff
refer
raisd

G
feathers
feever
finsih
folow
fiction

H
donkiys
doubble
drawer
dosen
detective

I
handsum
herrd
holiday
healthy
haevy

J
explore
elctrecity
enjine
enormous
ecstat

Complete the picture and add what other details you would like.
Completa este dibujo y agrega otros detalles que desees.

Level Orange 64 Bridges™

Incentive Contract Calendar

Month (Mes) _____

My parents and I decided that if I complete 15 days of *Bridges*™ and read _____ minutes a day, my incentive/reward will be:

(Si yo completo 15 días de *Bridges*™ y leo _____ minutos al día, mi recompensa será:)

_____

Child's Signature (Firma del Niño) _____
Parent's Signature (Firma del Padre) _____

	📓	📘			📓	📘	
Day 1 (Día 1)	☐	☐	____	Day 9	☐	☐	____
Day 2	☐	☐	____	Day 10	☐	☐	____
Day 3	☐	☐	____	Day 11	☐	☐	____
Day 4	☐	☐	____	Day 12	☐	☐	____
Day 5	☐	☐	____	Day 13	☐	☐	____
Day 6	☐	☐	____	Day 14	☐	☐	____
Day 7	☐	☐	____	Day 15	☐	☐	____
Day 8	☐	☐					

bridges

Parent: Initial the ____ for daily activities and reading your child completes.
Padre: (Marque ____ para las actividades y lectura que su niño complete.)

Child: Put a ✔ in the ☐ for the daily activities 📓 completed.
Pon ✔ en ☐ para las actividades diaria que hayas completado.

Put a ✔ in the ☐ for the daily reading 📘 completed.
Pon ✔ en ☐ para las actividades diarias de lectura que hayas completado.

Try Something New
Fun Activity Ideas

1. Draw a picture of your favorite friend, toy, or teacher during your favorite time of the year.
   Haz un dibujo de tu amigo, juguete o maestra favorita en tu época favorita del año.

2. Put together a collection of leaves from your neighborhood and label as many as you can.
   Junta hojas de tu vecindario y colócale el nombre a la mayor cantidad posible.

3. Write five questions that you would like to ask the president of the United States.
   Escribe cinco preguntas que te gustaría hacerle al presidente de los Estados Unidos.

4. Invent a new ice cream flavor. How is it made? What will you call it?
   Inventa un nuevo sabor de helado. ¿Cómo se prepara? ¿Cómo se llama?

5. Play football with a frisbee.
   Juega al fútbol con un frisbee.

6. Find out how to recycle in your town; then make and deliver flyers to inform your neighbors.
   Averigua cómo se recicla en tu pueblo. Luego fabrica volantes y repártelos para informar a tus vecinos.

7. Use a book on astronomy to help you look for stars and constellations.
   Usa un libro de astronomía que te ayude a buscar las estrellas y las constelaciones.

8. Write your answer to the following question: How would the world be different without Alexander Graham Bell?
   Escribe tu respuesta a la siguiente pregunta: ¿Cómo sería diferente el mundo si Alexander Graham Bell no hubiera existido?

9. Surprise your parents and weed a flower bed or garden, rake the leaves, do the dishes, etc.
   Sorprende a tus padres y desmaleza un parterre de flores o el jardín, rastrilla las hojas, lava los platos, etc.

10. Play flashlight tag, tonight!
    ¡Juega a la pesca de la luz esta misma noche!

11. Design a comic strip and draw it.
    Diseña una tira cómica y dibújala.

12. Paint a mural on butcher paper.
    Pinta un mural en papel de carnicería.

13. Set up a miniature golf course in your backyard.
    Haz una cancha de mini-golf en tu patio.

14. Play hockey using a broom.
    Juega al hockey usando una escoba.

Level Orange — Bridges™

Day 1

Equal Fractions. Use the fraction table on page 57 to find equal fractions. You could make your own fraction table!
Utiliza la tabla de fracciones de la página 57 para encontrar fracciones equivalentes.

1. $\dfrac{1}{3} = \dfrac{}{6}$
2. $\dfrac{4}{5} = \dfrac{}{10}$
3. $\dfrac{10}{10} = \dfrac{}{6}$
4. $\dfrac{}{5} = \dfrac{4}{10}$
5. $\dfrac{4}{16} = \dfrac{}{8}$
6. $\dfrac{12}{12} = \dfrac{}{10}$
7. $\dfrac{3}{6} = \dfrac{}{12}$
8. $\dfrac{9}{12} = \dfrac{}{4}$
9. $\dfrac{}{9} = \dfrac{4}{6}$
10. $\dfrac{0}{4} = \dfrac{}{2}$
11. $\dfrac{6}{8} = \dfrac{}{4}$
12. $\dfrac{1}{2} = \dfrac{}{10}$
13. $\dfrac{}{4} = \dfrac{4}{8}$
14. $\dfrac{3}{9} = \dfrac{}{3}$
15. $\dfrac{}{15} = \dfrac{2}{3}$
16. $\dfrac{2}{3} = \dfrac{}{12}$
17. $\dfrac{}{3} = \dfrac{6}{18}$
18. $\dfrac{}{15} = \dfrac{3}{5}$
19. $\dfrac{}{6} = \dfrac{2}{3}$
20. $\dfrac{}{8} = \dfrac{1}{4}$
21. $\dfrac{3}{6} = \dfrac{}{2}$
22. $\dfrac{1}{3} = \dfrac{}{9}$
23. $\dfrac{6}{9} = \dfrac{}{3}$
24. $\dfrac{}{6} = \dfrac{3}{18}$

What Does It Mean? Choose a word from the word bank and write it next to the correct meaning.
Escribe la palabra del Banco de Palabras al lado del significado correcto.

Word Bank
schedule
assistant
campaign
approximately
hollow
exchange
university
venture
artificial
publicity
harness
estate
reputation
genuine

1. not natural, not real _____
2. a timed plan for a project _____
3. a giving or taking of one thing for another _____
4. esteem in which a person is commonly held _____
5. a person who serves or helps _____
6. really being what it is said to be; true or real _____
7. a series of organized, planned actions _____
8. to make information commonly known _____
9. near in position _____
10. an educational institution of the highest level _____
11. having a cavity within it, not solid _____
12. something on which a risk is taken _____
13. one's property or possessions _____
14. connects an animal to a plow or vehicle _____

Day 1 Look at the homonyms you spelled on page 56. Choose five pairs of these and write a sentence for each one.

Elige cinco pares de homónimos‡ de la página 56 y escribe una oración‡ con cada par.

EXAMPLE: way/weigh
I could not see him; we were <u>way</u> down the road.
How much do you <u>weigh</u>?

1. _____
2. _____
3. _____
4. _____
5. _____

Every home should have a first-aid kit. This enables the family to have many types of bandages and medicines in one place, should they be needed.

Make a list of things you think should be in a first-aid kit. When you are finished, check with your parents to see if you have all the basic things listed for a first-aid kit. If your family has one, ask your parents to go through it with you.

Haz una lista de cosas que pienses que debería haber en un botiquín de primeros auxilios. Revisa con tus padres si las cosas básicas están en tu lista.

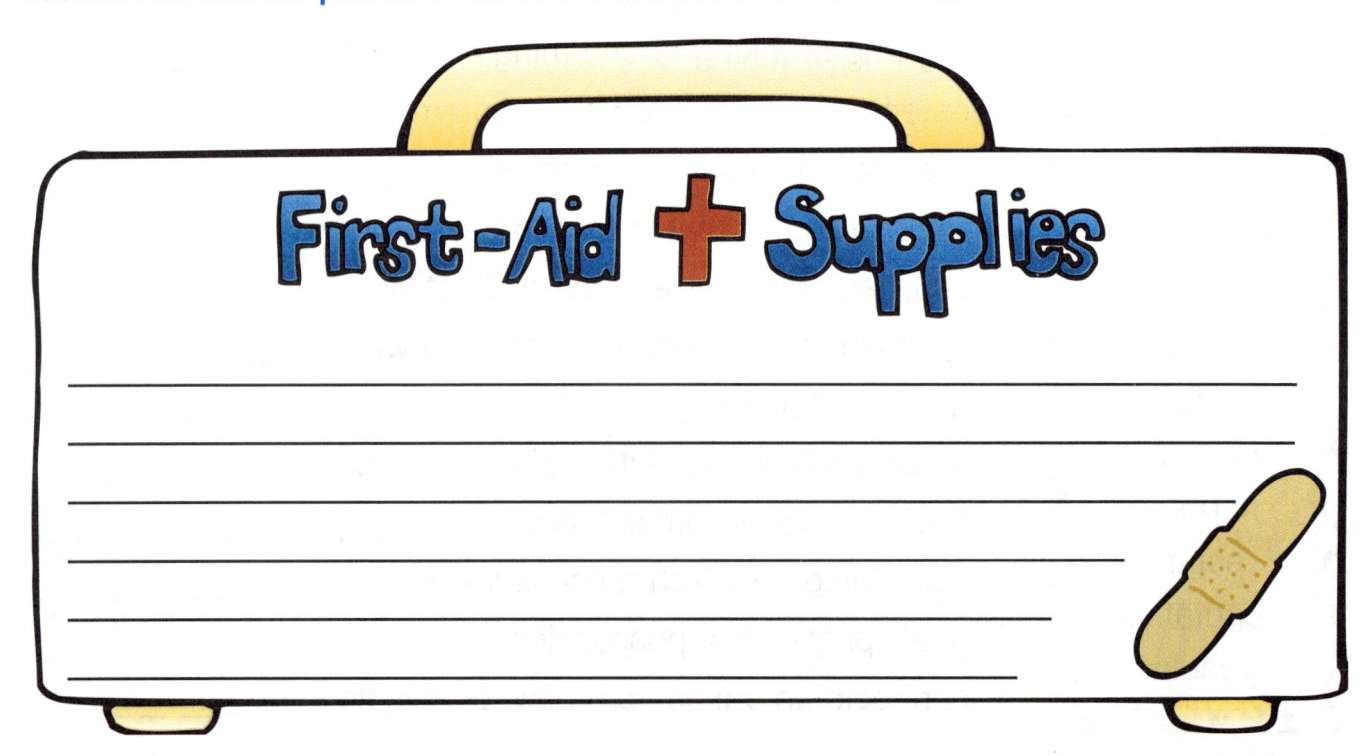

First-Aid + Supplies

Day 2

Adding Fractions.
Suma‡ estas fracciones.

$\frac{2}{3} + \frac{1}{3} = \frac{3}{3}$ ← add the numerator
← use the same denominator

1. $\frac{1}{3} + \frac{1}{3} =$
2. $\frac{1}{2} + \frac{1}{2} =$
3. $\frac{6}{12} + \frac{5}{12} =$
4. $\frac{6}{12} + \frac{7}{12} =$

5. $\frac{5}{8} + \frac{2}{8} =$
6. $\frac{3}{10} + \frac{4}{10} =$
7. $\frac{1}{6} + \frac{2}{6} =$
8. $\frac{11}{12} + \frac{11}{12} =$

9. $\frac{7}{10} + \frac{1}{10} =$
10. $\frac{1}{8} + \frac{6}{8} =$
11. $\frac{4}{9} + \frac{4}{9} =$
12. $\frac{7}{10} + \frac{6}{10} =$

13. $\frac{1}{4} + \frac{2}{4} =$
14. $\frac{4}{10} + \frac{5}{10} =$
15. $\frac{3}{8} + \frac{3}{8} =$
16. $\frac{2}{8} + \frac{4}{8} =$

17. $\frac{3}{6} + \frac{1}{6} =$
18. $\frac{4}{12} + \frac{5}{12} =$
19. $\frac{2}{8} + \frac{7}{8} =$
20. $\frac{8}{12} + \frac{5}{12} =$

21. $\frac{3}{12} + \frac{8}{12} =$
22. $\frac{3}{10} + \frac{3}{10} =$
23. $\frac{5}{9} + \frac{5}{9} =$
24. $\frac{5}{8} + \frac{7}{8} =$

Circle the abbreviations and titles in these sentences. Remember: Abbreviations are short forms of words and usually begin with capital letters and end with periods.
Encierra en un círculo las abreviaturas‡ de estas oraciones.

1. Dr. Cox is my family doctor.
2. Do you live on Rocksberry Rd.?
3. My teacher's name is Mrs. Wright.
4. On Mon. we are taking a trip to Fort Worth, TX.
5. Will Mr. Harris sell his company to your parents?
6. Rick's birthday and mine are both on Feb. 16.

Mister Slade
Mr. Slade

Now write the abbreviations for these words.
Escribe las abreviaturas para estas palabras.

7. street _____
8. avenue _____
9. postscript _____
10. Miss _____
11. January _____
12. Thursday _____

13. Vermont _____
14. Tuesday _____
15. Mister _____
16. tablespoon _____
17. circle _____
18. company _____

© Federal Education Publishing   Level Orange

Day 2

Choose four **compound** **words** and illustrate them.

Elige cuatro palabras compuestas e ilústralas.

EXAMPLE: starfish is star and fish.

Here are some to choose from, or you can choose some of your own: billfold, screwdriver, backyard, butterfly, rainbow, mushroom, supermarket, postman, undertake, windpipe, drawbridge, basketball.

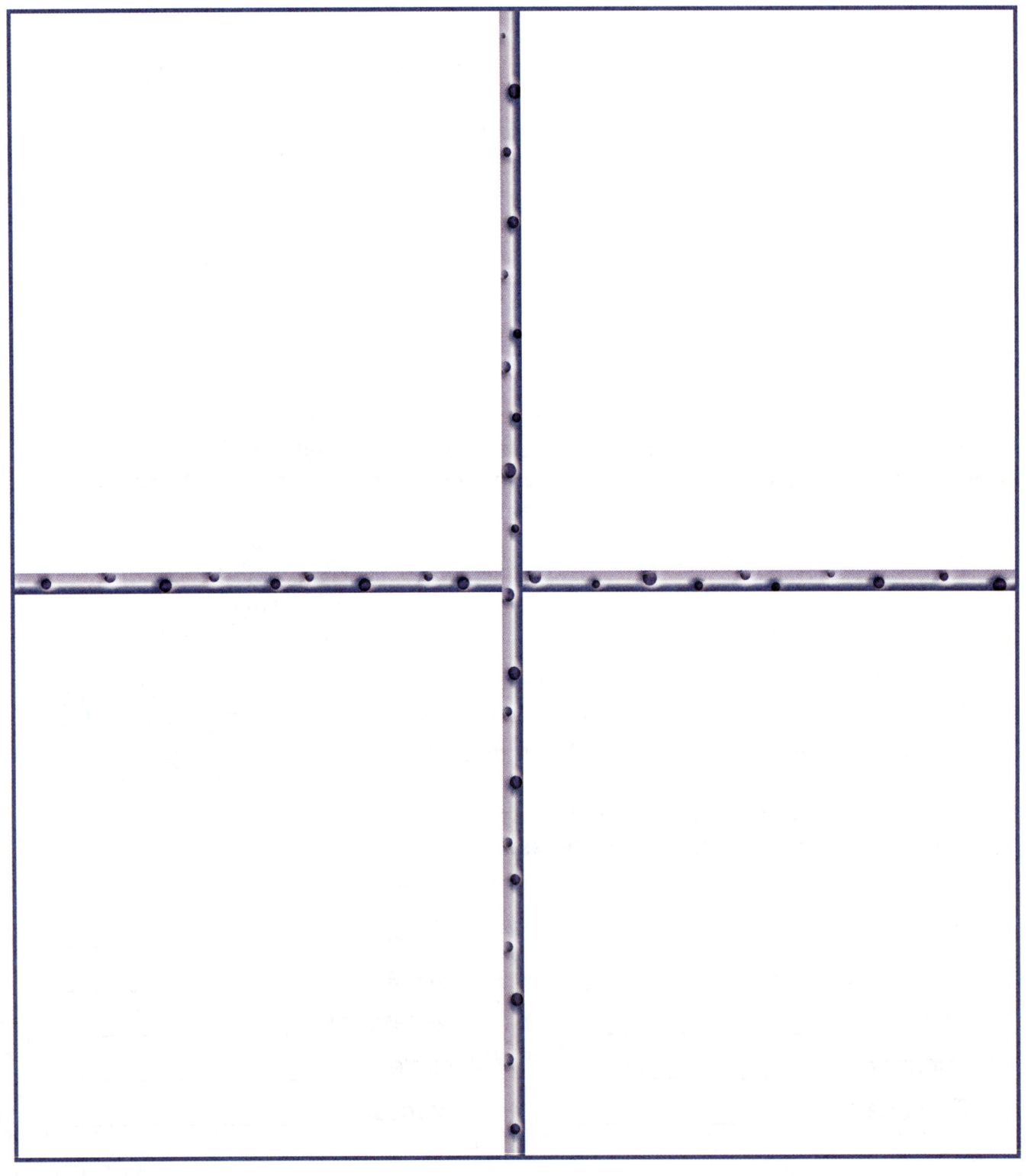

Level Orange   70   Bridges™

Understanding Polygons.
Responde estas preguntas sobre polígonos.
Closed figures that have straight lines are *polygons*.
Which of these are polygons? _____

1. 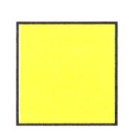 ▫ 2.  ● 3. 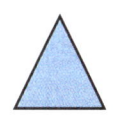 ▲ 4.  ▰ 5. 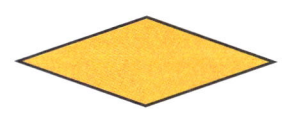 ◆

Why? _____

Where each side or point meets is called a *vertex*. Count and write the number of sides and the number of vertices each polygon has.

triangle	pentagon	quadrilateral	octagon
sides _____	sides _____	sides _____	sides _____
vertices _____	vertices _____	vertices _____	vertices _____

How are these shapes below alike? _____
How are they different? _____

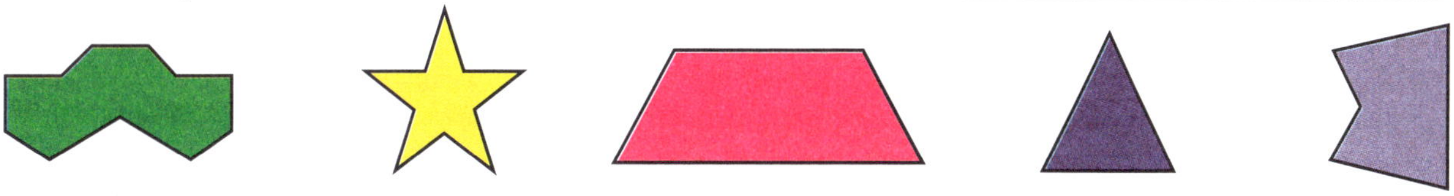

Write the book titles correctly. <u>Remember</u>: Underline the whole title and use capital letters at the beginning of all the important words and the last word in the title.
Escribe estos títulos de libros correctamente.

1. millions of cats _____
2. higher than the arrow _____
3. john paul jones _____
4. no flying in the house _____
5. ludo and the star horse _____
6. marvin k. mooney, will you please leave now?
   _____
7. an elephant is not a cat _____
8. one wide river to cross _____
9. the polar express _____
10. where the sidewalk ends _____

© Federal Education Publishing   71   Level Orange

Day 3

Neighborhood Survey. Conduct a survey with your neighborhood, friends, or relatives. Find out how many have pets they have. If possible, observe them with their pets. Do they keep their pets inside or outside? Are the pets left to find their own food, part of their food, or is their food provided for them? How much space do they have to move around in? In what conditions are their pets? Think of other questions you might ask. Record your information either in a report, chart, graph, table, or a picture.

Lleva a cabo una encuesta sobre mascotas. Anota la información en un reporte, tabla, gráfica o dibujo.

Level Orange

Day 4

Use what you know about polygons to make a pattern. Start with one polygon and flip, turn, or slide it to make a pattern.
Comienza con un polígono‡ y gíralo, voltéalo o córrelo para crear una patrón.

EXAMPLE:

or

Now try your hand at making some polygon patterns.

Review of Homonyms or Homophones. Write 10 sentences using some of these pairs of homonyms or homophones. Be sure to use both words, and underline the homonyms you use.
Escribe diez oraciones usando algunos de estos pares de homónimos‡.

EXAMPLE: Would you chop some wood?

1. no, know
2. ate, eight
3. see, sea
4. knight, night
5. new, knew
6. four, for
7. sun, son
8. tail, tale
9. sale, sail
10. so, sew
11. way, weigh
12. sent, cent
13. rode, road
14. pair, pear
15. their, there
16. hour, our
17. red, read
18. wear, where

© Federal Education Publishing   73   Level Orange

Day 4

Read this paragraph. Put in the missing punctuation marks. Don't forget capitals.

Inserta los signos de puntuación y las letras mayúsculas que falten en este párrafo.

do you ever wonder about the planet pluto it takes pluto 248 earth years to orbit the sun most of the time pluto is farther away from the sun than any other planet but for some time pluto had been closer to the sun than neptune because it was traveling inside neptune's orbit it remained in neptunes orbit until february 9 1999 pluto is now traveling out of neptunes orbit

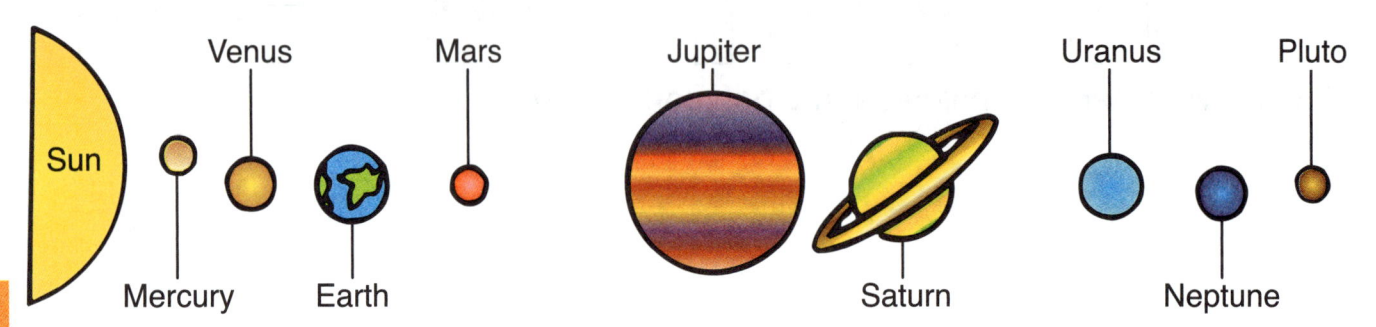

Sun   Venus   Mars   Jupiter   Uranus   Pluto
Mercury   Earth   Saturn   Neptune

See if you can find more information about Pluto. Did you know that some astronomers believe that it was once a moon of Neptune? Look in an encyclopedia to find out more.

Chart the weather and temperature for the month. You will need to check with the weatherman for the high and low temperatures for the day. Write down or draw the weather for the day. Include the high and low temperature.

Registra el clima y la temperatura durante un mes. Escribe o dibuja el clima de cada día.

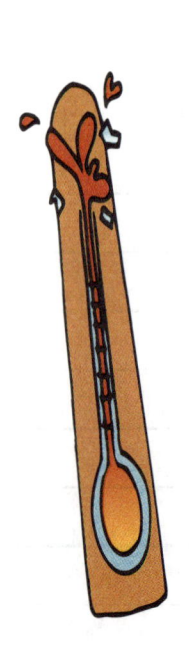

Sun.	Mon.	Tues.	Weds.	Thurs.	Fri.	Sat.

Level Orange   Bridges™

Day 5

Rename these fractions.
Simplifica estas fracciones.

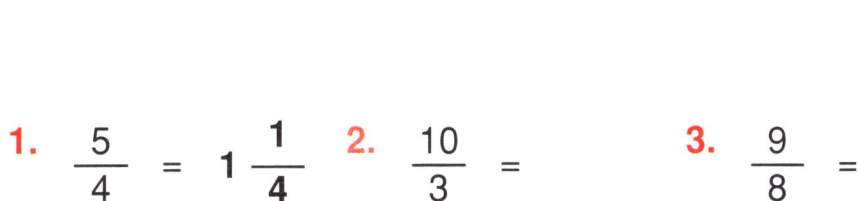

1. $\frac{5}{4}$ = $1\frac{1}{4}$
2. $\frac{10}{3}$ =
3. $\frac{9}{8}$ =
4. $\frac{8}{3}$ =
5. $\frac{5}{2}$ =
6. $\frac{7}{4}$ =
7. $\frac{10}{3}$ =
8. $\frac{11}{10}$ =
9. $\frac{10}{7}$ =
10. $\frac{19}{8}$ =
11. $\frac{25}{10}$ =
12. $\frac{9}{5}$ =
13. $\frac{31}{10}$ =
14. $\frac{23}{10}$ =
15. $\frac{17}{8}$ =
16. $\frac{13}{3}$ =
17. $\frac{25}{12}$ =
18. $\frac{28}{9}$ =
19. $\frac{36}{10}$ =
20. $\frac{9}{4}$ =
21. $\frac{13}{6}$ =
22. $\frac{215}{100}$ =
23. $\frac{76}{25}$ =
24. $\frac{100}{3}$ =

Name the parts of a letter.
Coloca el nombre de las partes de una carta.

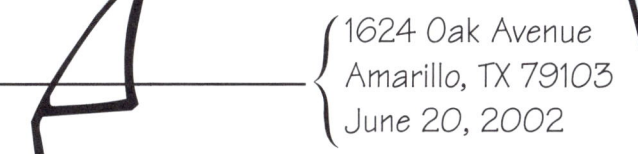

1. _____
2. _____
3. _____
4. _____
5. _____

1 — 1624 Oak Avenue
Amarillo, TX 79103
June 20, 2002

2 — Dear Patt,

3 — Today my friends and I went swimming in June's pool. We had a lot of fun.
I sure miss you. I wish your family hadn't moved. Have you made any new friends yet?
Please write to me as soon as you can.

4 — Your friend,

5 — Judy

© Federal Education Publishing — Level Orange

Day 5

Complete each sentence by circling the word that is spelled correctly; then write it in the blank space.
Encierra en un círculo la palabra que esté escrita correctamente. Escríbela en el espacio en blanco.

1. The big cat couldn't _____ from the trap.
   a. escape   b. iscape   c. eskape   d. acape   e. iccape
2. Mother paid $100.00 for _____.
   a. groseries   b. groceeries c. groceries   d. grcerees   e. grooseries
3. Anna is a very _____ person.
   a. kreative   b. creative   c. createive   d. crative   e. creetive
4. Have you ever seen a more _____ man?
   a. handsum   b. hansome   c. handsume   d. handcome   e. handsome
5. We love to _____ ride in the winter.
   a. sleigh   b. sleia   c. cleigh   d. slagh   e. sleeigh
6. I found the perfect _____ for my new dress.
   a. matterial   b. matirial   c. metariel   d. material   e. materiall
7. Scott's son got a _____ to Harvard University.
   a. schoolarship b. scholarship c. skullarship d. sholarship e. scholership
8. What would it take to _____ your appetite?
   a. satesfy   b. satisfi   c. satisffy   d. catisfy   e. satisfy
9. Richard, turn down the _____!
   a. volime   b. volumee   c. volume   d. volumme   e. valume
10. That was a _____ report, Amy.
    a. fantistic   b. fantastik   c. fanntastic d. fantastic e. fantestic
11. We saw a man fight an _____ in the show.
    a. aligator   b. alligator   c. allegator   d. alligetor e. alligater
12. Do you understand the _____?
    a. instructions b. enstructions c. instiructions d. instrucions e. instracteons

Electricity. Make a list of all the things around you that use electricity.
Haz una lista de cosas a tu alrededor que utilicen electricidad.

_____
_____
_____
_____
_____
_____
_____
_____

Level Orange   Bridges™

Day 6

Add and rename fractions where needed.
Suma‡ y simplifica estas fracciones.

EXAMPLE:

1. $\frac{3}{4} + \frac{2}{4} = \frac{5}{4}$ or $1\frac{1}{4}$
2. $\frac{9}{11} + \frac{2}{11} =$
3. $\frac{7}{12} + \frac{8}{12} =$
4. $\frac{9}{16} + \frac{9}{16} =$
5. $\frac{6}{10} + \frac{8}{10} =$
6. $\frac{10}{12} + \frac{14}{12} =$
7. $\frac{5}{10} + \frac{6}{10} =$
8. $\frac{12}{24} + \frac{13}{24} =$ 
9. $\frac{6}{8} + \frac{5}{8} =$
10. $\frac{4}{7} + \frac{5}{7} =$
11. $\frac{3}{4} + \frac{5}{4} =$
12. $\frac{6}{11} + \frac{7}{11} =$
13. $\frac{5}{15} + \frac{10}{15} =$
14. $\frac{8}{9} + \frac{6}{9} =$
15. $\frac{10}{16} + \frac{9}{16} =$
16. $\frac{15}{20} + \frac{15}{20} =$

Look at the the letter on page 75 to answer the following questions.
Mira la carta de la página 75 para contestar estas preguntas.

1. What does the heading tell you? _____

2. How many paragraphs are in the letter? _____
3. What is the signature? _____

4. What words in the letter have capitals? _____

5. Where are the commas in the letter? _____

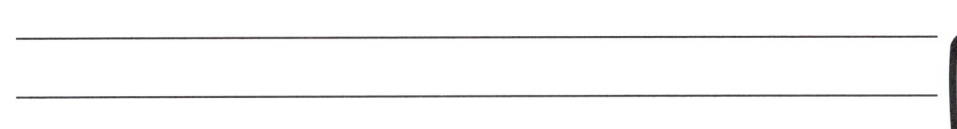

© Federal Education Publishing   Level Orange

Day 6

Electric Circuit Crossword Puzzle.
Crucigrama de circuito eléctrico.

Across
1. Electric currents from a battery flow in one direction from n _ _ _ _ _ _ _ to p _ _ _ _ _ _ _.
2. Electrical c _ _ _ _ _ _ means the flow of charged particles.
3. M _ _ _ _ _ are good conductors of electrical currents because electricity can flow through them easily.
4. The plastic or rubber coverings on wires are called i _ _ _ _ _ _ _ _ _.
5. In a lightbulb, when the switch is turned on or connected, the electricity flows through what we call a c _ _ _ _ _ c _ _ _ _ _ _.
6. When electricity flows through the wires on a toaster they become hot, and h _ _ _ from the wires toasts our bread.
7. L _ _ _ _ _ and thickness are the two things that determine the wires' resistance that causes them to become hot.
8. A _ _ _ _ _ _ _ _ _ such as electric stoves and toasters contain wires that are conductors of electricity.
9. A b _ _ _ _ _ _ is a cell storing an electrical charge and capable of furnishing an electrical current.
10. Copper and aluminum are good c _ _ _ _ _ _ _ _ of electricity because electricity can go through them easily due to their low resistance to the electrical current.

Down
1. A r _ _ _ _ _ _ _ _ is a tool used to control the amount of electrical current that goes through a circuit.
2. When wires, bulbs, and batteries are connected they make a path for electricity to flow through called an e _ _ _ _ _ _ _ _ _ c _ _ _ _ _ _.
3. Lightbulbs have a special wire in them called a f _ _ _ _ _ _ _.
4. The property of the filament that makes it light up when electricity flows through it is called the r _ _ _ _ _ _ _ _ _ to electricity.

Level Orange 78 Bridges™

Day 7

Subtracting Fractions.
Resta de fracciones.

$\frac{4}{5} - \frac{1}{5} = \frac{3}{5}$ ← subtract the numerators.
← keep the same denominators.

1. $\frac{2}{6} - \frac{1}{6} =$

2. $\frac{6}{8} - \frac{3}{8} =$

3. $\frac{11}{12} - \frac{7}{12} =$

4. $\frac{5}{10} - \frac{3}{10} =$

5. $\frac{8}{11} - \frac{3}{11} =$

6. $\frac{4}{5} - \frac{1}{5} =$

7. $\frac{3}{4} - \frac{2}{4} =$

8. $\frac{6}{7} - \frac{4}{7} =$

9. $\frac{5}{9} - \frac{2}{9} =$

10. $6\frac{8}{10}$
    $-3\frac{4}{10}$

11. $8\frac{4}{10}$
    $-3\frac{3}{10}$

12. $7\frac{2}{5}$
    $-3\frac{1}{5}$

13. $6\frac{7}{8}$
    $-3\frac{4}{8}$

14. $13\frac{3}{4}$
    $-9\frac{1}{4}$

15. $14\frac{10}{12}$
    $-7\frac{9}{12}$

16. $24\frac{7}{10}$
    $-12\frac{3}{10}$

17. $15\frac{8}{9}$
    $-7\frac{3}{9}$

Put all the punctuation marks and capital letters in this letter.
Agrégale los signos de puntuación y las mayúsculas a esta carta.

Mr. Greg Jones
1461 Condor St.
Lake Tona, OH

1461 condor st
lake tona oh
july 21 2002

dear david

    thank you for sending me the pictures of your trip it looks like you had a great time do you want me to send them back
    next week im going to kansas city to spend the rest of the summer with my dad i hope we will get along well
    write again when you can

        your friend
          greg

Level Orange

Day 7

Body Facts. Use the words in the Word Box to complete these sentences on "body facts."

Utiliza las palabras del Recuadro de Palabras para completar estas oraciones.

Word Box
- brain
- water
- calcium
- circulatory
- cells
- iron
- digestive
- eyes
- heart

1. Our bodies are made up of millions of tiny _____.
2. Our bodies are mostly _____, between 55 and 75 percent.
3. Our bodies have lots of metals and minerals in them, some of which are _____ and _____.
4. Our bodies have several systems that work together to help us. Our heart, blood vessels, and blood are part of our _____ system, which moves blood throughout our bodies.
5. Our salivary glands, esophagus, stomach, gallbladder, large intestines, and small intestines are part of our _____ system.
6. Our _____ is like a wonderful tool. It tells our _____ to beat and our _____ to blink.

Our Five Senses Can Sense Danger! Think about your five senses—touch, smell, sight, hearing, and taste. Now list all the ways your five senses can protect you or keep you from danger. Which sense do you trust most to keep you from danger?

Haz una lista de la forma en que tus cinco sentidos pueden protegerte del peligro.

_____
_____
_____
_____
_____
_____
_____
_____
_____
_____

Level Orange

Bridges™

Addition and Subtraction with Thousands

Suma‡ o resta.

1. 5,162
   − 2,678

2. 9,252
   − 5,003

3. 7,825
   − 3,148

4. 3,529
   + 7,506

5. 8,929
   + 4,050

6. 9,341
   − 6,037

7. 2,629
   + 7,536

8. 4,528
   + 1,257

9. 7,932
   − 5,847

10. 9,826
    + 1,329

11. 4,723
    + 5,297

12. 3,872
    − 1,799

13. 8,000
    − 4,587

14. 7,909
    + 5,360

15. 9,031
    − 5,592

16. 2,354
    + 5,967

Write a letter to a friend, grandparent, or someone else you would like to write. Be sure to put in all five parts of the letter. Remember: Letter writing uses the same steps as writing a story. Refer to page 57. Copy your letter to another sheet of paper.

Escríbele una carta a alguien. Incluye las cinco partes de una carta.

Day 8

Below are the stressed syllables of some spelling words. Write the other syllables and then write the words in cursive. Each blank stands for a letter.

Debajo se encuentran las sílabas‡ tónicas de algunas palabras. Escribe las otras sílabas y luego escribe las palabras en cursiva‡. Cada espacio en blanco representa una letra.

favor	amount	busy	accept	violin
paddle	piano	begin	dial	bacon
several	salad	wonderful	unlock	vegetable
~~parent~~	library	limit	into	depend

1. par´ ent   *parent*
2. li´ _ _ _ _ _
3. lim´ _ _
4. in´ _ _
5. _ _ pend´
6. ba´ _ _ _
7. di´ _ _
8. _ _ gin´
9. _ _ a´ _ _
10. pad´ _ _ _
11. sev´ _ _ _ _
12. sal´ _ _
13. won´ _ _ _ _ _ _
14. _ _ lock´
15. veg´ _ _ _ _ _ _
16. _ _ _ lin´
17. _ _ cept´
18. bus´ _
19. _ mount´
20. fa´ _ _ _

Self-Portrait Poem.

Sigue las instrucciones para escribir un poema sobre ti mismo.

1. Write your name.
2. Write two words that tell about you.
3. Write three words that tell what you like to do.
4. Write two more words that describe you.
5. Write your name again.

Try writing another "portrait poem" about a favorite person or pet in your life.

Level Orange — Bridges™

Day 9

It's about Time! <u>Remember</u>: There are 24 hours in a day. The times from midnight to noon are written a.m., and the times from noon to midnight are written p.m. Write down the times. Remember a.m. and p.m.

Escribe la hora. Recuerda poner a.m. y p.m.

1.　　　　　　　　2.　　　　　　　　3.

_____　_____　_____

4. Write the time 50 minutes later than clock 1. _____

5. Write the time 25 minutes earlier than clock 2. _____

6. Write the time 95 minutes later than clock 3. _____

7. How much earlier is clock 1 than clock 2? _____

8. How much later is clock 3 than clock 2? _____

9. If you add 12 hours to clock 1, what time is it? _____

10. What was the time 6 hours earlier on clock 2? _____

This envelope is not addressed correctly. Rewrite it correctly. <u>Remember</u>: The <u>return address</u> is the <u>address</u> of the person writing the letter, and the address is the address of the person to whom the letter is going.

Ponga correctamente la dirección en este sobre.

1461 condor st
mr greg jones
lake tona oh

mr david fisher
little creek id
route 2 box 3 f

Day 9

Who Did It?

Griffin and Trevor were playing baseball in their backyard with some friends. They had been playing all afternoon in the hot sun.

Trevor decided that he was tired of playing ball. He sat down on the back steps to watch the others. "Man, am I thirsty," he said. "I'm going in the house to get a drink." Several of the others decided that they were thirsty and went inside with Trevor. "Wait for me!" hollered Griffin. "I'm coming, too!"

The boys agreed to watch television instead of playing more baseball. Then the guys thought they had better go home because it was close to dinnertime. Griffin said he was hungry and was going to look in the kitchen for something to eat. Trevor ran after him to remind him that their mom said they were not to eat anything before dinner. About that time their mother came into the kitchen to fix dinner. "Who ate all the hot dogs?" she exclaimed. "They were right here on the counter." Griffin and Trevor looked at each other. "Not us, Mom," they said. "Somebody must have. Do you have any clues?"

They started looking around for clues. The mud off their shoes had left tracks on the floor but had come nowhere near where Mother had put the hot dogs. After their survey of the kitchen, they sat down to discuss the "case of the missing hot dogs." Then they heard what sounded like a satisfied meow from the den. The three of them walked into the den to find Tiger, their cat, finishing off the last hot dog. He licked both his paws clean and meowed loudly. "No wonder we didn't find any cat tracks in the kitchen where the hot dogs were," laughed Mother. "Tiger always keeps his paws very clean, unlike some boys I know."

After reading this story, write down at least five things you know about Trevor and Griffin.

Escribe por lo menos cinco cosas que sepas sobre Trevor y Griffin después de haber leído la historia.

1. _____

2. _____

3. _____

4. _____

5. _____

Level Orange   Bridges™

Day 10

Fractions to Tenths and the Decimal Equivalents for the Fraction

Remember: When working with fractions that have a denominator of 10, you can write them as fractions in tenths, or you can use the decimal equivalent. Do this activity by writing each both ways.

Escribe la fracción‡ correcta y/o el decimal en los espacios en blanco.

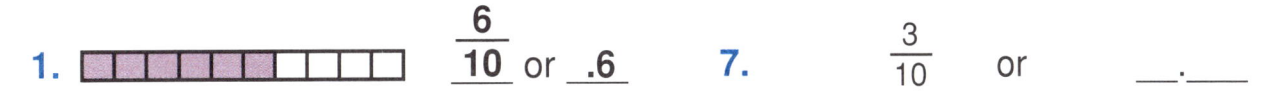

1. [bar] $\frac{6}{10}$ or .6
2. [bar]   ___ or ___
3. [bar]   ___ or ___
4. [bar]   ___ or ___
5. [bar]   ___ or ___
6. [bar]   ___ or ___

7. $\frac{3}{10}$ or ___.___
8. $1\frac{7}{10}$ or ___.___
9. $3\frac{5}{10}$ or ___.___
10. 1.9 or _____
11. .8 or _____
12. 3.4 or _____

On page 81, you wrote a letter to someone. Today, address an envelope and send the letter to them. Be sure to put your address in the upper left-hand corner and the address of the person to whom you're sending the letter in the center. Don't forget to put a stamp in the upper right-hand corner. Use the space below to practice.

Coloca la dirección a un sobre y envía la carta que has escrito en la página 81.

Date_____

Name_____

© Federal Education Publishing   Level Orange

Day 10

Write an analogy to finish these sentences. <u>Remember</u>: An analogy is a comparison between two pairs of words. Try to think of the relationship between the two words given and then think of another word that has the same kind of relationship to the third word.

Escribe una analogía‡ para finalizar estas oraciones.

EXAMPLE: <u>Story</u> is to <u>read</u> as <u>song</u> is to <u>sing</u>.

1. <u>Brother</u> is to <u>boy</u> as <u>sister</u> is to _____.
2. <u>Princess</u> is to <u>queen</u> as <u>prince</u> is to _____.
3. <u>Milk</u> is to <u>drink</u> as <u>hamburger</u> is to _____.
4. <u>Arrow</u> is to <u>bow</u> as <u>bullet</u> is to _____.
5. <u>Car</u> is to <u>driver</u> as <u>plane</u> is to _____.
6. <u>Ceiling</u> is to <u>room</u> as <u>lid</u> is to _____.
7. <u>Paper</u> is to <u>tear</u> as <u>glass</u> is to _____.
8. <u>Large</u> is to <u>huge</u> as <u>small</u> is to _____.
9. <u>Wrist</u> is to <u>hand</u> as <u>ankle</u> is to _____.
10. <u>Father</u> is to <u>uncle</u> as <u>mother</u> is to _____.
11. <u>Cupboard</u> is to <u>dishes</u> as <u>library</u> is to _____.
12. <u>Hard</u> is to <u>difficult</u> as <u>easy</u> is to _____.
13. <u>Moon</u> is to <u>earth</u> as <u>earth</u> is to _____.
14. <u>Time</u> is to <u>clock</u> as <u>date</u> is to _____.

Exercising Parts of the Body. Make a list of 5 or 6 exercises. Some examples are running, hopping, sit-ups, jumping jacks, touching your toes, push-ups, jumping, skipping, playing sports, gymnastics, and swinging your arms. Try them. Which parts of the body are affected? Write down the results. Try this exercise. Take an ordinary spring-centered clothespin. Hold the ends between your thumb and one of your fingers. How many times can you open and close it in 30 to 40 seconds?

Haz una lista de 5 ó 6 ejercicios físicos. Trata de hacerlos. Escribe qué partes de tu cuerpo se ven afectadas.

_____
_____
_____
_____
_____
_____

Level Orange
Bridges™

Day 11

Use what you know about <u>fractions</u> <u>to</u> <u>tenths</u> and their <u>decimal equivalents</u> to work with <u>hundredths</u>. <u>Remember</u>: When a whole object is divided into 100 equal parts, each part is <u>one</u> <u>hundredth</u> ($\frac{1}{100}$ or .01). Write the fraction as a decimal.

Escribe la fracción‡ como decimal.

1. $\frac{49}{100}$ = .**49**
2. $\frac{25}{100}$ = .___
3. $\frac{20}{100}$ = .___
4. $\frac{52}{100}$ = .___
5. $\frac{86}{100}$ = .___
6. $\frac{37}{100}$ = .___
7. $\frac{4}{100}$ = .___
8. $\frac{9}{100}$ = .___

Now write the mixed number as a decimal.

Escribe la fracción mixta como decimal.

9. $1\frac{93}{100}$ = __.__
10. $7\frac{15}{100}$ = __.__
11. $9\frac{13}{100}$ = __.__
12. $15\frac{47}{100}$ = __.__
13. $46\frac{89}{100}$ = __.__
14. $35\frac{6}{100}$ = __.__
15. $94\frac{7}{100}$ = __.__
16. $625\frac{12}{100}$ = __.__
17. $12\frac{5}{100}$ = __.__
18. $81\frac{1}{100}$ = __.__
19. $37\frac{87}{100}$ = __.__
20. $10\frac{11}{100}$ = __.__

Adjectives are words that tell about or describe nouns and pronouns. Circle the adjective(s) in these sentences. Write the noun(s) or pronoun(s) described at the end of the sentence.

Encierra en un círculo los adjetivos‡ de estas oraciones. Escribe los sustantivos‡ o pronombres‡ descritos.

1. A (beautiful) light flashed across the (cloudy) sky.   *light   sky*
2. Her golden hair was very long. _____
3. On the tall mountain we found blue and yellow flowers. _____
4. He was brave after the accident. _____
5. It is fun, but it is also dangerous to skydive. _____
6. Our brown dog had six cute puppies. _____

Now fill in the blanks with adjectives.

Completa los espacios en blanco con adjetivos.

7. My _____ pencil is never in my desk.
8. The _____ students were having a _____ time.
9. Lions are _____ animals that we can see in the zoo.
10. The _____, _____ ride was making me sick.
11. My brother, Jack, sang a _____ song when we were camping.
12. _____, _____ snakes were wiggling around in the box.

© Federal Education Publishing — 87 — Level Orange

Day 11

Fill in the blanks below with health terms from the box.

Completa los espacios en blanco con los términos sobre la salud del Recuadro de Palabras.

> nutrients, healthy, sleep, exercise, liquids, water,
> cleanliness, checkups, energy, food groups.

1. _____ are basic nourishing ingredients in good foods that we eat.
2. _____ helps us to strengthen our muscles. It helps our heart and lungs grow, too.
3. _____ help us prevent tooth decay and maintain good health.
4. Meat, fruits and vegetables, milk, and breads and cereals make up the basic four _____ _____ that keep us healthy.
5. Being healthy means feeling good and having the _____ to work and play.
6. Vitamins and minerals are kinds of _____ that we get from food.
7. Being _____ means feeling good and not being sick.
8. Sugar, starch, and fats are _____ that the body uses for fuel to give us _____.
9. We need to drink a lot of _____ because our body is approximately 60 to 70 percent _____.
10. Plenty of _____ helps give our body time to grow and repair itself. Children need 10 to 11 hours of it because they are not finished growing.
11. _____ is a way of fighting germs and staying healthy.
12. We need health _____ by a doctor or dentist at least once a year.

Are you confused?
¿Estás confundido?

1. Are any of the lines curved?
   _____

2. Which line is the longest?
   _____

3. Which vase is wider at the top and bottom? _____

4. Which line is longer, a or b?
   _____

5. Is the hat taller than it is wide?
   _____

Level Orange 88 Bridges™

Day 12

Decimals and Money. <u>Remember</u>: 100 pennies = 1 dollar. One penny is 1/100 of a dollar, or $.01, so 49 pennies = $.49. We can compute money by adding, subtracting, multiplying, and dividing—just watch the decimals. Look at the signs. Use a separate piece of paper to show your work.

Puedes calcular dinero sumando, restando multiplicando y dividiendo. Solamente observa los decimales.

EXAMPLE:

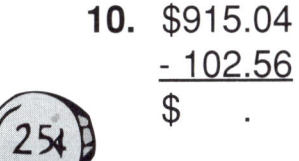

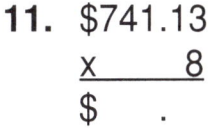

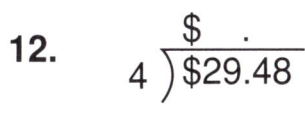

```
                                                              $3.95
   $57.34        $62.89       $12.45                      5 )$19.75
  +62.89        -34.91       x    3                          -15
  ───────       ───────      ───────                          47
  $120.23       $27.98       $37.35                          -45
                                                              25
                                                             -25
                                                               0
```

1. $409.75
   − 249.83
   $.

2. $14.74
   x   3
   $.

3. $492.00
   − 349.50
   $.

4. $.
   4)$12.92

5. $162.49
   + 186.32
   $.

6. $.
   7)$49.77

7. $601.89
   + 403.23
   $.

8. $9.57
   x   6
   $.

9. $668.45
   + 171.63
   $.

10. $915.04
    − 102.56
    $.

11. $741.13
    x   8
    $.

12. $.
    4)$29.48

Write nouns to go with these adjectives.
Escribe sustantivos‡ que concuerden con estos adjetivos‡.

1. two, red _apples_
2. fluffy, yellow _____
3. cold, wet _____
4. dark, strange _____
5. wild, dangerous _____
6. black, furry _____
7. big, heavy _____
8. fancy, little _____

9. pink, small _____
10. smooth, green _____
11. fat, juicy _____
12. loud, shrill _____
13. fourteen, blue _____
14. long, thick _____
15. cozy, warm _____
16. sharp, silver _____

© Federal Education Publishing   Level Orange

Day 12

Add a prefix and a suffix to the following words; then choose five of the words and write a sentence with them.

Agrega un prefijo‡ y un sufijo a las siguientes palabras. Elige cinco de las palabras y escribe oraciones con ellas.

1. _____ print _____
2. _____ light _____
3. _____ poison _____
4. _____ courage _____
5. _____ agree _____
6. _____ spell _____
7. _____ lock _____
8. _____ port _____
9. _____ cook _____
10. _____ appoint _____
11. _____ record _____
12. _____ health _____

Sentences:

1. _____
2. _____
3. _____
4. _____
5. _____

What's for Breakfast, Lunch, and Dinner? This is your day to plan the meals. You can have anything you want to eat for the day. It can be for the whole family or just yourself. Plan and write down your menu for breakfast, lunch, and dinner. You can even schedule a few snacks.

Escribe un menu para el desayuno, el almuerzo y la cena.

_____
_____
_____
_____
_____
_____
_____
_____

Level Orange

Day 13

Multiplying Multiples of 10 and 100.
Multiplicación de múltiplos‡ de 10 y de 100.
To use shortcuts to find the product of multiples of 10 or 100, write the product for the basic fact and count the zeros in the factors.
  10 x 8 = 80 (1 zero)   10 x 80 = 800 (2 zeros)   10 x 800 = 8,000 (3 zeros)

Multiples of tens:

1. 10 x 5 = ____
2. 7 x 10 = ____
3. 39 x 10 = ____
4. 30 x 30 = ____
5. 54 x 10 = ____
6. 10 x 21 = ____
7. 710 x 10 = ____
8. 9 x 10 = ____
9. 70 x 30 = ____
10. 40 x 40 = ____
11. 85 x 10 = ____
12. 341 x 10 = ____

Multiples of hundreds:

13. 900
    x 40

14. 600
    x 10

15. 230
    x 20

16. 700
    x 80

17. 500
    x 50

18. 600
    x 90

19. 440
    x30

20. 700
    x 60

Adjectives can be used to compare. Write these adjectives. Add -er and -est.
Escribe estos adjetivos‡. Agrega –er y –est.

EXAMPLE: red   redder   reddest

1. hot   _____   _____
2. nice   _____   _____
3. warm   _____   _____
4. hard   _____   _____
5. easy   _____   _____
6. few   _____   _____

Now write a story. Use as many of the adjectives above as you can. Underline the adjectives.
Escribe una historia. Utiliza la mayor cantidad posible de adjetivos. Subráyalos.

_____
_____
_____
_____
_____

© Federal Education Publishing   Level Orange

Day 13

Idioms. Choose 4 <u>idioms and illustrate them</u>. Here are some to choose from, or you can use your own.

Ilustra cuatro modismos‡. Elige uno de estos o utiliza uno propio.

- Lend a hand.
- She's a ball of fire.
- He's got rocks in his head.
- She gave him a dirty look.
- I got it straight from the horse's mouth.
- You won the game by the skin of your teeth.
- Time flies.
- Keep a stiff upper lip.
- The boys were shooting the breeze.
- I'd really like to catch her eye.
- I was dog tired.

Level Orange

Bridges™

Day 14

Place Value. A place-value chart can help us read as well as figure out large numbers.
Utiliza la tabla de valores posicionales para leer y escribir estos números.

Hundred Millions	Ten Millions	Millions	Hundred Thousands	Ten Thousands	Thousands	Hundreds	Tens	Ones
	8	6	5	3	7	1	4	3

Using the place-value chart to help you, read and write the following numbers.

1. Eighty-six million five hundred thirty-seven thousand one hundred forty-three
   __86,537,143__.

2. Seven hundred eighty-nine million four hundred ninety-six thousand three hundred twenty-one _____.

3. One hundred sixty million seven hundred six thousand one hundred twenty-nine _____.

4. Seventy-one million four hundred eleven thousand eight hundred ninety-nine _____.

5. One hundred million three hundred seventy-five thousand _____.

6. Ninety million two hundred fifty-seven thousand four hundred forty-three _____.

7. 1,369,000 _____
8. 375,403,101 _____
9. 894,336,045 _____
10. 284,300,070 _____

Overworked And. Rewrite the paragraph and leave out all the occurrences of and that you can. Write in cursive and be sure to put capitals and periods where they need to go.
Vuelve a escribir este párrafo. Elimina la palabra and todas las reces que sea posible.

   My friend and I visited Cardiff, Wales, and we learned that Cardiff is the capital and largest port of Wales and the city lies on the River Taff near the Bristol Channel and Cardiff is near the largest coal mines in Great Britain and it is one of the great coal-shipping ports of the world.

How many times were you able to leave and out of the paragraph? _____

© Federal Education Publishing   93   Level Orange

Day 14

The following words are often misspelled. Write each word three times, then have someone give you a test on another piece of paper.
Escribe cada palabra tres veces y luego haz que alguien te evalúe.

EXAMPLE:
1. although   *although*   *although*   *although*
2. arithmetic _____
3. trouble _____
4. bought _____
5. chocolate _____
6. aunt _____
7. handkerchief _____
8. piece _____
9. vacation _____
10. practice _____
11. receive _____
12. getting _____
13. lessons _____
14. weather _____
15. surprise _____

Categorizing the People in Your Family. Include some aunts, uncles, and cousins. Categorize them according to age, height, weight, hair color, hair length, eye color, etc. What do they have in common? What are some of their differences? Then draw a picture of them. Use another sheet of paper.
Categoriza a las personas de tu familia. ¿En qué se parecen? ¿En qué se diferencian‡?

family member	age	height	weight	hair color

Level Orange   Bridges™

Day 15

Multiplying 2-digit Numbers.
Multiplica.

1. 39
   x 69

2. 72
   x 18

3. 85
   x 36

4. 23
   x 87

5. 46
   x 77

6. 57
   x 49

7. 41
   x 73

8. 48
   x 95

9. 88
   x 66

10. 68
    x 92

11. 507
    x 13

12. 456
    x 32

13. 640
    x 21

14. 576
    x 45

Write S behind the word pairs that are synonyms, A for antonyms, or H for homonyms.
Escribe S para los pares de palabras que sean sinónimos‡, A para los antónimos‡ y H para los homónimos‡.

EXAMPLE:
tie • bind __S__
high • low __A__
here • hear __H__

1. weep • cry ____
2. wonderful • terrible ____
3. look • glare ____
4. huge • large ____
5. away • toward ____
6. walk • stroll ____
7. never • always ____
8. bear • bare ____
9. ask • told ____
10. cymbal • symbol ____
11. many • numerous ____
12. end • begin ____

13. hair • hare ____
14. move • transport ____
15. problem • solution ____
16. idea • thought ____
17. claws • clause ____
18. I'll • isle ____
19. add • subtract ____
20. try • attempt ____
21. that • this ____
22. doe • dough ____
23. enough • ample ____
24. board • bored ____
25. day • date ____
26. capital • capitol ____
27. leave • arrive ____

© Federal Education Publishing   95   Level Orange

Day 15

Do this crossword puzzle. Read the clues to help you decide what words go in the boxes. Lee las pistas y decide qué palabras van en los recuadros.

Down
1. birds with webbed feet
3. plays the piano
5. gave money
6. holds up the gate
8. boards for building
9. frilly
11. do it again to a story
12. hair by the eye
13. another name for a mule

Across
2. red from the sun
4. won't bend easily
5. eat outside
6. beginning of a word
7. decay of food
10. very large; great
14. nothing in it
15. cook in

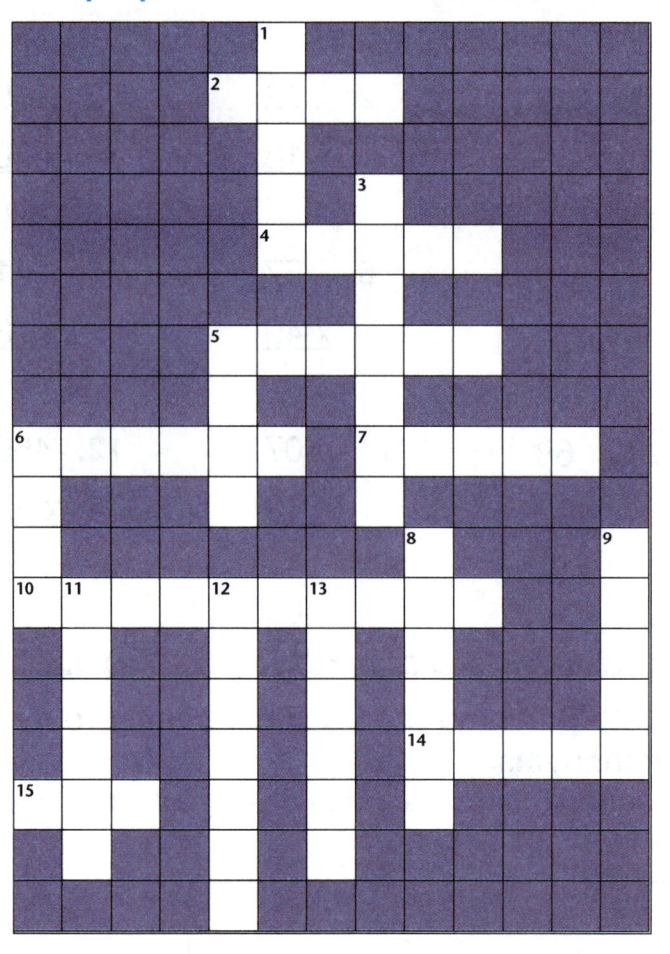

Finish drawing the illusion. Is it a face or a vase? It's both! (Look until you see them.)
Termina de dibujar la ilusión. ¿Es un rostro o una vasija? ¡Es ambos!

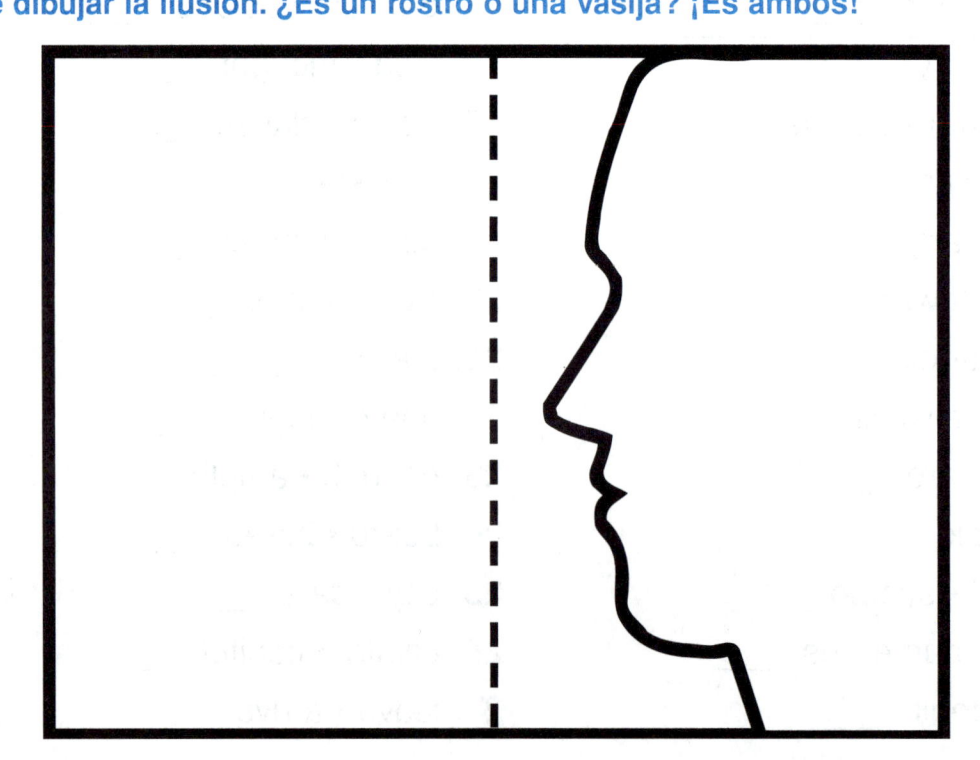

Level Orange

High-Frequency Word List

a	cut	hand	looking	president	to
about	decided	happened	lost	pretty	today
above	did	hard	mad	probably	told
across	didn't	has	made	ready	took
afraid	died	have	make	red	top
after	do	having	many	ride	toward
against	does	he	may	room	tree
all	dogs	head	maybe	running	trees
almost	doing	hear	money	said	tried
an	done	heard	more	same	trip
and	door	he's	morning	sea	true
animals	down	high	most	second	try
answer	dream	hill	mother	see	turn
are	during	him	move	seen	turned
as	each	himself	Mr.	sentence	TV
ask	earth	his	must	several	two
baby	enough	horse	my	she	up
basketball	ever	hour	myself	ship	upon
be	example	how	near	show	use
beautiful	face	however	need	side	usually
been	family	hurt	night	since	very
began	far	I	no	sleep	walk
being	fast	if	not	small	walked
best	father	I'm	nothing	snow	was
better	feet	in	now	so	wasn't
black	few	into	of	some	water
boat	fight	is	oh	soon	way
body	find	it	ok	start	we
book	first	its	on	story	were
both	fish	it's	once	street	what
boy	five	job	one	study	when
broke	for	jump	only	summer	where
but	four	just	or	sun	which
by	Friday	kind	other	sure	white
called	from	knew	out	teachers	who
can	funny	know	outside	than	whole
candy	gas	land	over	that	will
car	gave	later	own	the	with
care	gets	learn	page	their	without
cars	goes	let	paper	them	won't
change	got	life	people	then	words
circus	grade	light	picture	there	would
city	grader	like	planet	these	year
clothes	group	likes	plants	they	you
coming	grow	little	play	thing	young
could	had	live	playing	this	your
country	half	long	point	time	you're

© Federal Education Publishing   97   Level Orange

Words to Sound out, Read, and Spell

aboard	banana	cattle	confirm	delayed	dried
accept	bathe	cedar	confusion	delicate	dry
accident	bathroom	ceiling	conjunction	delivery	due
account	battery	center	connect	demand	dumb
ache	battle	century	conquer	dentist	dump
actress	beauty	certain	constant	describe	eagle
additional	bedtime	certainly	contain	desert	eardrum
advice	beet	chalk	continue	deserve	earlier
advise	behave	chamber	contribution	despite	earliest
affect	believe	champion	conversation	dessert	early
afford	between	character	convince	detective	earthquake
agency	bicycle	charcoal	copper	determination	echo
agree	birthday	cheerful	correctly	determine	echoing
agriculture	blindfold	chemist	correspond	development	editor
alligator	boathouse	cherish	cottage	diamond	education
aloud	bookcase	chicken	council	dictionary	effort
alphabet	boring	chief	couple	difference	either
already	borrow	chocolate	coupling	different	eldest
although	boulevard	choice	courage	difficult	electric
among	bowl	choicest	cousin	dignity	electricity
ancient	breathless	choose	cowboy	dining	enemies
ankle	bridge	chose	cozier	direct	enemy
announcement	bridle	chuckled	cozy	director	engine
anxious	brief	circle	cradle	disagree	enormous
appearance	brow	circuses	crawl	disappear	enthusiasm
appreciate	bruise	claim	crazy	disappoint	entrance
approach	bucket	climate	cream	disaster	environment
approval	build	closet	creative	discover	envy
approximately	built	clue	creature	discovery	equal
apron	bulb	clumsier	crew	disease	equipment
aren't	burglar	clumsiest	crossroads	distance	escape
aroma	bury	clumsy	crow	distant	especially
arranged	bushel	clutch	cube	distrust	estate
arrival	busiest	coach	cure	divide	eventually
article	business	coal	curious	divided	evidence
assistant	busy	coast	current	division	exact
association	cabin	coil	curtain	dizziest	except
assortment	cabinet	collect	custom	dizzy	exchange
assume	camera	collection	customer	doctor	excitement
attend	campaign	comfort	dairy	does	excuse
attention	canoes	comfortable	dangerous	doesn't	exercise
attic	captain	comical	data	dollar	exercising
audience	caption	commander	daughter	donkeys	existence
auditorium	caravan	committee	dawn	doubt	expect
author	cardboard	community	debt	downstairs	expensive
avenue	carefully	companion	decision	downtown	experience
backward	carpenter	company	declare	doze	explanation
baggage	carpet	concerns	defense	dozen	explore
balcony	cartwheel	conference	definite	drawer	factories
balloon	category	confess	degree	drew	factory

Level Orange   98   Bridges™

Words to Sound out, Read, and Spell

familiar	governor	important	lightning	moisture	pause
famous	graceful	impossible	limb	moment	peace
fancy	graduated	increase	limping	month	peak
fantastic	graph	index	linen	moonlight	pear
farewell	grateful	indicate	lion	motion	peddle
faultless	gratitude	innocent	liquid	mountain	peek
favor	great	inquire	listen	museum	perfect
favorite	grief	insect	litter	musician	performance
features	groan	inspiring	lonelier	nation	perhaps
fiction	groceries	instance	loneliest	nature	petal
field	grocery	instant	lonely	nearby	piano
financial	grow	instead	loosen	neat	picnic
flapped	grown	institutions	losing	necklace	picnicking
flapping	grown-up	instructions	loss	necktie	picturing
flattered	guarantee	intention	lumber	needle	piece
flavor	guard	interest	machine	neighbor	pigeon
flock	guilty	interjection	machinery	nervous	plain
footprint	habit	international	mail	newsreel	plane
forecast	hadn't	interview	male	northwest	plantation
forenoon	hail	introduction	mankind	notebook	platform
forest	handkerchief	investigate	mansion	notice	pleasant
fortunate	handsome	island	market	noun	pleasure
fortune	happiness	jelly	marry	oasis	plural
forward	harness	jewelry	marvelous	obey	pocket
foster	haunt	judgment	material	object	poison
foundation	hawk	juice	meadow	occur	poisonous
fountain	he's	junior	meal	ocean	police
fourth	headquarters	justice	mean	offer	policing
frequent	health	kettle	meant	office	polish
fright	heartily	kindness	measure	often	polite
fuel	heavy	kingdom	measured	opposite	political
furious	height	kneel	measuring	orchard	pollution
furnace	histories	knit	medal	ordinary	porch
furniture	history	knob	medicine	original	position
future	hobby	know	medium	orphan	possess
gable	holiday	knowledge	mention	ounce	possible
gain	homemade	known	merchant	outlook	postscript
gallon	honor	label	message	package	potato
garage	honorable	laid	method	paddle	potatoes
geese	hoof	language	midst	pair	pound
generation	hospital	lantern	mineral	pajamas	poverty
genuine	hotel	laughter	minus	palm	powder
germ	huge	lecture	minute	pane	practically
glare	human	length	mirror	partial	practice
glaring	humor	lettuce	miserable	particular	practicing
glorious	iceberg	level	mission	pass	praise
gnaw	idea	lever	mistake	passage	precious
goodness	imagine	library	mixture	past	prefer
goose	impatient	lie	model	pasture	prejudice
government	import	lied	modern	pattern	preposition

© Federal Education Publishing   Level Orange

Words to Sound out, Read, and Spell

preserve	relief	separate	steal	throughout	vegetable
pressure	remarkable	serious	steel	thumb	versus
price	remember	serve	stew	ticket	victory
pricing	repair	service	sting	tied	view
principal	repeat	settlement	stomach	tiger	violin
private	replace	severe	straight	tight	vision
privilege	replied	shadow	strain	toast	volume
proceed	reply	sharpener	street	toe	waist
professional	report	she'll	stressed	together	wait
professor	reputation	shield	stripe	tomato	walnut
promise	rescue	shine	stroke	tongue	warehouse
prompt	resign	shone	struggle	tool	warn
prop	respect	shoulder	stumble	toothbrush	wasn't
prosperous	response	shouldn't	success	topic	waste
protect	restore	shown	successes	topsoil	we're
prove	retreat	sigh	suggest	total	wealthy
provide	reward	sight	suitcase	tractor	weary
prune	rise	signal	sunburn	traffic	weather
publicity	road	silence	sunshine	transportation	weight
puddle	rocket	simple	superintendent	treasure	welcome
pupil	route	singular	supply	treatment	weren't
purpose	rude	sleigh	supplying	tremendous	wheat
purse	ruin	slept	support	trial	where's
quality	safety	slice	suspect	trouble	whether
quart	sailor	slight	suspicious	tune	whirl
quarter	saint	slim	sweater	typewriter	whistle
question	salad	slippery	sweet	unfold	whistling
quiet	salary	smooth	sword	unhappy	who's
quite	salute	snake	syllable	uniform	whom
radish	satisfaction	soar	synonym	union	widow
railroad	satisfy	society	teach	universal	wilderness
rather	Saturday	soldier	teapot	university	windshield
reach	sawdust	sorrow	teaspoon	unknown	wise
real	scarce	south	teenagers	unlike	wolf
reappear	scarcest	soybean	teeth	unload	woman
rearrange	scene	spare	telephone	unlock	women
recall	schedule	sparrow	television	unlucky	wonderful
recess	scholarship	specific	tennis	upstairs	world
recognition	science	speech	terrible	urge	worm
recommend	scissors	spell	terrific	urged	worried
record	season	spinach	territory	urgent	worry
recover	secret	splendid	thaw	useless	worrying
recovery	secretary	spoon	there's	usual	worth
reference	seldom	sprinkle	they've	vacant	wouldn't
refrigerator	selfish	squeeze	thief	vain	wreck
region	senator	standard	thigh	valuable	wrestle
regular	senior	staring	thirsty	vanish	wrist
reindeer	sense	statement	thought	variety	you've
relate	sensible	station	thousand	various	yourself
relative	sentencing	statue	thread	vary	yourselves

Level Orange

Bridges™

Glossary

a breve (ă) — el sonido a en bat.

a larga (ā) — el sonido a en cake.

abreviatura (abbreviation) — forma corta de una palabra. Por ejemplo: dic. por diciembre, Dr. por doctor. Las abreviaturas finalizan con un punto y muchas veces comienzan con mayúscula.

adjetivo (adjective) — una palabra que califica a un sustantivo o pronombre. Los adjetivos pueden describir cuántos, de qué tipo o cuál. En la oración "El hombre delgado cepillaba tres perros con un peine azul", tres, delgado y azul son adjetivos.

adverbio (adverb) — una palabra que modifica o califica a un verbo, adjetivo u otro adverbio. Los adverbios pueden indicar cómo, cuándo y dónde. En inglés, muchos finalizan en –ly, en español, muchos finalizan en –mente.

analogía (analogy) — una comparación entre dos pares de palabras. Por ejemplo, "la manzana es al árbol como la leche a la vaca" es una analogía que compara de dónde provienen dos cosas.

antónimo (antonym) — una palabra que significa lo opuesto a otra palabra. Contento y triste son antónimos.

área (area) — la medida de la superficie de un objeto. Calculamos el área multiplicando el largo por el ancho del objeto. El área se mide en unidades cuadradas. Entonces si el área de la superficie de una mesa mide 4 pies de largo y 3 pies de ancho, tendrá 12 pies cuadrados (3 x 4 = 12).

cambio físico (physical change) — ocurre cuando una sustancia cambia pero no se forma una nueva. Por ejemplo, un cambio físico ocurre cuando el agua se convierte en hielo.

cambio químico (chemical change) — ocurre cuando dos o más sustancias se combinan y forman una nueva sustancia. Por ejemplo, hierro más oxígeno forma óxido.

categorizar (categorize/categorizing) — agrupar ítems basándose en aspectos que tienen en común. Por ejemplo, se puede incluir manzanas, peras y bananas en una categoría que se denomine "Frutas".

circunferencia (circumference) — la distancia alrededor de un círculo. Para encontrar la circunferencia de un círculo se debe multiplicar el diámetro por 3.14.

cociente (quotient) — el resultado de un problema de división.

comillas (" ") (quotation marks) — las comillas se sitúan antes y después de lo que una persona está diciendo y, además, en los títulos de historias, poemas y canciones.

contracción (contraction) — una combinación reducida de dos palabras que incluye un apóstrofe en el lugar dónde se han omitido letras. "Didn't" es una contracción de "did not".

cursiva (cursive) — una forma de escritura en la que las letras están unidas: *esto es letra cursiva*.

diferencia (difference) — la respuesta a un problema de sustracción.

doble negación (double negative) — el uso de dos palabras negativas, como "not" o "no", cuando se necesita solamente una. Por ejemplo: "He did not have no breakfast," debería escribirse "He had no breakfast" o "He did not have any breakfast."

e breve (ĕ) — el sonido e en pet.

e larga (ē) — el sonido e en sleep.

estimar (estimate) — realizar una buena aproximación.

examen de desarrollo (essay test) — un examen en el que deben contestarse las preguntas en oraciones y párrafos.

examen objetivo (objective test) — un examen en dónde se debe responder verdadero o falso, multiple choice, unir, etc., en vez de desarrollar una respuesta.

Glossary

forma estándar / notación estándar (standard form / standard notation) — la forma habitual de escribir un número. 538 ó 6,700 están escritos en notación estándar.

fracción (fraction) — un número que representa parte de un total. 1/2 2/10 y 2/3 son fracciones.

frase preposicional (prepositional phrase) — una preposición y su objeto. En la oración "El gusano está en la manzana", "en la manzana" es la frase preposicional.

grupos consonánticos (blends) — dos consonantes que se juntan para formar un cierto sonido. Pl, br, gr, cl y sp son todos grupos consonánticos.

homófonos (homophones) — ver homónimos.

homónimos (también homófonos) (homonyms or homophones) — palabras que suenan o se escriben igual pero tienen un significado distinto. Por ejemplo: see y sea en inglés, echo y hecho en español.

i breve (ĭ) — el sonido i en pit.

i larga (ī) — el sonido i en ice.

idea principal (main idea) — la idea principal indica de qué trata una historia.

lluvia de ideas (brainstorm) — lanzar ideas.

modismo (idiom) — un dicho de una lengua que significa algo diferente a lo que las palabras realmente dicen. Por ejemplo, "llueven sapos y culebras" significa que está lloviendo muy fuerte, no que están cayendo animales del cielo.

múltiplo (multiple) — un número exactamente divisible por otro número. Por ejemplo: 6, 12, 18, 24, 30 son todos múltiplos de 6.

número negativo (negative number) — un número menor a 0.

número positivo (positive number) — un número mayor a cero.

o breve (ŏ) — el sonido o en pot.

o larga (ō) — el sonido o en boat.

objeto directo (direct objects) — sustantivos o pronombres que completan o reciben la acción del verbo. En la oración "Él tiró la pelota," pelota es el objeto directo.

oración (sentence) — un grupo de palabras que expresa un pensamiento completo. Una oración comienza con mayúscula y, generalmente, finaliza con un punto (.), signo de interrogación (?), o signo de exclamación (!)

oración principal (topic sentence) — una oración que indica la idea principal de un párrafo.

palabra base (o palabra raíz) (base word or root word) — una palabra a la que puede agregársele un prefijo o un sufijo. Por ejemplo, "thank" sería la palabra base en "unthankful" y "gracia" sería la palabra base en "desgraciado".

palabra compuesta (compound word) — una palabra formada por dos palabras más pequeñas como, por ejemplo, "farmhouse" o "lightbulb" en inglés, "portalámpara" o "cubrecama" en español.

palabra raíz (o palabra base) (root word or base word) — una palabra a la que puede agregársele un prefijo o un sufijo. Por ejemplo "thank" sería la palabra base en "unthankful" y "gracia" sería la palabra base en "desgraciado".

perímetro (perimeter) — la distancia alrededor de un objeto, o el largo de todos sus lados. Para obtener el perímetro, se debe sumar el largo de todos los lados.

plural (plural) — más de uno.

polígono (polygon) — una figura cerrada por cuatro líneas rectas.

porcentaje (percent) — una porción de 100. Por ejemplo, 15% significa lo mismo que 15/100 ó 15 de 100.

predicado (predicate) — indica al lector algo sobre el sujeto de una oración.

Glossary

prefijo (prefix) —una sílaba que se agrega al principio de una palabra base para formar una nueva palabra. En la palabra "untie", -un es un prefijo, en la palabra "insatisfecho", -in es un prefijo.

preposición (preposition) — palabras como en, bajo y sobre, que muestran relaciones entre otras palabras. Por ejemplo "El gusano está en la manzana."

producto (product) — el resultado de un problema de multiplicación.

pronombre (pronoun) — una palabra que reemplaza a un sustantivo. Yo, él, ellos, alguien y nosotros son todos pronombres.

pronombre posesivo (possessive pronoun) — un pronombre que muestra posesión. Suyo, nuestro y suyos son pronombres posesivos.

pronombre subjetivo (subject pronoun) — pronombres como yo, tu, él, nosotros y ellos pueden ser el sujeto de una oración.

reagrupar (regroup) — en matemática, se reagrupa cuando se "toma prestado" diez de una columna para usarlo en otra. Por ejemplo, en el problema 22-17 se mueve 1 grupo de 10 de la columna de las decenas a la columna de las unidades, para poder restar 7 a 12. Entonces queda 1 decena en la columna de las decenas y 1 menos 1 es cero.

redondear (round(ing) numbers) — una manera de estimar números para que sea más fácil utilizarlos para resolver un problema. Por ejemplo, podría redondearse el número 9 "para arriba" a 10 o el número 103 "para abajo" a 100 ó 6.72 a 7 para ayudar a realizar rápidamente un estimativo.

schwa — el sonido "uh"

sílaba (syllable) — una combinación de letras que se pronuncian como una unidad y se utilizan para dividir palabras. "Perro" tiene dos sílabas (pe-rro), "camello" tiene tres sílabas (ca-me-llo) y "elefante" tiene cuatro (e-le-fan-te).

sílaba tónica (stressed syllable) — una sílaba que se enfatiza más que las otras cuando se pronuncia una palabra. Por ejemplo, cuando se dice fútbol, se pone un poco más de énfasis en la sílaba "fút" que en "bol". Pruébalo de una manera diferente y escucha como suena.

simplificación (fracciones) (reduce (fractions)) — escribir una fracción en su forma más simple, en la que el divisor común máximo del nominador y el denominador sea 1. Por ejemplo, en la fracción 6/9, tanto 6 como 9 pueden dividirse por 3, lo que da como resultado 2/3. 2 y 3 sólo pueden dividirse por el número 1, por lo tanto 2/3 es la forma más simple de escribir 6/9.

singular — uno.

sinónimo (synonym) — una palabra que significa prácticamente lo mismo que otra. Feliz y contento son sinónimos.

sufijos (suffixes) — una sílaba que se agrega al final de una palabra base para formar una nueva palabra. En la palabra "helpless", "less" es un sufijo, en la palabra "cordialmente", "-mente" es un sufijo.

sujeto (subject) — indica sobre qué o quién es la oración.

suma (sum) — el resultado de un problema de adición.

sustantivo (noun) — una palabra que nombra a una persona, lugar, cosa o idea. Mamá, castillo, tenedor y justicia son sustantivos.

sustantivo común (common noun) — un sustantivo que no es el nombre específico de una persona, lugar o cosa. Bebé, tienda, equipo e independencia son todos sustantivos comunes. Los sustantivos comunes no se escriben con mayúscula, salvo que sean la primera palabra de una oración.

sustantivo posesivo (possessive noun) — un sustantivo que muestra posesión. Por ejemplo, en la frase "the dog's dish", "dog's" es un posesivo porque indica que el plato (dish) pertenece al perro (dog). Para formar un

Glossary

sustantivo singular posesivo se agrega 's — dog's dish. Un sustantivo plural posesivo se forma agregando s' — dogs' dish (lo que significa que el plato es usado por más de un perro).

sustantivo propio (proper noun) — el nombre específico de una persona, lugar o cosa. Por ejemplo, Rob, New York, y Oreo son todos sustantivos propios. Los sustantivos propios siempre comienzan con mayúscula.

término de la preposición (object of a preposition) — el sustantivo o pronombre que sigue a una preposición. En la oración "El gusano está en la manzana", manzana es el término de la preposición en.

transformar a número mixto (fracciones) (renaming fractions) — convertir una fracción con un numerador mayor que su denominador en un número entero y una fracción. Por ejemplo, 10/6 puede transformarse a número mixto como 1 4/6 ó 1 2/3.

transportar (suma / multiplicación) (carry [addition/multiplication]) — como reagrupar, cuando uno transporta, mueve un número de una columna a otra. Por ejemplo, en 15 + 16, se suma 5 +6, lo que da por resultado 11. Piensa en 11 como 10 + 1. Para finalizar el problema se pone el 1 en el lugar de las unidades y luego se "transporta" el 10 a la columna de las decenas, donde ahora figuran 3 decenas, o 30. Por lo tanto, el resultado es 31.

u breve (ŭ) — el sonido "u" en cup.

u larga (ū) — el sonido "u" en blue.

valor relativo (place value) — se refiere al valor de un número basado en su posición dentro de un número mayor. Por ejemplo, en el número 245, el 5 se encuentra en el lugar de las unidades y representa 5 unidades, el 4 ocupa el lugar de las decenas y representa 40 ó 4 decenas y el 2 está ubicado en el lugar de las centenas, representando 200 ó 2 centenas.

verbo (verb) — palabras que muestran una acción o un estado. Saltar, pensar, ir, es y poder son todos verbos.

verbo 'to be' ('to be" verb) — una forma del verbo que significa ser, estar o existir: is, am, are, was, were, be, being, been.

verbo activo (action verb) — una palabra para algo que se realiza. Por ejemplo: correr, gritar o dormir son verbos activos.

verbo irregular (irregular verb) — los verbos regulares muestran que la acción sucedió en el pasado agregando –ed a la palabra base. Para mostrar el tiempo pasado en los verbos irregulares, se debe cambiar la ortografía. Por ejemplo, el tiempo pasado de "run" es "ran", no "runned" y el tiempo pasado de "go" es "went".

verbos auxiliares (helping verb) — verbos que "ayudan" al verbo principal. El verbo principal muestra la acción. En la oración "El puede ir mañana", ir es el verbo principal y puede es el verbo auxiliar.

verbos copulativos (state-of-being verbs) — indican lo que algo o alguien es o hace. Son verbos copulativos: ser, parecer y semejar.

verbos en tiempo pasado (past tense verbs) — palabras que describen acciones que ya sucedieron. Escribió, caminó, olió y miró, son todos verbos en tiempo pasado.

verbos en tiempo presente (present tense verbs) —verbos que ocurren ahora. Escribe, camina y mira son todos verbos en tiempo presente.

vocal sorda (silent vowel) — una vocal como "e" al final de "cake" que no tiene sonido cuando se pronuncia la palabra.

Level Orange — Bridges™

Answer Pages

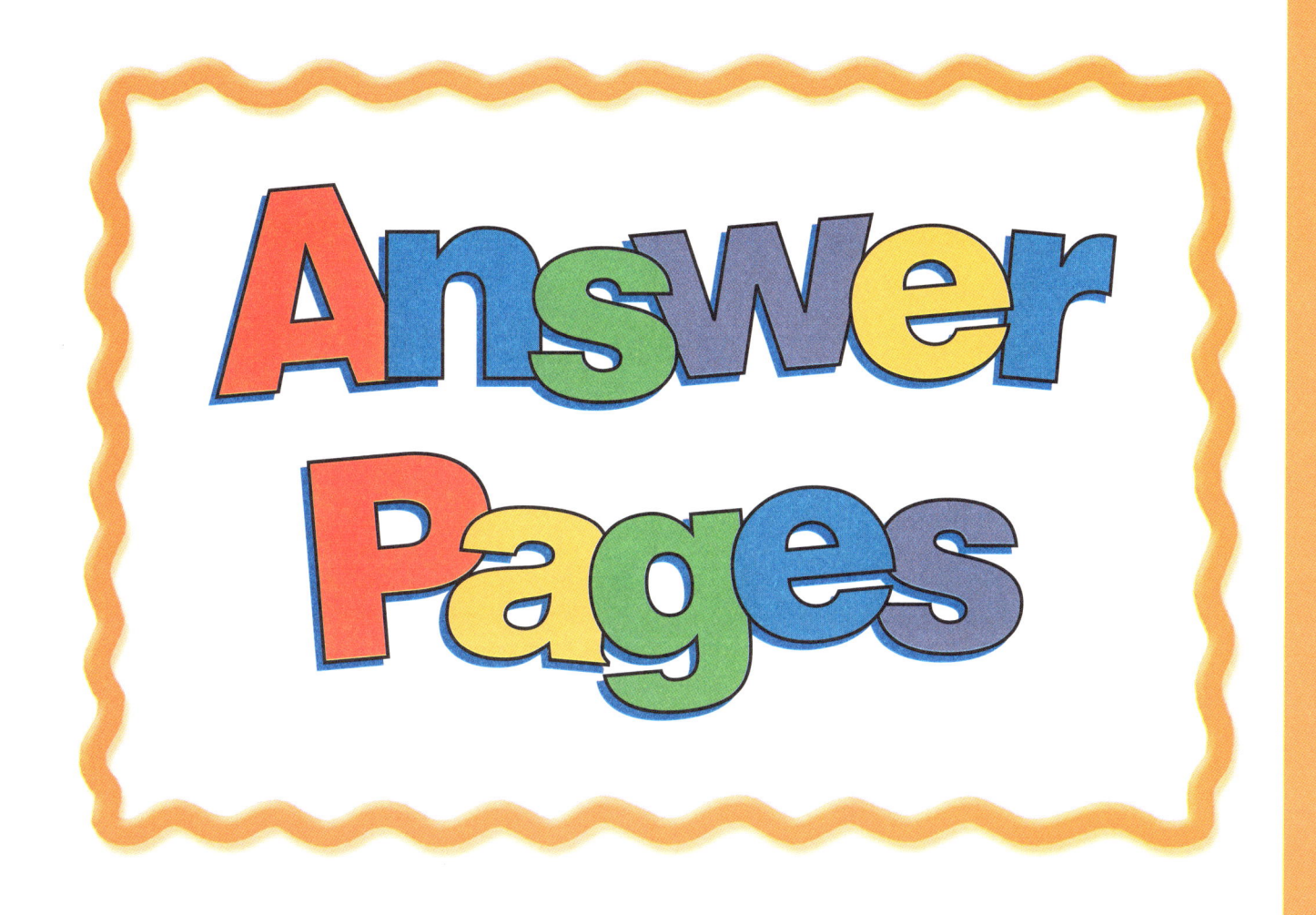

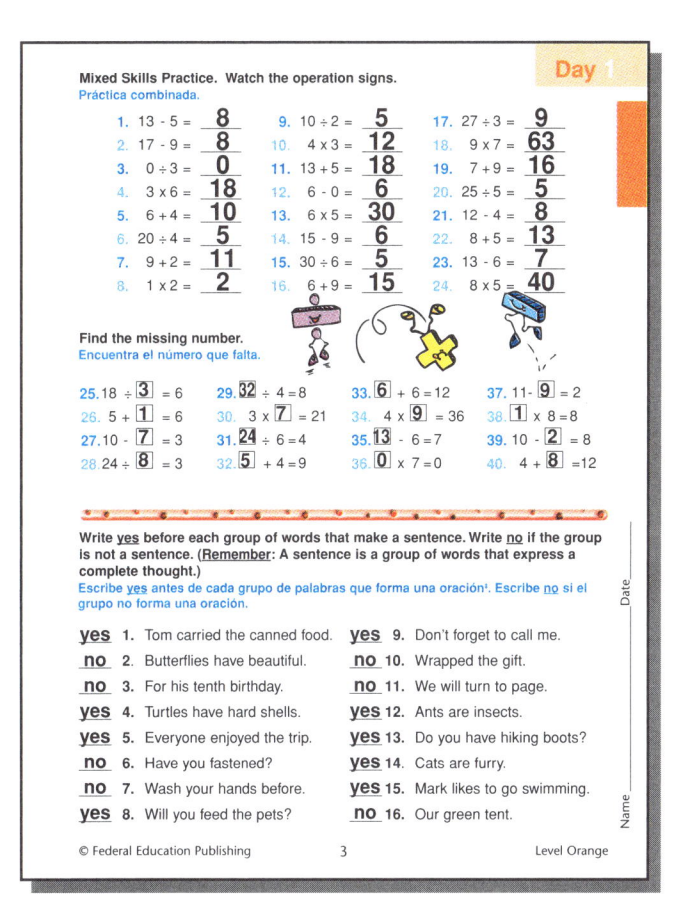

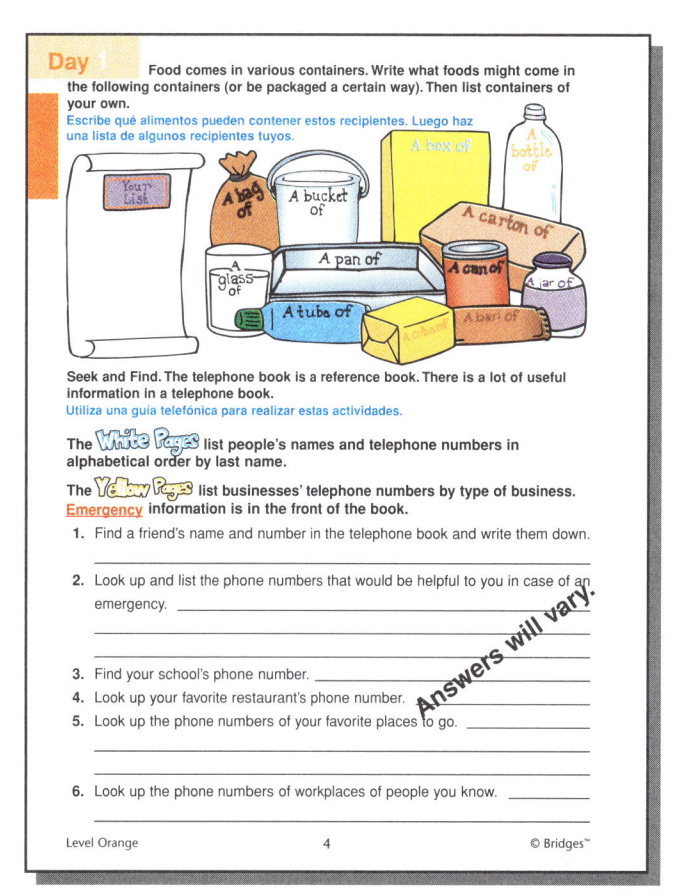

Page 3

Mixed Skills Practice. Watch the operation signs.
Práctica combinada.

1. 13 - 5 = **8**
2. 17 - 9 = **8**
3. 0 ÷ 3 = **0**
4. 3 × 6 = **18**
5. 6 + 4 = **10**
6. 20 ÷ 4 = **5**
7. 9 + 2 = **11**
8. 1 × 2 = **2**
9. 10 ÷ 2 = **5**
10. 4 × 3 = **12**
11. 13 + 5 = **18**
12. 6 - 0 = **6**
13. 6 × 5 = **30**
14. 15 - 9 = **6**
15. 30 ÷ 6 = **5**
16. 6 + 9 = **15**
17. 27 ÷ 3 = **9**
18. 9 × 7 = **63**
19. 7 + 9 = **16**
20. 25 ÷ 5 = **5**
21. 12 - 4 = **8**
22. 8 + 5 = **13**
23. 13 - 6 = **7**
24. 8 × 5 = **40**

Find the missing number.
Encuentra el número que falta.

25. 18 ÷ **3** = 6
26. 5 + **1** = 6
27. 10 - **7** = 3
28. 24 ÷ **8** = 3
29. **32** ÷ 4 = 8
30. 3 × **7** = 21
31. **24** ÷ 6 = 4
32. **5** + 4 = 9
33. **6** + 6 = 12
34. 4 × **9** = 36
35. **13** - 6 = 7
36. **0** × 7 = 0
37. 11 - **9** = 2
38. **1** × 8 = 8
39. 10 - **2** = 8
40. 4 + **8** = 12

Write yes before each group of words that make a sentence. Write no if the group is not a sentence. (Remember: A sentence is a group of words that express a complete thought.)
Escribe yes antes de cada grupo de palabras que forma una oración. Escribe no si el grupo no forma una oración.

- **yes** 1. Tom carried the canned food.
- **no** 2. Butterflies have beautiful.
- **no** 3. For his tenth birthday.
- **yes** 4. Turtles have hard shells.
- **yes** 5. Everyone enjoyed the trip.
- **no** 6. Have you fastened?
- **no** 7. Wash your hands before.
- **yes** 8. Will you feed the pets?
- **yes** 9. Don't forget to call me.
- **no** 10. Wrapped the gift.
- **no** 11. We will turn to page.
- **yes** 12. Ants are insects.
- **yes** 13. Do you have hiking boots?
- **yes** 14. Cats are furry.
- **yes** 15. Mark likes to go swimming.
- **no** 16. Our green tent.

Page 4

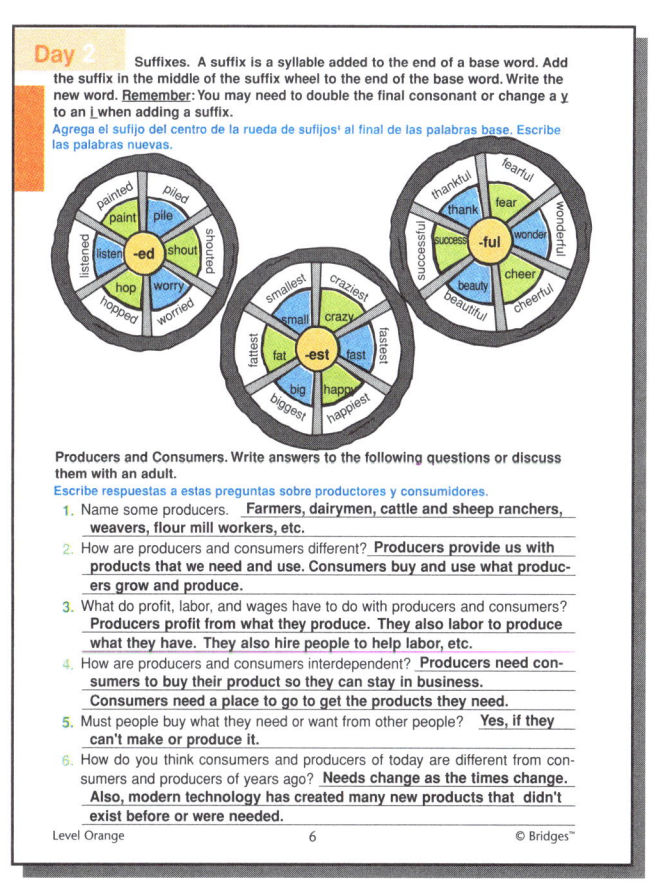

Food comes in various containers. Write what foods might come in the following containers (or be packaged a certain way). Then list containers of your own.
Escribe qué alimentos pueden contener estos recipientes. Luego haz una lista de algunos recipientes tuyos.

Seek and Find. The telephone book is a reference book. There is a lot of useful information in a telephone book.
Utiliza una guía telefónica para realizar estas actividades.

The **White Pages** list people's names and telephone numbers in alphabetical order by last name.
The **Yellow Pages** list businesses' telephone numbers by type of business.
Emergency information is in the front of the book.

1. Find a friend's name and number in the telephone book and write them down.
2. Look up and list the phone numbers that would be helpful to you in case of an emergency.
3. Find your school's phone number.
4. Look up your favorite restaurant's phone number.
5. Look up the phone numbers of your favorite places to go.
6. Look up the phone numbers of workplaces of people you know.

Answers will vary.

Page 5

Add or subtract these 3- or 4-digit numbers.
Suma o resta.

1. 681 + 145 = **826**
2. 569 - 247 = **322**
3. 3,744 - 1,378 = **2,366**
4. 8,171 + 7,445 = **15,616**
5. 1,355 + 1,927 = **3,282**
6. 248 + 48 = **296**
7. 143 + 219 = **362**
8. 2,830 - 519 = **2,311**
9. 9,873 + 828 = **10,701**
10. 5,893 + 3,072 = **8,965**
11. 304 - 172 = **132**
12. 4,918 + 3,928 = **8,846**
13. 6,219 - 4,356 = **1,863**
14. 2,456 + 1,529 = **3,985**
15. 1,375 + 6,518 = **7,893**
16. 428 - 119 = **309**
17. 2,709 + 1,282 = **3,991**
18. 7,645 - 564 = **7,081**
19. 1,680 - 354 = **1,326**
20. 6,142 - 2,525 = **3,617**

Add the correct word—their or there. Remember: their means "they own" or "have," and there means "in or at the place," or it can begin a sentence.
Agrega la palabra correcta: their o there.

1. **There** must be something wrong with that cow.
2. The Hills were training **their** horse to jump.
3. We are going to **their** farm tomorrow.
4. Please put the boxes over **there**.
5. **There** will be sixteen people at the party.
6. Will you please sit here, not **there**?
7. **Their** barn burned down yesterday.
8. They will put **their** animals in Mr. Jack's barn tonight.

Write four sentences about your school. Use their in two of them and there in the other two.
Escribe cuatro oraciones sobre tu escuela. Utiliza their en dos oraciones y there en otras dos.

9. _____
10. _____
11. _____
12. _____

Sentences will vary.

Page 6

Suffixes. A suffix is a syllable added to the end of a base word. Add the suffix in the middle of the suffix wheel to the end of the base word. Write the new word. **Remember:** You may need to double the final consonant or change a y to an i when adding a suffix.
Agrega el sufijo del centro de la rueda de sufijos al final de las palabras base. Escribe las palabras nuevas.

Producers and Consumers. Write answers to the following questions or discuss them with an adult.
Escribe respuestas a estas preguntas sobre productores y consumidores.

1. Name some producers. **Farmers, dairymen, cattle and sheep ranchers, weavers, flour mill workers, etc.**
2. How are producers and consumers different? **Producers provide us with products that we need and use. Consumers buy and use what producers grow and produce.**
3. What do profit, labor, and wages have to do with producers and consumers? **Producers profit from what they produce. They also labor to produce what they have. They also hire people to help labor, etc.**
4. How are producers and consumers interdependent? **Producers need consumers to buy their product so they can stay in business. Consumers need a place to go to get the products they need.**
5. Must people buy what they need or want from other people? **Yes, if they can't make or produce it.**
6. How do you think consumers and producers of today are different from consumers and producers of years ago? **Needs change as the times change. Also, modern technology has created many new products that didn't exist before or were needed.**

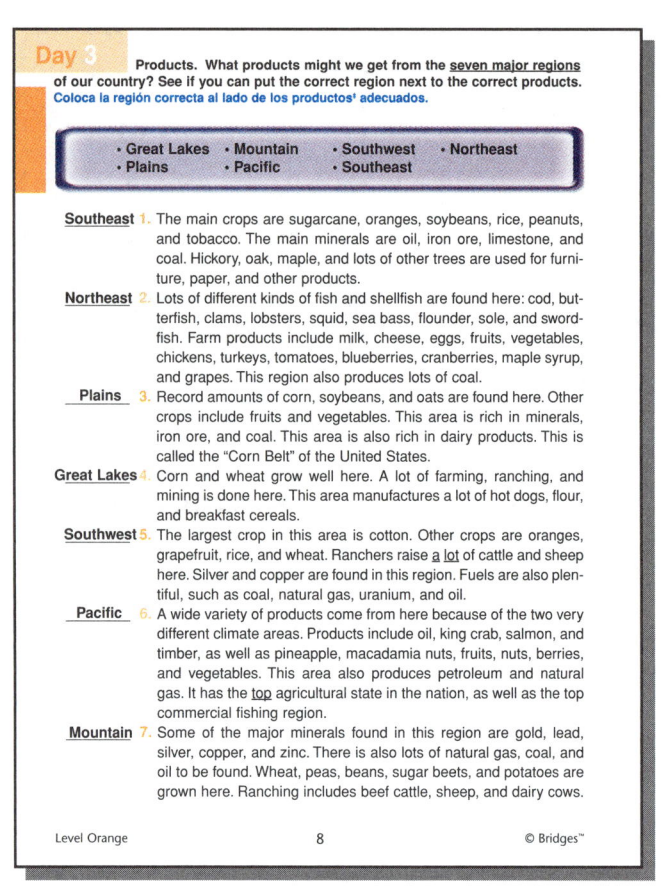

Page 7

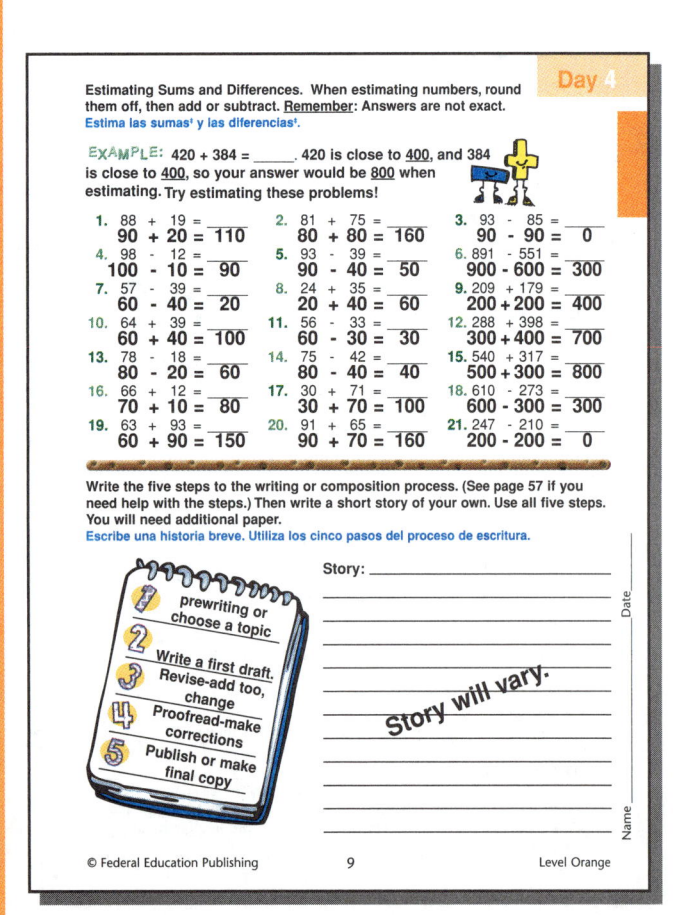

Understanding Thousands. Write each number in standard form.
Escribe cada número en forma estándar.

1. 8 thousands, 3 tens, 9 ones — **8,039**
2. 1 thousand, 7 tens, 5 ones — **1,075**
3. 6,000 + 300 + 10 + 2 — **6,312**
4. 2,000 + 900 + 80 + 9 — **2,989**
5. 3 thousands, 8 hundreds, 4 tens, 1 one — **3,841**
6. 6 thousands, 9 hundreds, 9 tens, 6 ones — **6,996**
7. 5,000 + 700 + 3 — **5,703**
8. 1,000 + 400 + 10 — **1,410**
9. 7 thousands, 1 hundred, 7 ones — **7,107**
10. 0 thousands, 4 hundreds, 7 tens — **470**
11. 9,000 + 900 + 90 + 9 — **9,999**
12. 7,000 + 900 + 5 — **7,905**
13. 2 thousands, 9 hundreds, 6 tens, 2 ones — **2,962**
14. 4 thousands, 5 tens — **4,050**
15. 1,000 + 8 — **1,008**
16. 3,000 + 10 + 5 — **3,015**

Read the following paragraph and answer the questions.
Lee el párrafo y contesta las preguntas.

Kangaroos are furry, hopping mammals that live only in Australia. Antelope kangaroos live on the plains in the north. Gray kangaroos live mostly in the grasslands and forests of eastern and southern Australia. Red kangaroos make their home in the deserts and dry grasslands in the central part of the country, and most wallaroos live in dry, rocky hills.

1. What is the main idea of this paragraph?
   Where kangaroos live in Australia
   Answers may vary.

2. List some of the important details of the paragraph.
   Kangaroos are furry, hopping mammals.
   There are several kinds of kangaroos and they live in different places. (Child could list the kinds of kangaroos and where they are found.)

Page 8

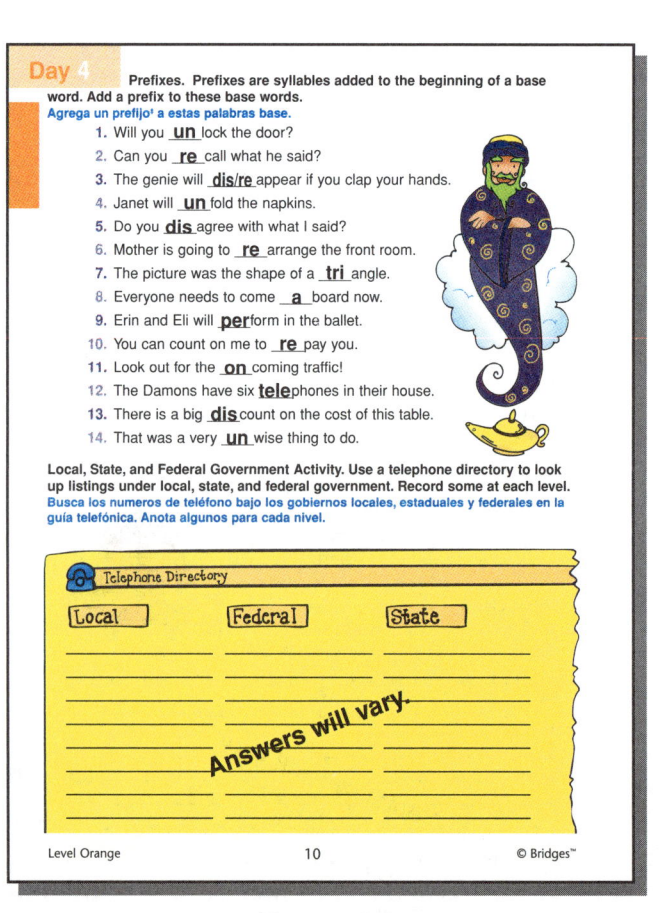

Products. What products might we get from the seven major regions of our country? See if you can put the correct region next to the correct products.
Coloca la región correcta al lado de los productos adecuados.

• Great Lakes • Mountain • Southwest • Northeast
• Plains • Pacific • Southeast

Southeast 1. The main crops are sugarcane, oranges, soybeans, rice, peanuts, and tobacco. The main minerals are oil, iron ore, limestone, and coal. Hickory, oak, maple, and lots of other trees are used for furniture, paper, and other products.

Northeast 2. Lots of different kinds of fish and shellfish are found here: cod, butterfish, clams, lobsters, squid, sea bass, flounder, sole, and swordfish. Farm products include milk, cheese, eggs, fruits, vegetables, chickens, turkeys, tomatoes, blueberries, cranberries, maple syrup, and grapes. This region also produces lots of coal.

Plains 3. Record amounts of corn, soybeans, and oats are found here. Other crops include fruits and vegetables. This area is rich in minerals, iron ore, and coal. This area is also rich in dairy products. This is called the "Corn Belt" of the United States.

Great Lakes 4. Corn and wheat grow well here. A lot of farming, ranching, and mining is done here. This area manufactures a lot of hot dogs, flour, and breakfast cereals.

Southwest 5. The largest crop in this area is cotton. Other crops are oranges, grapefruit, rice, and wheat. Ranchers raise a lot of cattle and sheep here. Silver and copper are found in this region. Fuels are also plentiful, such as coal, natural gas, uranium, and oil.

Pacific 6. A wide variety of products come from here because of the two very different climate areas. Products include oil, king crab, salmon, and timber, as well as pineapple, macadamia nuts, fruits, nuts, berries, and vegetables. This area also produces petroleum and natural gas. It has the top agricultural state in the nation, as well as the top commercial fishing region.

Mountain 7. Some of the major minerals found in this region are gold, lead, silver, copper, and zinc. There is also lots of natural gas, coal, and oil to be found. Wheat, peas, beans, sugar beets, and potatoes are grown here. Ranching includes beef cattle, sheep, and dairy cows.

Page 9

Estimating Sums and Differences. When estimating numbers, round them off, then add or subtract. Remember: Answers are not exact.
Estima las sumas y las diferencias.

EXAMPLE: 420 + 384 = ____. 420 is close to 400, and 384 is close to 400, so your answer would be 800 when estimating. Try estimating these problems!

1. 88 + 19 = ; 90 + 20 = **110**
2. 81 + 75 = ; 80 + 80 = **160**
3. 93 - 85 = ; 90 - 90 = **0**
4. 98 - 12 = ; 100 - 10 = **90**
5. 93 - 39 = ; 90 - 40 = **50**
6. 891 - 551 = ; 900 - 600 = **300**
7. 57 - 39 = ; 60 - 40 = **20**
8. 24 + 35 = ; 20 + 40 = **60**
9. 209 + 179 = ; 200 + 200 = **400**
10. 64 + 39 = ; 60 + 40 = **100**
11. 56 - 33 = ; 60 - 30 = **30**
12. 288 + 398 = ; 300 + 400 = **700**
13. 78 - 18 = ; 80 - 20 = **60**
14. 75 - 42 = ; 80 - 40 = **40**
15. 540 + 317 = ; 500 + 300 = **800**
16. 66 + 12 = ; 70 + 10 = **80**
17. 30 + 71 = ; 30 + 70 = **100**
18. 610 - 273 = ; 600 - 300 = **300**
19. 63 + 93 = ; 60 + 90 = **150**
20. 91 + 65 = ; 90 + 70 = **160**
21. 247 - 210 = ; 200 - 200 = **0**

Write the five steps to the writing or composition process. (See page 57 if you need help with the steps.) Then write a short story of your own. Use all five steps. You will need additional paper.
Escribe una historia breve. Utiliza los cinco pasos del proceso de escritura.

1. prewriting or choose a topic
2. Write a first draft.
3. Revise-add too, change
4. Proofread-make corrections
5. Publish or make final copy

Story: *Story will vary.*

Page 10

Prefixes. Prefixes are syllables added to the beginning of a base word. Add a prefix to these base words.
Agrega un prefijo a estas palabras base.

1. Will you **un** lock the door?
2. Can you **re** call what he said?
3. The genie will **dis/re** appear if you clap your hands.
4. Janet will **un** fold the napkins.
5. Do you **dis** agree with what I said?
6. Mother is going to **re** arrange the front room.
7. The picture was the shape of a **tri** angle.
8. Everyone needs to come **a** board now.
9. Erin and Eli will **per** form in the ballet.
10. You can count on me to **re** pay you.
11. Look out for the **on** coming traffic!
12. The Damons have six **tele** phones in their house.
13. There is a big **dis** count on the cost of this table.
14. That was a very **un** wise thing to do.

Local, State, and Federal Government Activity. Use a telephone directory to look up listings under local, state, and federal government. Record some at each level.
Busca los números de teléfono bajo los gobiernos locales, estaduales y federales en la guía telefónica. Anota algunos para cada nivel.

Telephone Directory

Local	Federal	State

Answers will vary.

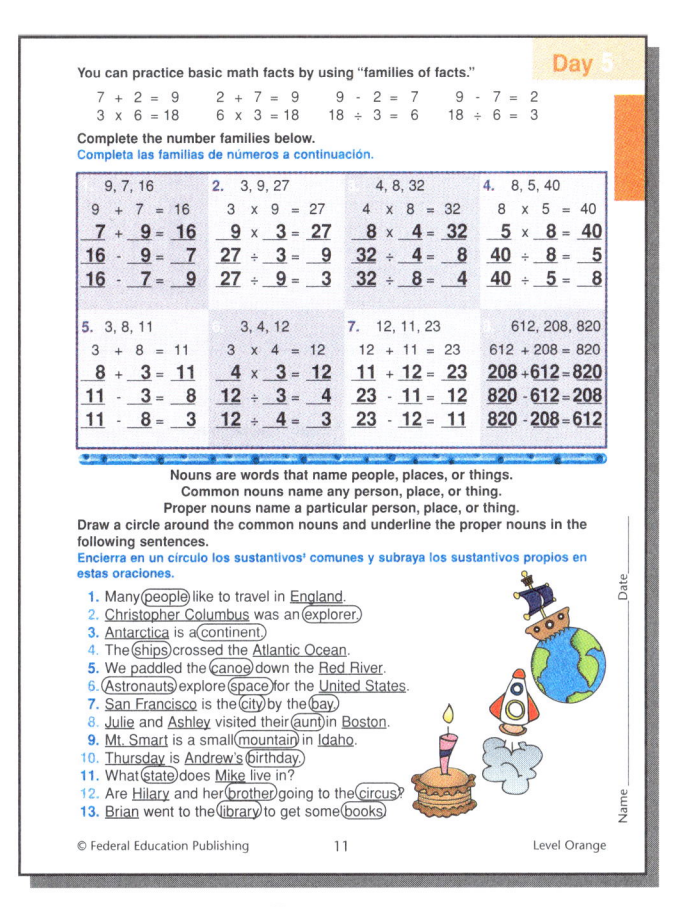

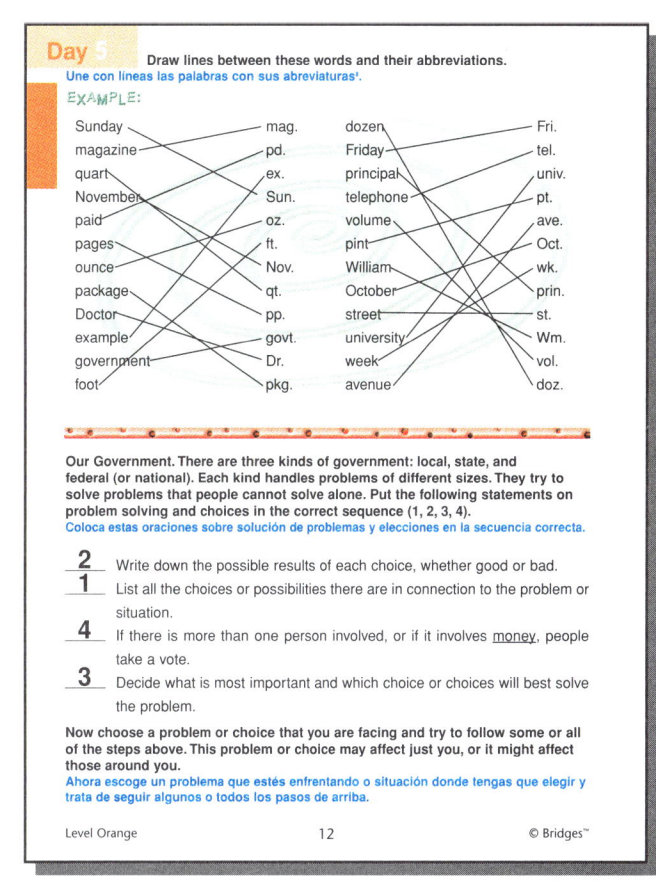

Page 11

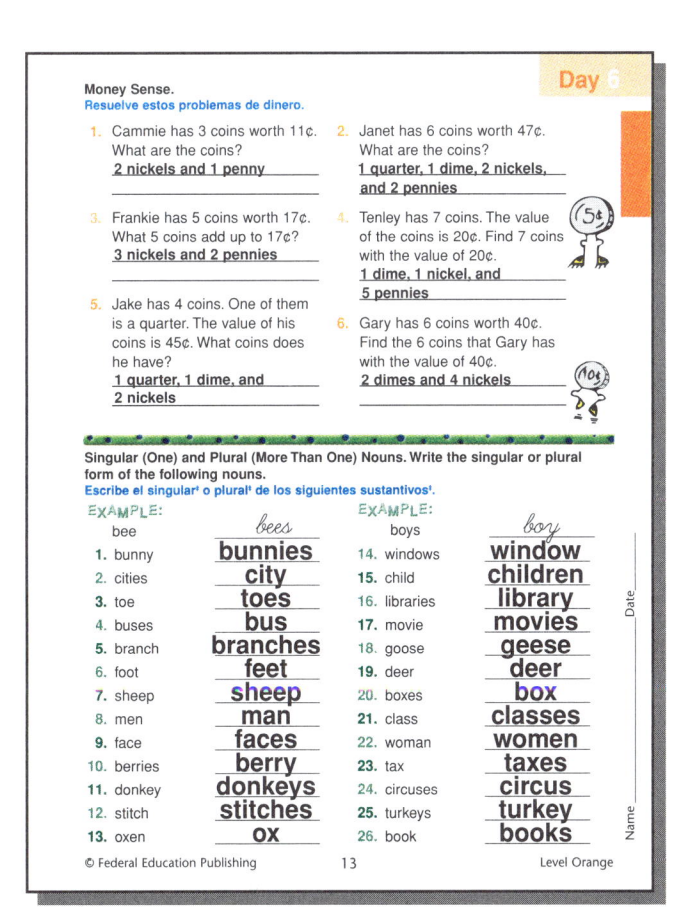

Day 5

You can practice basic math facts by using "families of facts."

7 + 2 = 9   2 + 7 = 9   9 − 2 = 7   9 − 7 = 2
3 × 6 = 18   6 × 3 = 18   18 ÷ 3 = 6   18 ÷ 6 = 3

Complete the number families below.
Completa las familias de números a continuación.

9, 7, 16	2. 3, 9, 27	4, 8, 32	4. 8, 5, 40
9 + 7 = 16	3 × 9 = 27	4 × 8 = 32	8 × 5 = 40
7 + 9 = 16	9 × 3 = 27	8 × 4 = 32	5 × 8 = 40
16 − 9 = 7	27 ÷ 3 = 9	32 ÷ 4 = 8	40 ÷ 8 = 5
16 − 7 = 9	27 ÷ 9 = 3	32 ÷ 8 = 4	40 ÷ 5 = 8
5. 3, 8, 11	3, 4, 12	7. 12, 11, 23	612, 208, 820
3 + 8 = 11	3 × 4 = 12	12 + 11 = 23	612 + 208 = 820
8 + 3 = 11	4 × 3 = 12	11 + 12 = 23	208 + 612 = 820
11 − 3 = 8	12 ÷ 3 = 4	23 − 11 = 12	820 − 612 = 208
11 − 8 = 3	12 ÷ 4 = 3	23 − 12 = 11	820 − 208 = 612

Nouns are words that name people, places, or things.
Common nouns name any person, place, or thing.
Proper nouns name a particular person, place, or thing.

Draw a circle around the common nouns and underline the proper nouns in the following sentences.
Encierra en un círculo los sustantivos comunes y subraya los sustantivos propios en estas oraciones.

1. Many (people) like to travel in England.
2. Christopher Columbus was an (explorer).
3. Antarctica is a (continent).
4. The (ships) crossed the Atlantic Ocean.
5. We paddled the (canoe) down the Red River.
6. (Astronauts) explore (space) for the United States.
7. San Francisco is the (city) by the (bay).
8. Julie and Ashley visited their (aunt) in Boston.
9. Mt. Smart is a small (mountain) in Idaho.
10. Thursday is Andrew's (birthday).
11. What (state) does Mike live in?
12. Are Hilary and her (brother) going to the (circus)?
13. Brian went to the (library) to get some (books).

Page 12

Day 5

Draw lines between these words and their abbreviations.
Une con líneas las palabras con sus abreviaturas.

EXAMPLE:
Sunday — Sun.
magazine — mag.
quart — qt.
November — Nov.
paid — pd.
pages — pp.
ounce — oz.
package — pkg.
Doctor — Dr.
example — ex.
government — govt.
foot — ft.

dozen — doz.
Friday — Fri.
principal — prin.
telephone — tel.
volume — vol.
pint — pt.
William — Wm.
October — Oct.
street — st.
university — univ.
week — wk.
avenue — ave.

Our Government. There are three kinds of government: local, state, and federal (or national). Each kind handles problems of different sizes. They try to solve problems that people cannot solve alone. Put the following statements on problem solving and choices in the correct sequence (1, 2, 3, 4).
Coloca estas oraciones sobre solución de problemas y elecciones en la secuencia correcta.

2 Write down the possible results of each choice, whether good or bad.
1 List all the choices or possibilities there are in connection to the problem or situation.
4 If there is more than one person involved, or if it involves money, people take a vote.
3 Decide what is most important and which choice or choices will best solve the problem.

Now choose a problem or choice that you are facing and try to follow some or all of the steps above. This problem or choice may affect just you, or it might affect those around you.
Ahora escoge un problema que estés enfrentando o situación donde tengas que elegir y trata de seguir algunos o todos los pasos de arriba.

Page 13

Money Sense.
Resuelve estos problemas de dinero.

1. Cammie has 3 coins worth 11¢. What are the coins?
   2 nickels and 1 penny

2. Janet has 6 coins worth 47¢. What are the coins?
   1 quarter, 1 dime, 2 nickels, and 2 pennies

3. Frankie has 5 coins worth 17¢. What 5 coins add up to 17¢?
   3 nickels and 2 pennies

4. Tenley has 7 coins. The value of the coins is 20¢. Find 7 coins with the value of 20¢.
   1 dime, 1 nickel, and 5 pennies

5. Jake has 4 coins. One of them is a quarter. The value of his coins is 45¢. What coins does he have?
   1 quarter, 1 dime, and 2 nickels

6. Gary has 6 coins worth 40¢. Find the 6 coins that Gary has with the value of 40¢.
   2 dimes and 4 nickels

Singular (One) and Plural (More Than One) Nouns. Write the singular or plural form of the following nouns.
Escribe el singular o plural de los siguientes sustantivos.

EXAMPLE: bee — bees
EXAMPLE: boys — boy

1. bunny — **bunnies**
2. cities — **city**
3. toe — **toes**
4. buses — **bus**
5. branch — **branches**
6. foot — **feet**
7. sheep — **sheep**
8. men — **man**
9. face — **faces**
10. berries — **berry**
11. donkey — **donkeys**
12. stitch — **stitches**
13. oxen — **ox**
14. windows — **window**
15. child — **children**
16. libraries — **library**
17. movie — **movies**
18. goose — **geese**
19. deer — **deer**
20. boxes — **box**
21. class — **classes**
22. woman — **women**
23. tax — **taxes**
24. circuses — **circus**
25. turkeys — **turkey**
26. book — **books**

Page 14

Day 6

Which word referent should be used in place of the word or words in parentheses? Write it in the blank. he, she, you, it, they, him, her, them, then, here, us, and there are all word referents.
Usa he, she, you, it, they, him, her, them, then, here, us, o there para reemplazar las

Barbara and Ashley were best friends. (Barbara and Ashley) **They** had decided to go on a trip together this summer. With maps and brochures scattered all over Barbara's floor, (Barbara and Ashley) **they** started looking for a place to go. One brochure described an interesting place. (The brochure) **It** was about Yellowstone Park. "Let's go (Yellowstone) **there**!" cried Ashley. "(Yellowstone) **It** would be a fun place to go. I think we should ask my brother to go with us," said Barbara. " (My brother) **He** could do a lot of the driving for (Barbara and Ashley) **us**."

Tom's car was packed and ready to go the next morning. (The car) **It** was a new 4x4 Ranger. (Barbara, Ashley, and Tom) **They** would have taken Barbara's car, but (Barbara's) **her** car had a flat tire.

After driving for two days the travelers got to Yellowstone Park. Tom shouted, "At last we are (at Yellowstone) **here**!" (Tom) **He** was tired of driving. (The trip) **It** turned out to be a fun trip for (Ashley, Barbara, and Tom) **them**.

Points of Interest.
What makes the state, town, or country that you live in an interesting place? Write an advertisement to get people to visit or even live in your state, town, or country. What are the points of interest? What makes it special and different from other places?
Escribe lo que hace que tu estado, pueblo o país sea un lugar interesante.

Answers will vary.

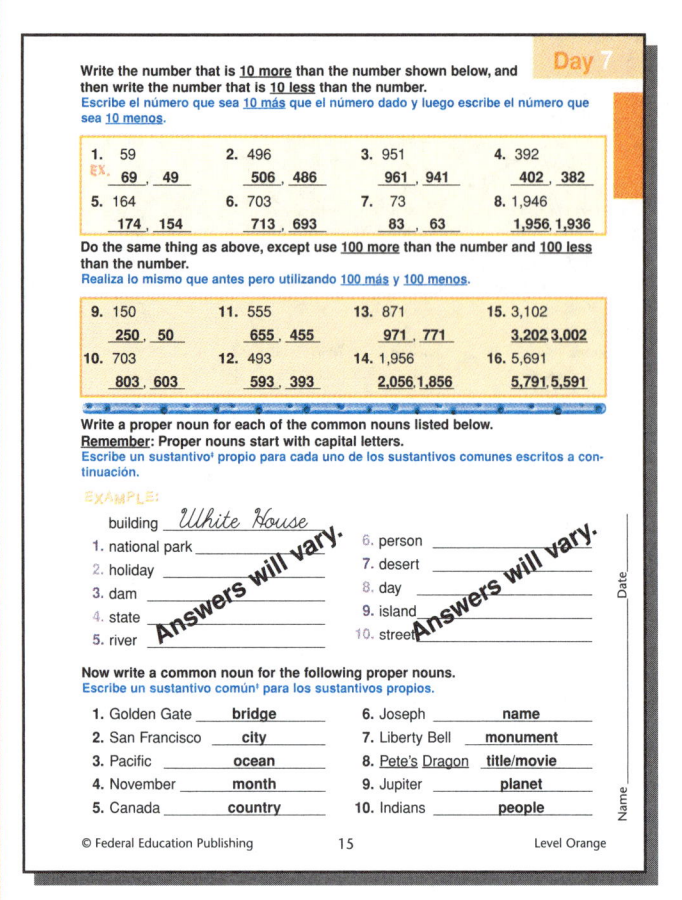

Page 15

Day 7

Write the number that is 10 more than the number shown below, and then write the number that is 10 less than the number.
Escribe el número que sea 10 más que el número dado y luego escribe el número que sea 10 menos.

1. 59 EX. **69** , **49**	2. 496 **506** , **486**	3. 951 **961** , **941**	4. 392 **402** , **382**
5. 164 **174** , **154**	6. 703 **713** , **693**	7. 73 **83** , **63**	8. 1,946 **1,956** , **1,936**

Do the same thing as above, except use 100 more than the number and 100 less than the number.
Realiza lo mismo que antes pero utilizando 100 más y 100 menos.

9. 150 **250** , **50**	11. 555 **655** , **455**	13. 871 **971** , **771**	15. 3,102 **3,202** , **3,002**
10. 703 **803** , **603**	12. 493 **593** , **393**	14. 1,956 **2,056** , **1,856**	16. 5,691 **5,791** , **5,591**

Write a proper noun for each of the common nouns listed below.
Remember: Proper nouns start with capital letters.
Escribe un sustantivo propio para cada uno de los sustantivos comunes escritos a continuación.

EXAMPLE: building **White House**

1. national park _____
2. holiday _____
3. dam _____
4. state _____
5. river _____
6. person _____
7. desert _____
8. day _____
9. island _____
10. street _____

Answers will vary.

Now write a common noun for the following proper nouns.
Escribe un sustantivo común para los sustantivos propios.

1. Golden Gate — **bridge**
2. San Francisco — **city**
3. Pacific — **ocean**
4. November — **month**
5. Canada — **country**
6. Joseph — **name**
7. Liberty Bell — **monument**
8. Pete's Dragon — **title/movie**
9. Jupiter — **planet**
10. Indians — **people**

Page 16

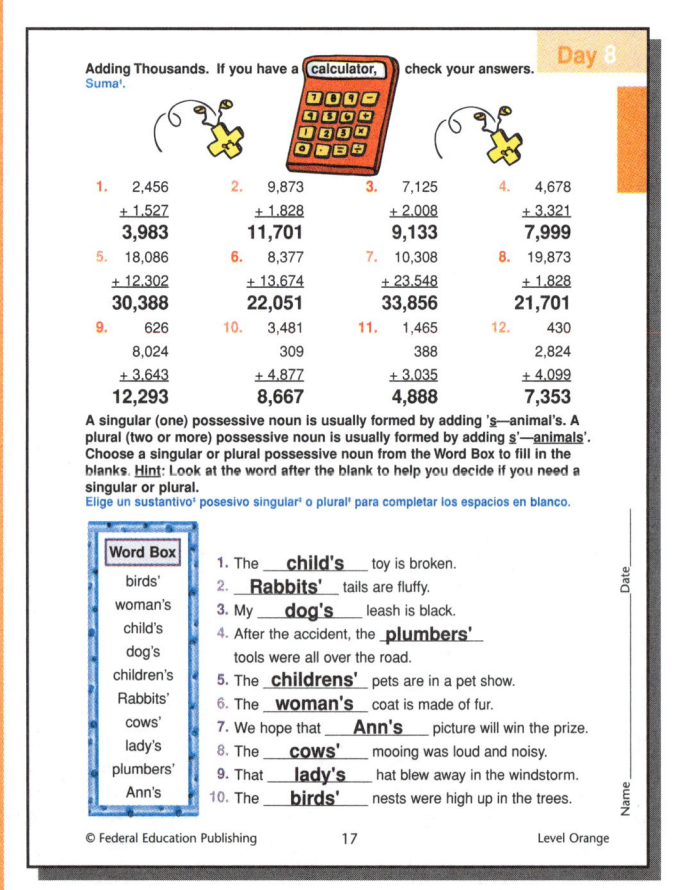

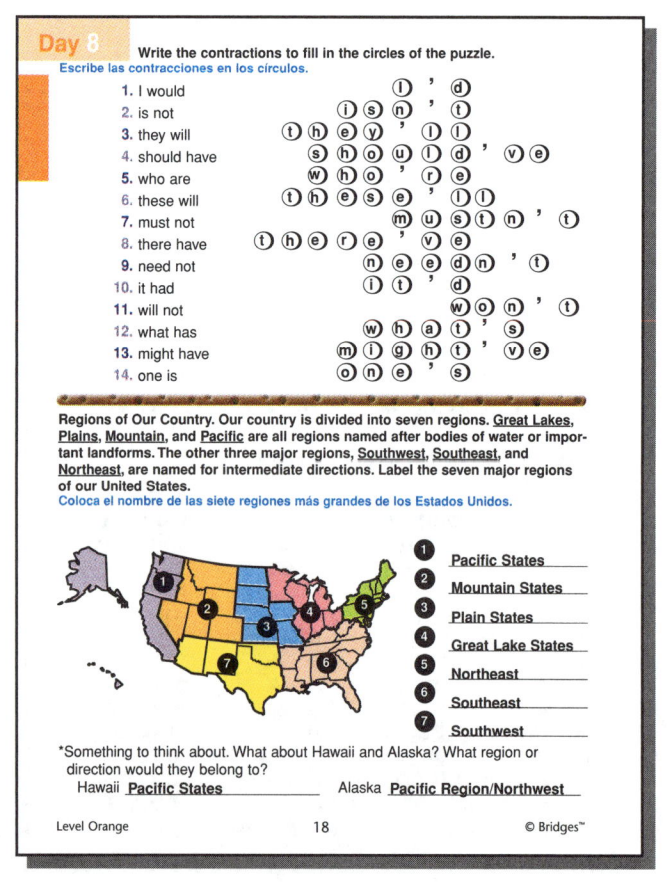

Day 7

Write about fathers; then draw a picture. Fathers should always… Father should never… If I were a father I would want to always…
Escribe sobre tu padre y luego haz un dibujo.

Stories will vary.

Draw your picture here!

Page 17

Day 8

Adding Thousands. If you have a calculator, check your answers.
Suma.

1. 2,456 + 1,527 = **3,983**	2. 9,873 + 1,828 = **11,701**	3. 7,125 + 2,008 = **9,133**	4. 4,678 + 3,321 = **7,999**
5. 18,086 + 12,302 = **30,388**	6. 8,377 + 13,674 = **22,051**	7. 10,308 + 23,548 = **33,856**	8. 19,873 + 1,828 = **21,701**
9. 626 + 8,024 + 3,643 = **12,293**	10. 3,481 + 309 + 4,877 = **8,667**	11. 1,465 + 388 + 3,035 = **4,888**	12. 430 + 2,824 + 4,099 = **7,353**

A singular (one) possessive noun is usually formed by adding 's—animal's. A plural (two or more) possessive noun is usually formed by adding s'—animals'. Choose a singular or plural possessive noun from the Word Box to fill in the blanks. **Hint:** Look at the word after the blank to help you decide if you need a singular or plural.
Elige un sustantivo posesivo singular o plural para completar los espacios en blanco.

Word Box: birds', woman's, child's, dog's, children's, Rabbits', cows', lady's, plumbers', Ann's

1. The **child's** toy is broken.
2. **Rabbits'** tails are fluffy.
3. My **dog's** leash is black.
4. After the accident, the **plumbers'** tools were all over the road.
5. The **childrens'** pets are in a pet show.
6. The **woman's** coat is made of fur.
7. We hope that **Ann's** picture will win the prize.
8. The **cows'** mooing was loud and noisy.
9. That **lady's** hat blew away in the windstorm.
10. The **birds'** nests were high up in the trees.

Page 18

Day 8

Write the contractions to fill in the circles of the puzzle.
Escribe las contracciones en los círculos.

1. I would — **I'd**
2. is not — **isn't**
3. they will — **they'll**
4. should have — **should've**
5. who are — **who're**
6. these will — **these'll**
7. must not — **mustn't**
8. there have — **there've**
9. need not — **needn't**
10. it had — **it'd**
11. will not — **won't**
12. what has — **what's**
13. might have — **might've**
14. one is — **one's**

Regions of Our Country. Our country is divided into seven regions. Great Lakes, Plains, Mountain, and Pacific are all regions named after bodies of water or important landforms. The other three major regions, Southwest, Southeast, and Northeast, are named for intermediate directions. Label the seven major regions of our United States.
Coloca el nombre de las siete regiones más grandes de los Estados Unidos.

1. Pacific States
2. Mountain States
3. Plain States
4. Great Lake States
5. Northeast
6. Southeast
7. Southwest

*Something to think about. What about Hawaii and Alaska? What region or direction would they belong to?
Hawaii **Pacific States**   Alaska **Pacific Region/Northwest**

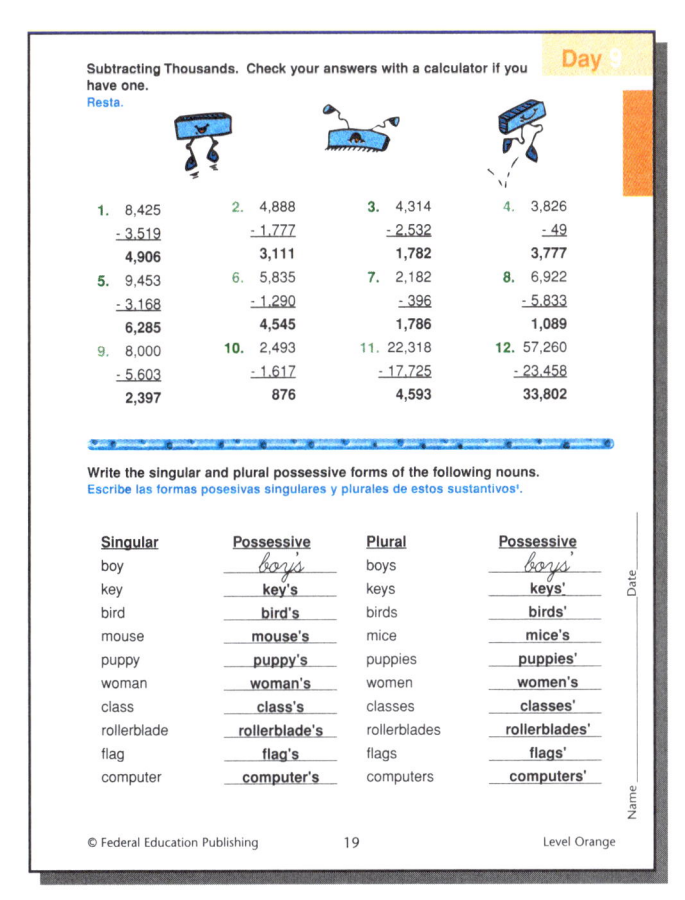

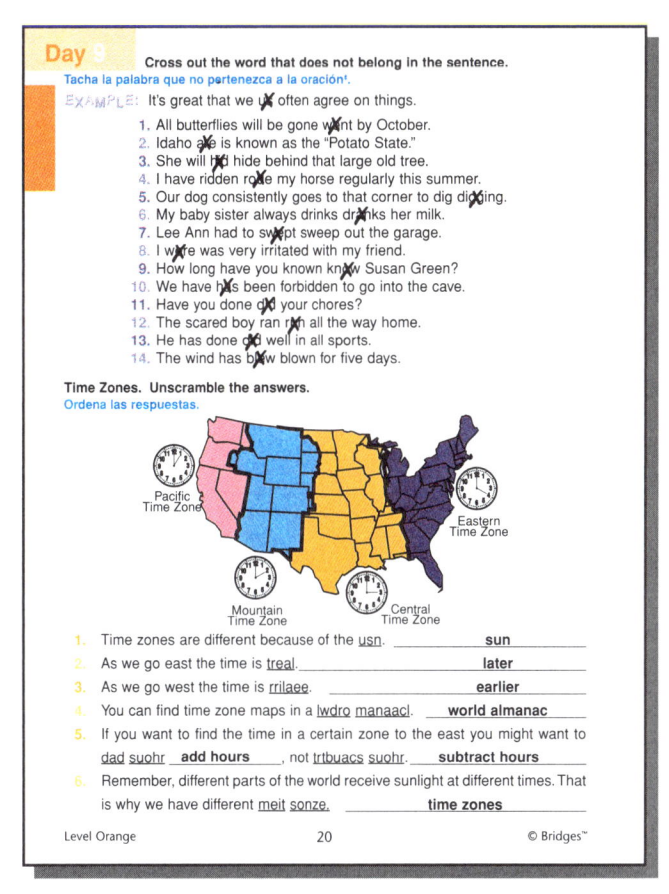

Page 19

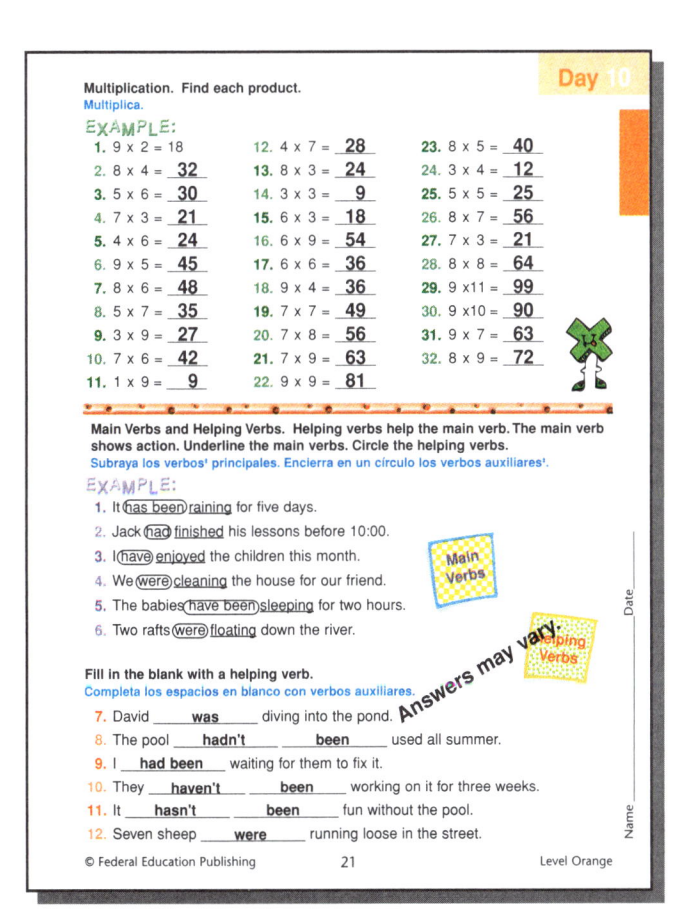

Subtracting Thousands. Check your answers with a calculator if you have one.
Resta.

1.	8,425 - 3,519 **4,906**	2.	4,888 - 1,777 **3,111**	3.	4,314 - 2,532 **1,782**	4.	3,826 - 49 **3,777**
5.	9,453 - 3,168 **6,285**	6.	5,835 - 1,290 **4,545**	7.	2,182 - 396 **1,786**	8.	6,922 - 5,833 **1,089**
9.	8,000 - 5,603 **2,397**	10.	2,493 - 1,617 **876**	11.	22,318 - 17,725 **4,593**	12.	57,260 - 23,458 **33,802**

Write the singular and plural possessive forms of the following nouns.
Escribe las formas posesivas singulares y plurales de estos sustantivos.

Singular	Possessive	Plural	Possessive
boy	boy's	boys	boys'
key	key's	keys	keys'
bird	bird's	birds	birds'
mouse	mouse's	mice	mice's
puppy	puppy's	puppies	puppies'
woman	woman's	women	women's
class	class's	classes	classes'
rollerblade	rollerblade's	rollerblades	rollerblades'
flag	flag's	flags	flags'
computer	computer's	computers	computers'

Page 20

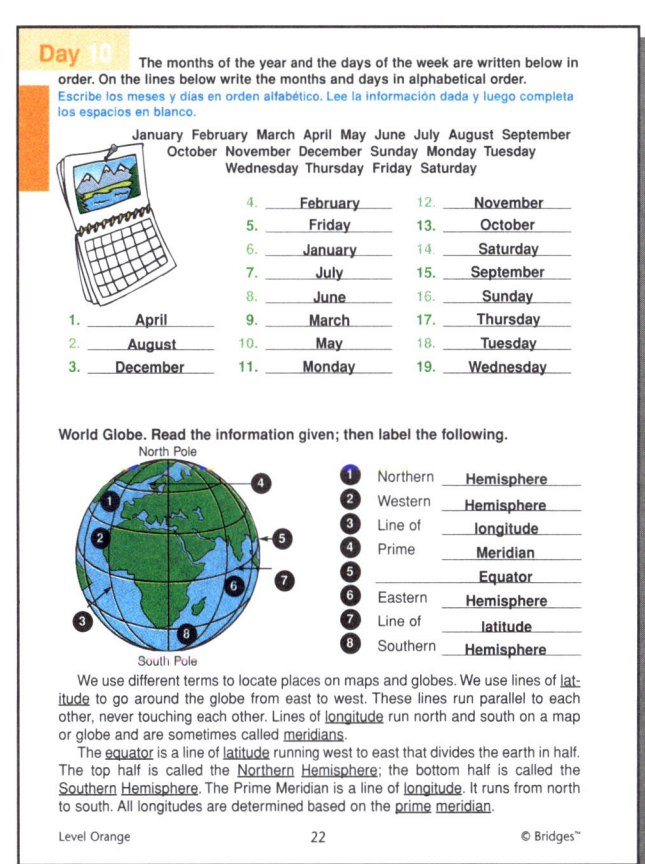

Cross out the word that does not belong in the sentence.
Tacha la palabra que no pertenezca a la oración.
EXAMPLE: It's great that we ~~often~~ agree on things.

1. All butterflies will be gone ~~went~~ by October.
2. Idaho ~~are~~ is known as the "Potato State."
3. She will ~~hid~~ hide behind that large old tree.
4. I have ridden ~~rode~~ my horse regularly this summer.
5. Our dog consistently goes to that corner to dig ~~digging~~.
6. My baby sister always drinks ~~dranks~~ her milk.
7. Lee Ann had to ~~swept~~ sweep out the garage.
8. I ~~wife~~ was very irritated with my friend.
9. How long have you known ~~know~~ Susan Green?
10. We have ~~has~~ been forbidden to go into the cave.
11. Have you done ~~did~~ your chores?
12. The scared boy ran ~~ran~~ all the way home.
13. He has done ~~did~~ well in all sports.
14. The wind has ~~blew~~ blown for five days.

Time Zones. Unscramble the answers.
Ordena las respuestas.

1. Time zones are different because of the usn. **sun**
2. As we go east the time is treal. **later**
3. As we go west the time is rrilaee. **earlier**
4. You can find time zone maps in a lwdro manaacl. **world almanac**
5. If you want to find the time in a certain zone to the east you might want to dad suohr **add hours**, not trtbuacs suohr. **subtract hours**
6. Remember, different parts of the world receive sunlight at different times. That is why we have different meit sonze. **time zones**

Page 21

Multiplication. Find each product.
Multiplica.
EXAMPLE: 1. 9 x 2 = 18

2. 8 x 4 = **32**	12. 4 x 7 = **28**	23. 8 x 5 = **40**
3. 5 x 6 = **30**	13. 8 x 3 = **24**	24. 3 x 4 = **12**
4. 7 x 3 = **21**	14. 3 x 3 = **9**	25. 5 x 5 = **25**
5. 4 x 6 = **24**	15. 6 x 3 = **18**	26. 8 x 7 = **56**
6. 9 x 5 = **45**	16. 6 x 9 = **54**	27. 7 x 3 = **21**
7. 8 x 6 = **48**	17. 6 x 6 = **36**	28. 8 x 8 = **64**
8. 5 x 7 = **35**	18. 9 x 4 = **36**	29. 9 x11 = **99**
9. 3 x 9 = **27**	19. 7 x 7 = **49**	30. 9 x10 = **90**
10. 7 x 6 = **42**	20. 7 x 8 = **56**	31. 9 x 7 = **63**
11. 1 x 9 = **9**	21. 7 x 9 = **63**	32. 8 x 9 = **72**
	22. 9 x 9 = **81**	

Main Verbs and Helping Verbs. Helping verbs help the main verb. The main verb shows action. Underline the main verbs. Circle the helping verbs.
Subraya los verbos principales. Encierra en un círculo los verbos auxiliares.
EXAMPLE:
1. It (has been) raining for five days.
2. Jack (had) finished his lessons before 10:00.
3. I (have) enjoyed the children this month.
4. We (were) cleaning the house for our friend.
5. The babies (have been) sleeping for two hours.
6. Two rafts (were) floating down the river.

Answers may vary.

Fill in the blank with a helping verb.
Completa los espacios en blanco con verbos auxiliares.

7. David **was** diving into the pond.
8. The pool **hadn't been** used all summer.
9. I **had been** waiting for them to fix it.
10. They **haven't been** working on it for three weeks.
11. It **hasn't been** fun without the pool.
12. Seven sheep **were** running loose in the street.

Page 22

The months of the year and the days of the week are written below in order. On the lines below write the months and days in alphabetical order.
Escribe los meses y días en orden alfabético. Lee la información dada y luego completa los espacios en blanco.

January February March April May June July August September October November December Sunday Monday Tuesday Wednesday Thursday Friday Saturday

1. April	4. February	12. November
2. August	5. Friday	13. October
3. December	6. January	14. Saturday
	7. July	15. September
	8. June	16. Sunday
	9. March	17. Thursday
	10. May	18. Tuesday
	11. Monday	19. Wednesday

World Globe. Read the information given; then label the following.

1. Northern **Hemisphere**
2. Western **Hemisphere**
3. Line of **longitude**
4. Prime **Meridian**
5. **Equator**
6. Eastern **Hemisphere**
7. Line of **latitude**
8. Southern **Hemisphere**

We use different terms to locate places on maps and globes. We use lines of latitude to go around the globe from east to west. These lines run parallel to each other, never touching each other. Lines of longitude run north and south on a map or globe and are sometimes called meridians.

The equator is a line of latitude running west to east that divides the earth in half. The top half is called the Northern Hemisphere; the bottom half is called the Southern Hemisphere. The Prime Meridian is a line of longitude. It runs from north to south. All longitudes are determined based on the prime meridian.

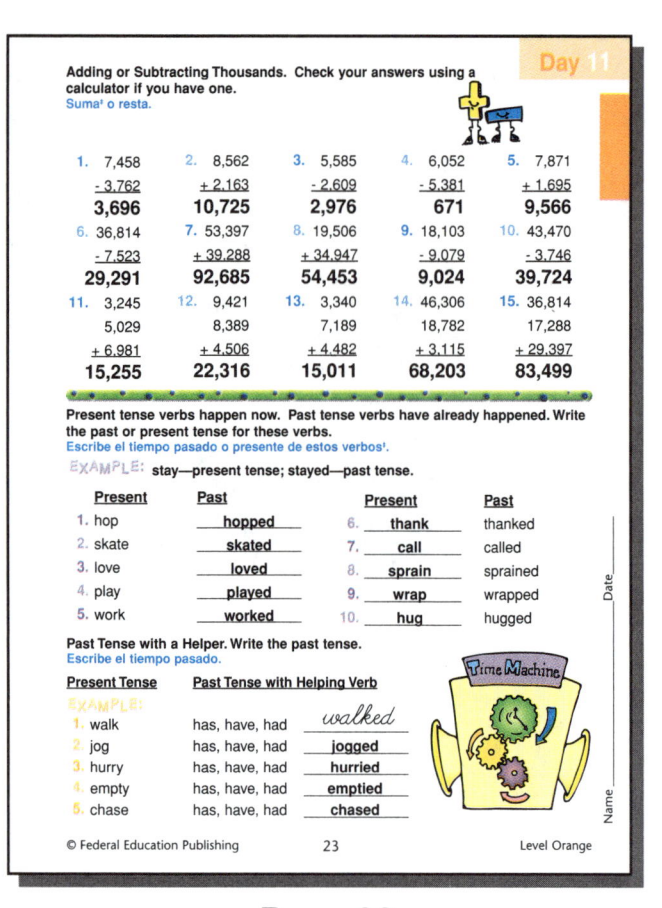

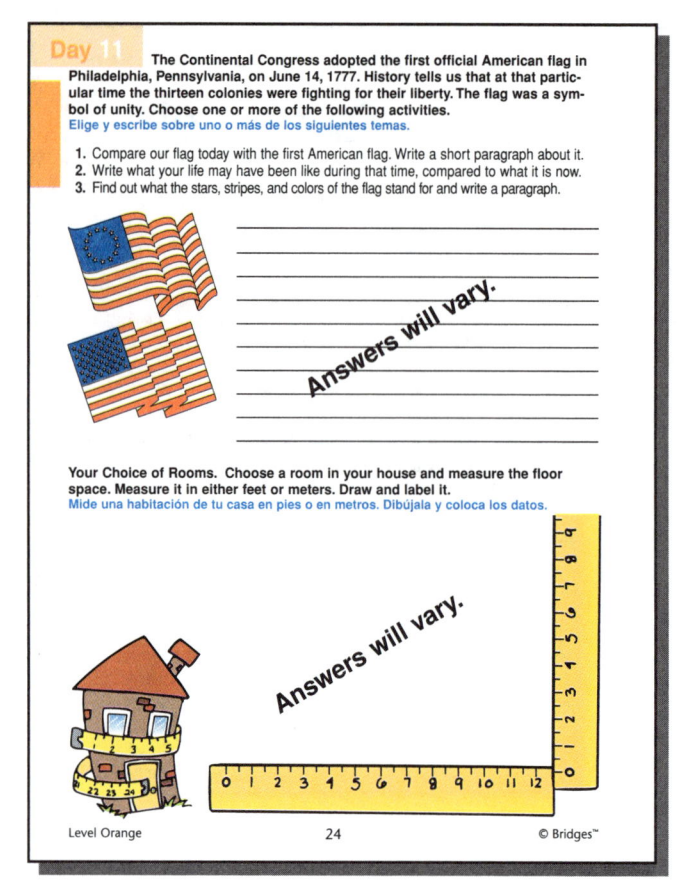

Page 23

Adding or Subtracting Thousands. Check your answers using a calculator if you have one.
Suma¹ o resta.

1. 7,458
  - 3,762
  3,696
	2. 8,562
	  + 2,163
	  10,725
		3. 5,585
		  - 2,609
		  2,976
			4. 6,052
			  - 5,381
			  671
				5. 7,871
				  + 1,695
				  9,566

6. 36,814
  - 7,523
  29,291
	7. 53,397
	  + 39,288
	  92,685
		8. 19,506
		  + 34,947
		  54,453
			9. 18,103
			  - 9,079
			  9,024
				10. 43,470
				  - 3,746
				  39,724

11. 3,245
  5,029
  + 6,981
  15,255
	12. 9,421
	  8,389
	  + 4,506
	  22,316
		13. 3,340
		  7,189
		  + 4,482
		  15,011
			14. 46,306
			  18,782
			  + 3,115
			  68,203
				15. 36,814
				  17,288
				  + 29,397
				  83,499

Present tense verbs happen now. Past tense verbs have already happened. Write the past or present tense for these verbs.
Escribe el tiempo pasado o presente de estos verbos¹.

EXAMPLE: stay—present tense; stayed—past tense.

Present	Past		Present	Past
1. hop	hopped	6.	thank	thanked
2. skate	skated	7.	call	called
3. love	loved	8.	sprain	sprained
4. play	played	9.	wrap	wrapped
5. work	worked	10.	hug	hugged

Past Tense with a Helper. Write the past tense.
Escribe el tiempo pasado.

Present Tense	Past Tense with Helping Verb
EXAMPLE: 1. walk	has, have, had *walked*
2. jog	has, have, had jogged
3. hurry	has, have, had hurried
4. empty	has, have, had emptied
5. chase	has, have, had chased

Page 24

The Continental Congress adopted the first official American flag in Philadelphia, Pennsylvania, on June 14, 1777. History tells us that at that particular time the thirteen colonies were fighting for their liberty. The flag was a symbol of unity. Choose one or more of the following activities.
Elige y escribe sobre uno o más de los siguientes temas.

1. Compare our flag today with the first American flag. Write a short paragraph about it.
2. Write what your life may have been like during that time, compared to what it is now.
3. Find out what the stars, stripes, and colors of the flag stand for and write a paragraph.

Answers will vary.

Your Choice of Rooms. Choose a room in your house and measure the floor space. Measure it in either feet or meters. Draw and label it.
Mide una habitación de tu casa en pies o en metros. Dibújala y coloca los datos.

Answers will vary.

Page 25

Division. Find each quotient.
Divide.

1. 20 ÷ 4 = **5**
2. 28 ÷ 4 = **7**
3. 14 ÷ 7 = **2**
4. 0 ÷ 2 = **0**
5. 42 ÷ 6 = **7**
6. 30 ÷ 5 = **6**
7. 32 ÷ 4 = **8**
8. 25 ÷ 5 = **5**
9. 81 ÷ 9 = **9**
10. 49 ÷ 7 = **7**
11. 18 ÷ 6 = **3**
12. 63 ÷ 7 = **9**
13. 40 ÷ 5 = **8**
14. 36 ÷ 9 = **4**
15. 72 ÷ 9 = **8**
16. 54 ÷ 6 = **9**
17. 48 ÷ 6 = **8**
18. 32 ÷ 8 = **4**
19. 45 ÷ 9 = **5**
20. 36 ÷ 6 = **6**
21. 54 ÷ 9 = **6**
22. 48 ÷ 8 = **6**
23. 63 ÷ 9 = **7**
24. 99 ÷ 9 = **11**

Fill in the blanks with the past tense verb.
Hint: You will have to change the spelling.
Completa los espacios en blanco con los verbos¹ en tiempo pasado.

Past Tense

1. Bells <u>ring</u>. Bells <u>rang</u>.
2. We <u>eat</u>. We <u>ate</u>.
3. I <u>wear</u> it. I <u>wore</u> it.
4. You <u>make</u> some. You <u>made</u> some.
5. They <u>sing</u>. They <u>sang</u>.
6. I <u>throw</u>. I <u>threw</u>.
7. I <u>say</u>. I <u>said</u>.
8. They <u>take</u>. They <u>took</u>.

Fill in the blank with the past tense of the verb.
Completa los espacios en blanco con los verbos en tiempo pasado¹.

9. Sam <u>knew</u> he wanted to stay in touch with Kit. (know)
10. Katie <u>wrote</u> a letter to Ron. (write)
11. He <u>brought</u> his friend with him. (bring)
12. The men <u>began</u> to dig the ditch. (begin)
13. That little girl <u>broke</u> her doll again. (break)
14. I <u>drove</u> her new car to the play. (drive)

Page 26

Replace the word <u>said</u> in these sentences with another word that fits the meaning.
Reemplaza la palabra said en estas oraciones por otra palabra que coincida con el significado.

EXAMPLE:
1. The man (said) <u>yelled</u>, "Get that cat out of here!"
2. Margaret (said) _____, "Please, don't do that."
3. Mother always (said) _____, "A stitch in time saves nine."
4. "This is my country," (said) _____ the man with a tall hat.
5. "Is it time to go home so soon?" (said) _____ Mike.
6. "I don't like vegetables in soups," (said) _____ Dad.
7. "My sore throat still hurts," (said) _____ Nicholas.
8. The weatherman (said) _____ that it will be windy today.
9. The boy with a mouth full of candy (said) _____ he wanted more.
10. I called Megan on the phone, and she (said) _____, "There's no school today."
11. The shopkeeper (said) _____, "Do you want red or orange socks?"
12. Kristine Jones (said) _____ her mother makes the best cookies.

Answers will vary.

According to the encyclopedia, the sun was born about 4,600,000,000 years ago. What else do you know about the sun? Read and then write some interesting facts about the sun. You may want to write about the things you like to do during hot weather when the sun shines.
Lee y luego escribe sobre hechos interesantes acerca del sol.

Answers will vary.

Level Orange   112   Bridges™

Page 27

Multiplication with Three Factors. Find the product of the three factors.
Encuentra el producto de estos tres factores.

EXAMPLE: 6 x 1 x 3 = __18__ — 6 x 1 x 3 = 6 x 1 = 6 x 3 = 18

1. 2 x 4 x 2 = __16__
2. 3 x 3 x 5 = __45__
3. 4 x 2 x 2 = __16__
4. 2 x 5 x 1 = __10__
5. 4 x 2 x 4 = __32__
6. 2 x 3 x 7 = __42__
7. 0 x 9 x 9 = __0__
8. 3 x 2 x 3 = __18__
9. 3 x 3 x 3 = __27__
10. 5 x 2 x 2 = __20__
11. 4 x 2 x 5 = __40__
12. 2 x 3 x 6 = __36__
13. 1 x 2 x 3 = __6__
14. 3 x 3 x 0 = __0__
15. 3 x 5 x 0 = __0__
16. 1 x 3 x 5 = __15__
17. 2 x 3 x 4 = __24__
18. 2 x 2 x 3 = __12__
19. 4 x 3 x 2 = __24__
20. 8 x 1 x 8 = __64__
21. 3 x 3 x 8 = __72__
22. 3 x 5 x 1 = __15__
23. 6 x 3 x 1 = __18__
24. 4 x 1 x 3 = __12__

Write four sentences using the word **are**. Write four sentences using the word **our**.
Escribe cuatro oraciones usando la palabra are y cuatro usando la palabra our.

1. Our house is almost finished.
2. When are you going to live in it?
3. _Sentences will vary._
4.
5.
6.
7.
8.

Now write two sentences using **it's** and **its**.
Remember: **It's** is a contraction of **it is**, and **its** is a possessive pronoun.
Escribe dos oraciones usando it's e its.

1. _Sentences will vary._
2.
3.
4.

Page 28

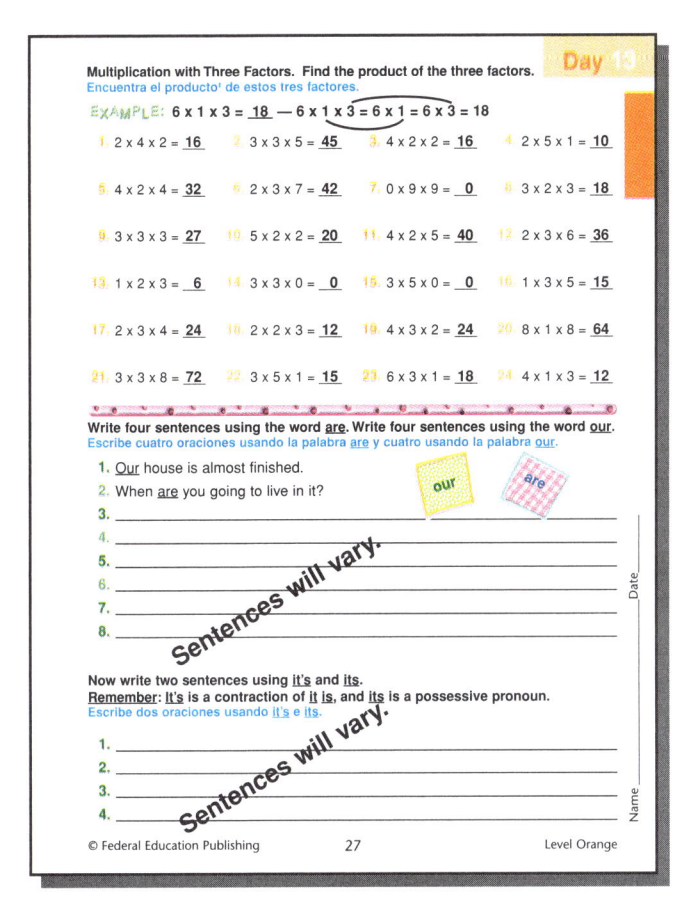

A Trip to Outer Space. We're planning a big trip into outer space! You are invited to come along, too. You can even invite a few friends. What will you pack? Why? Where shall we go? What needs to be done? What do you think will happen? What will it be like? Think, then write!
¡Lee, piensa y luego escribe!

Story will vary.

Page 29

Problem Solving.
Solución de problemas.

1. Jennifer bought a package of candy for $2.50. The tax was 19¢. She used a coupon for 42¢ off the price of the candy. How much did she pay? __$2.27__
2. Elsie worked at a grocery store keeping the shelves full. She worked 4 hours on Wednesday and 5 hours on Friday. She earned $5 an hour. How much did she earn that week? __$45.00__
3. Randy bought a box of cookies for $1.98. He used a 20¢ coupon on "Double Coupon Day." On this particular day, the store took off double the coupon's value. How much did Randy pay for that box of cookies? __$1.58__
4. Bradley bought a shirt for $5 off the original price of $24. The tax was $1.40. How much did Bradley pay? __$20.40__
5. Gayle bought a 6-pack of canned orange juice for $2.89. The store had a special for 74¢ off the original price. The tax was 60¢. How much did Gayle spend? __$2.75__

Match the word to the meaning.
Une la palabra con su significado.

EXAMPLE:
1. honorable — a kind of light
2. current — occupation, source of livelihood
3. knowledge — to make clearly known
4. suspicion — good reputation
5. exact — usual, familiar, common
6. lantern — very large, great
7. profession — leaving no room for error
8. universal — now in progress
9. agriculture — uninhabited region
10. declare — all the people born about the same time
11. wilderness — information, awareness, understanding
12. ordinary — humorous, funny
13. comical — understood by all
14. tremendous — the science and art of farming
15. generation — suspecting or being suspected

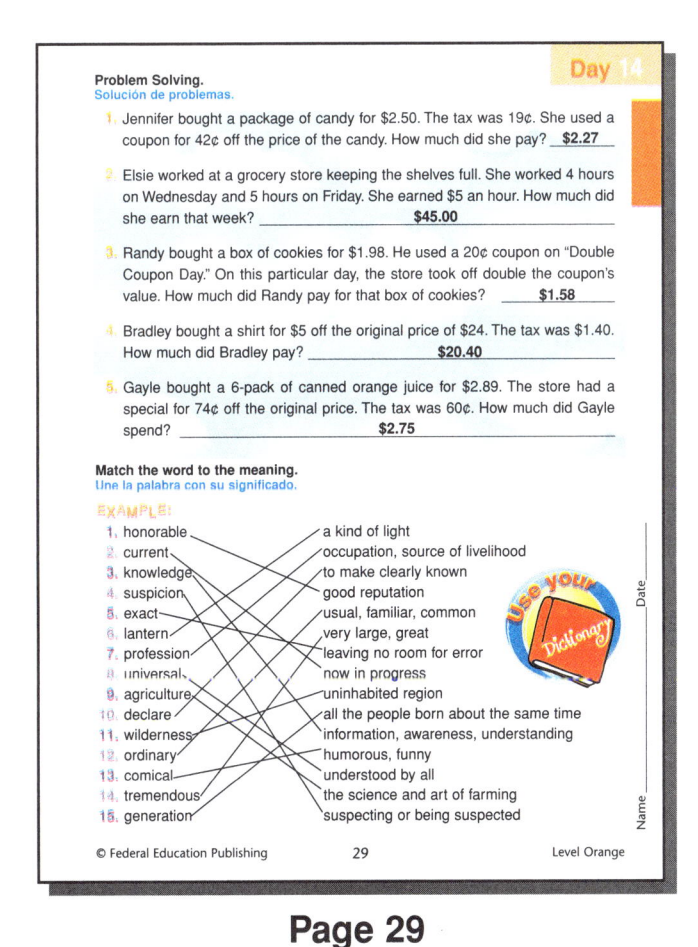

Page 30

Here are some words you should know how to spell. Read the meanings below and write the word by its meaning.
Escribe la palabra en el espacio en blanco al lado del significado correcto.

| gnaw | doubt | knit | gnat | glisten | plain |
| pause | pedal | scene | tow | comfort | admire |

1. make something with long needles out of yarn — __knit__
2. to have high regard for, with wonder and delight — __admire__
3. a lever worked with the foot — __pedal__
4. shine or sparkle — __glisten__
5. to not believe; to feel unsure — __doubt__
6. a short stop or wait — __pause__
7. to pull by a rope or chain — __tow__
8. freedom from hardship; to ease — __comfort__
9. flatland; not fancy — __plain__
10. part of a play; show strong feelings in front of others — __scene__
11. to bite at something or wear away — __gnaw__
12. small fly or insect — __gnat__

Continents. Have you ever really looked at the shapes of the continents on a world map? It almost seems as if the continents are part of a big puzzle. Trace the world map below. Then cut out the following major continents and islands: North and South America, Australia, Europe-Asia, Greenland, and Africa. Try to fit all of the continents together so that no (or very little) space exists between them.
Encuentra un mapa del mundo y luego traza y corta los continentes más grandes y las islas. Intenta armar el mapa.

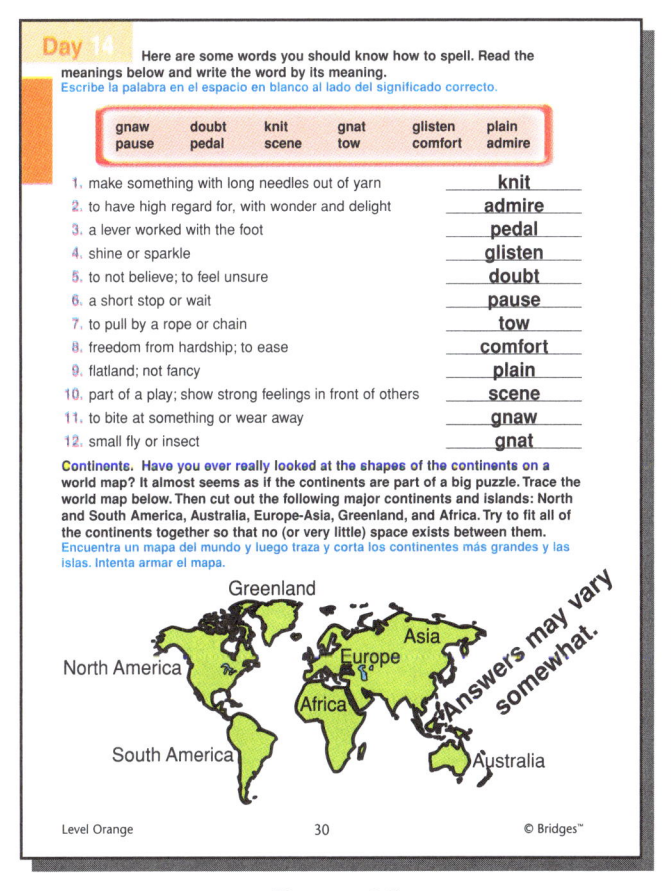

Answers may vary somewhat.

Page 31

Day 15

Divide to find the quotient.
Divide para encotrar el cociente.

1. 4)28 = 7
2. 5)40 = 8
3. 7)49 = 7
4. 6)30 = 5
5. 8)72 = 9
6. 9)45 = 5
7. 8)32 = 4
8. 3)15 = 5
9. 7)56 = 8
10. 6)24 = 4
11. 7)14 = 2
12. 6)54 = 9
13. 9)9 = 1
14. 7)28 = 4
15. 6)42 = 7
16. 8)56 = 7
17. 7)35 = 5
18. 6)48 = 8
19. 9)81 = 9
20. 8)24 = 3
21. 8)40 = 5
22. 9)72 = 8
23. 7)63 = 9
24. 7)42 = 6

You have been out of school for a few weeks now. Write a story telling what you have been doing for the past few weeks. Be sure to follow the five steps of the writing process.
Escribe una historia sobre lo que has hecho las últimas semanas.

Story will vary.

Page 32

Day 15

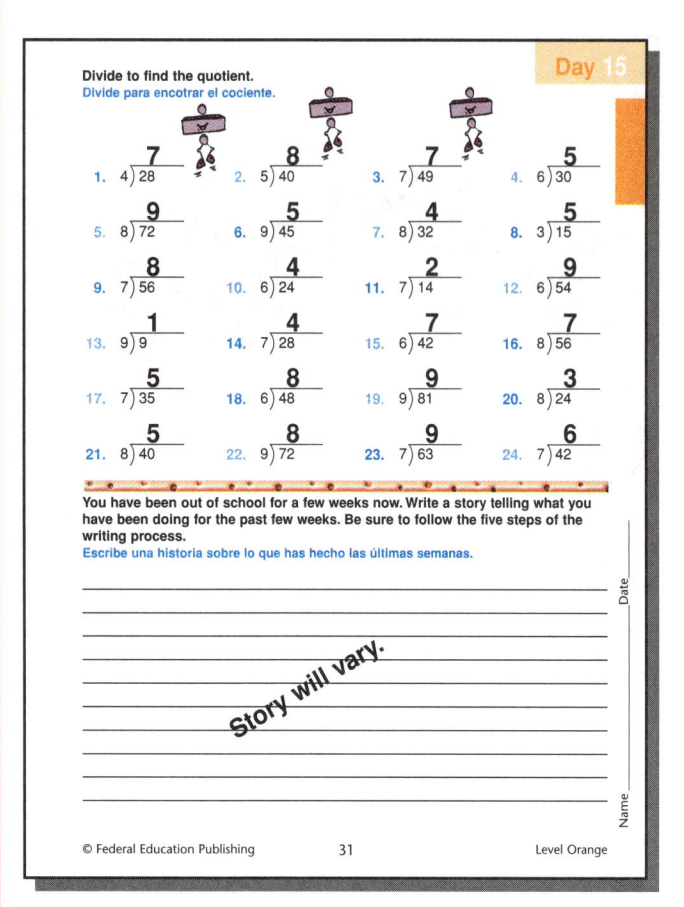

Below are the days of the week and the months of the year spelled with dictionary symbols. Write the words to the side. Don't forget capital letters.
A continuación se encuentran los días y meses escritos en símbolos de diccionario. Escribe las palabras al lado.

1. /ā′prₑl/ — April
2. /jan′ūre′ē/ — January
3. /mun′dā/ — Monday
4. /sep tem′bₑr/ — September
5. /dē sem′bər/ — December
6. /sat′ər dā/ — Saturday
7. /mā/ — May
8. /feb′rüer′ē/ — February
9. /tūz′dā/ — Tuesday
10. /frī′dā/ — Friday
11. /märch/ — March
12. /wenz′dā/ — Wednesday
13. /jūn/ — June
14. /sun′dā/ — Sunday
15. /nō vem′bər/ — November
16. /o′gest/ — August
17. /thərz′dā/ — Thursday
18. /ok tō bər/ — October
19. /jūlī′/ — July

Rocks. Rocks are found almost everywhere. There is much to see and learn about rocks. Geologists are scientists who study rocks. All rocks are made up of one or more minerals. Scientists have discovered over 2,000 minerals. Rocks are changed by water, plants, and other forces of nature. Below are words you need to know when talking about rocks. Look up each word in the dictionary and write down a short definition for it.
Busca en el diccionario estas palabras sobre rocas y escribe una definición breve para cada una.

1. igneous
2. sedimentary
3. metamorphic
4. mineral
5. crystal
6. lava
7. magma
8. anthracite
9. bituminous
10. coal

Answers will vary.

Page 35

Day 1

Write the rest of the number families.
Termina de escribir las familias de números.

1. 6 × 9 = 54 / 9 × 6 = 54 / 54 ÷ 6 = 9 / 54 ÷ 9 = 6
2. 7 × 8 = 56 / 8 × 7 = 56 / 56 ÷ 8 = 7 / 56 ÷ 7 = 8
3. 6 × 7 = 42 / 7 × 6 = 42 / 42 ÷ 6 = 7 / 42 ÷ 7 = 6
4. 63 ÷ 9 = 7 / 63 ÷ 7 = 9 / 7 × 9 = 63 / 9 × 7 = 63
5. 48 ÷ 6 = 8 / 48 ÷ 8 = 6 / 6 × 8 = 48 / 8 × 6 = 48
6. 72 ÷ 8 = 9 / 72 ÷ 9 = 8 / 9 × 8 = 72 / 8 × 9 = 72
7. 6 × 9 = 54 / 9 × 6 = 54 / 54 ÷ 6 = 9 / 54 ÷ 9 = 6
8. 32 ÷ 8 = 4 / 32 ÷ 4 = 8 / 4 × 8 = 32 / 8 × 4 = 32
9. 36 ÷ 4 = 9 / 36 ÷ 9 = 4 / 9 × 4 = 36 / 4 × 9 = 36
10. 9 × 7 = 63 / 7 × 9 = 63 / 63 ÷ 9 = 7 / 63 ÷ 7 = 9
11. 5 × 9 = 45 / 9 × 5 = 45 / 45 ÷ 9 = 5 / 45 ÷ 5 = 9
12. 90 ÷ 9 = 10 / 90 ÷ 10 = 9 / 9 × 10 = 90 / 10 × 9 = 90

Prefixes and suffixes. Remember: Prefixes are added to the beginning of a base word. Suffixes are added to the end of a base word. Add a prefix to these words. Use mis-, un-, and re-. Write the whole word.
Agrega un prefijo a estas palabras. Usa mis-, un- y re-

1. lucky — unlucky
2. spell — misspell
3. build — rebuild
4. judge — misjudge
5. fill — refill
6. able — unable

Add a suffix to these words. Use -er, -less, -ful, and -ed. Write the whole word.
Agrega un sufijo a estas palabras. Utiliza –er, -less y –ed.

7. use — useful, useless
8. care — careful, careless
9. sing — singer
10. spell — spelled, speller
11. hope — hopeless, hopeful, hoped
12. teach — teacher
13. paint — painter, painted
14. report — reporter, reported

Now write two sentences using words of your choice from each of the two word lists above.
Escribe dos oraciones usando palabras de la lista de arriba.

1.
2.

Sentences will vary.

Page 36

Day 1

Opinions. Everyone has an opinion on most things that happen around them. People will listen to your opinion more often if you state clearly and plainly why you feel as you do.

Write your opinion on one of the following topics or choose one of your own to write about.
Escribe tu opinión sobre uno de estos temas o sobre uno que elijas.

1. People should always wear seatbelts.
2. Children should be able to eat anything they want.
3. Schoolchildren should never have homework to do.
4. We should always help other people, whether they are in our country or not.

Answers will vary.

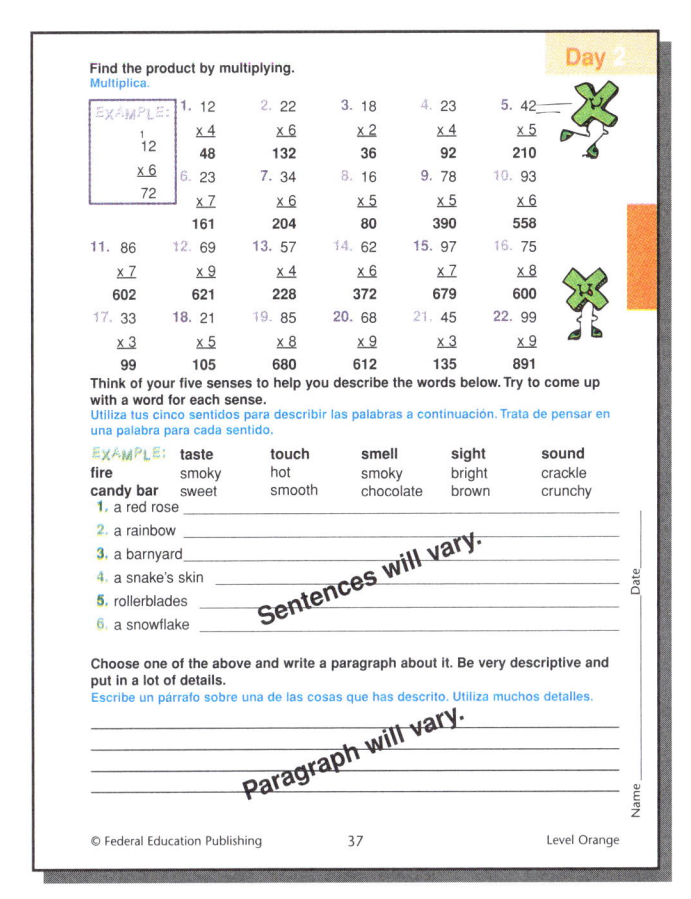

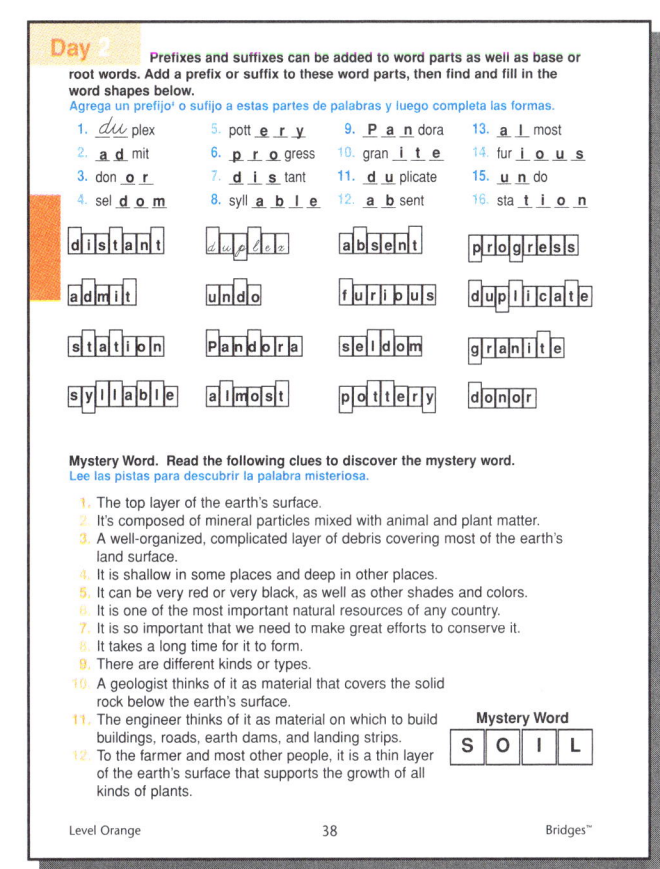

Page 37

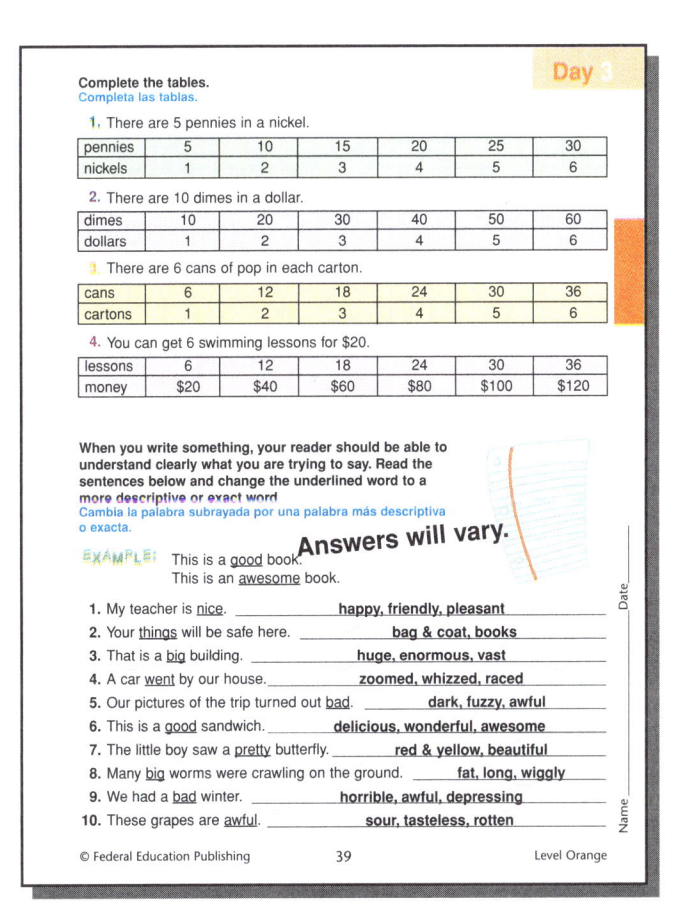

Find the product by multiplying.
Multiplica.

EXAMPLE:
12
x 6
72

1. 12 x 4 = 48	2. 22 x 6 = 132	3. 18 x 2 = 36	4. 23 x 4 = 92	5. 42 x 5 = 210
6. 23 x 7 = 161	7. 34 x 6 = 204	8. 16 x 5 = 80	9. 78 x 5 = 390	10. 93 x 6 = 558
11. 86 x 7 = 602	12. 69 x 9 = 621	13. 57 x 4 = 228	14. 62 x 6 = 372	15. 97 x 7 = 679	16. 75 x 8 = 600
17. 33 x 3 = 99	18. 21 x 5 = 105	19. 85 x 8 = 680	20. 68 x 9 = 612	21. 45 x 3 = 135	22. 99 x 9 = 891

Think of your five senses to help you describe the words below. Try to come up with a word for each sense.
Utiliza tus cinco sentidos para describir las palabras a continuación. Trata de pensar en una palabra para cada sentido.

EXAMPLE:
	taste	touch	smell	sight	sound
fire	smoky	hot	smoky	bright	crackle
candy bar	sweet	smooth	chocolate	brown	crunchy

1. a red rose
2. a rainbow
3. a barnyard
4. a snake's skin
5. rollerblades
6. a snowflake

Sentences will vary.

Choose one of the above and write a paragraph about it. Be very descriptive and put in a lot of details.
Escribe un párrafo sobre una de las cosas que has descrito. Utiliza muchos detalles.

Paragraph will vary.

Page 38

Prefixes and suffixes can be added to word parts as well as base or root words. Add a prefix or suffix to these word parts, then find and fill in the word shapes below.
Agrega un prefijo o sufijo a estas partes de palabras y luego completa las formas.

1. **du** plex
2. **ad** mit
3. don **or**
4. sel **dom**
5. pott **ery**
6. **pro** gress
7. **dis** tant
8. syll **able**
9. **Pan** dora
10. gran **ite**
11. **du** plicate
12. **ab** sent
13. **al** most
14. fur **ious**
15. **un** do
16. sta **tion**

distant, duplex, absent, progress
admit, undo, furious, duplicate
station, Pandora, seldom, granite
syllable, almost, pottery, donor

Mystery Word. Read the following clues to discover the mystery word.
Lee las pistas para descubrir la palabra misteriosa.

1. The top layer of the earth's surface.
2. It's composed of mineral particles mixed with animal and plant matter.
3. A well-organized, complicated layer of debris covering most of the earth's land surface.
4. It is shallow in some places and deep in other places.
5. It can be very red or very black, as well as other shades and colors.
6. It is one of the most important natural resources of any country.
7. It is so important that we need to make great efforts to conserve it.
8. It takes a long time for it to form.
9. There are different kinds or types.
10. A geologist thinks of it as material that covers the solid rock below the earth's surface.
11. The engineer thinks of it as material on which to build buildings, roads, earth dams, and landing strips.
12. To the farmer and most other people, it is a thin layer of the earth's surface that supports the growth of all kinds of plants.

Mystery Word
S O I L

Page 39

Complete the tables.
Completa las tablas.

1. There are 5 pennies in a nickel.

pennies	5	10	15	20	25	30
nickels	1	2	3	4	5	6

2. There are 10 dimes in a dollar.

dimes	10	20	30	40	50	60
dollars	1	2	3	4	5	6

3. There are 6 cans of pop in each carton.

cans	6	12	18	24	30	36
cartons	1	2	3	4	5	6

4. You can get 6 swimming lessons for $20.

lessons	6	12	18	24	30	36
money	$20	$40	$60	$80	$100	$120

When you write something, your reader should be able to understand clearly what you are trying to say. Read the sentences below and change the underlined word to a more descriptive or exact word.
Cambia la palabra subrayada por una palabra más descriptiva o exacta.

Answers will vary.

EXAMPLE: This is a good book.
This is an awesome book.

1. My teacher is nice. — happy, friendly, pleasant
2. Your things will be safe here. — bag & coat, books
3. That is a big building. — huge, enormous, vast
4. A car went by our house. — zoomed, whizzed, raced
5. Our pictures of the trip turned out bad. — dark, fuzzy, awful
6. This is a good sandwich. — delicious, wonderful, awesome
7. The little boy saw a pretty butterfly. — red & yellow, beautiful
8. Many big worms were crawling on the ground. — fat, long, wiggly
9. We had a bad winter. — horrible, awful, depressing
10. These grapes are awful. — sour, tasteless, rotten

Page 40

Most words spelled backwards don't mean anything, but some do. Here are clues for some words that become different words when they are written backwards.
Lee estas pistas de palabras que se convierten en palabras diferentes si se escriben al revés.

1. Spell a word backwards for something you cook in, and you will have a word that means siesta. **pan** & **nap**
2. Spell a word backwards for a name, and you will have something you turn on to get water. **Pat** & **tap**
3. Spell a word backwards for something you catch a fish in, and you will have a number. **net** & **ten**
4. Spell a word backwards for something to carry things in, and you will get a word that tells what you like to do with your friends. **bag** & **gab**
5. Spell a word backwards for something a train needs, and you will get a word for someone who is not honest. **rail** & **liar**
6. Spell a word for "victory" backwards, and you will have a word that means "at once." **won** & **now**
7. Spell a word backwards for something to catch a mouse in, and you will get a word that means something less than whole. **trap** & **part**
8. Spell a word backwards for a tool that cuts wood, and you will get a word that is a verb. **saw** & **was**
9. Spell a word backwards for a flying mammal, and you will get a word that means "a bill or check." **bat** & **tab**
10. Spell a word backwards for the end of your pen, and you will have a word that means a hole in the ground. **tip** & **pit**
11. Spell a word backwards that means something you bathe in, and you will have a word that means "other than." **tub** & **but**
12. Spell a word backwards for "an instrument used in doing work," and you will get a word that means "things taken in a robbery." **tool** & **loot**
13. Spell a word backwards for something that means "to have life," and you will get a word that means "wicked." **live** & **evil**
14. Spell a word backwards for a word that means "a girl," and you will have a word that means "to fall behind." **gal** & **lag**

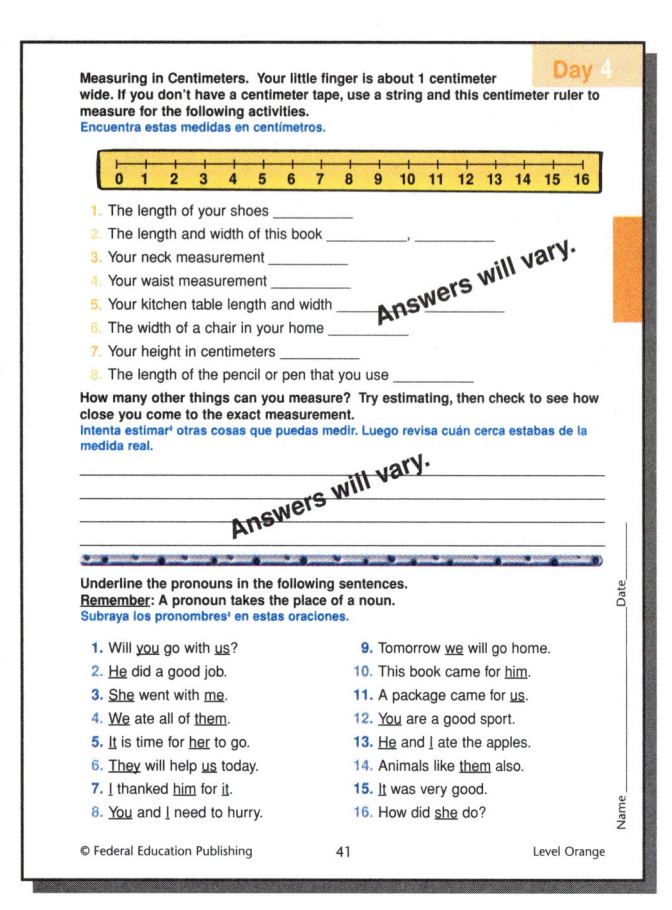

Page 41

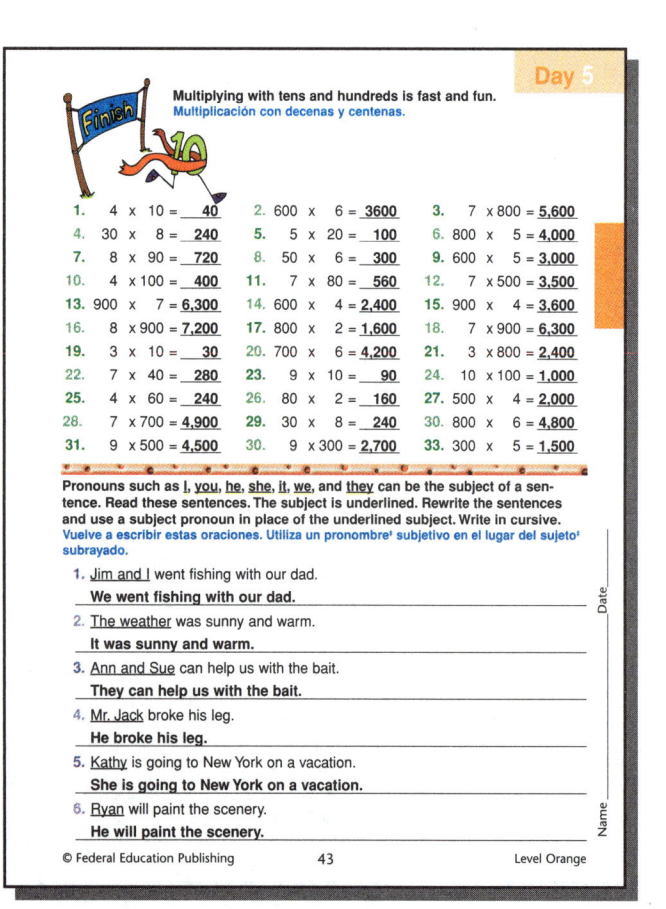

Measuring in Centimeters. Your little finger is about 1 centimeter wide. If you don't have a centimeter tape, use a string and this centimeter ruler to measure for the following activities.
Encuentra estas medidas en centímetros.

1. The length of your shoes _____
2. The length and width of this book _____, _____
3. Your neck measurement _____
4. Your waist measurement _____
5. Your kitchen table length and width _____
6. The width of a chair in your home _____
7. Your height in centimeters _____
8. The length of the pencil or pen that you use _____

Answers will vary.

How many other things can you measure? Try estimating, then check to see how close you come to the exact measurement.
Intenta estimar otras cosas que puedas medir. Luego revisa cuán cerca estabas de la medida real.

Answers will vary.

Underline the pronouns in the following sentences.
Remember: A pronoun takes the place of a noun.
Subraya los pronombres en estas oraciones.

1. Will you go with us?
2. He did a good job.
3. She went with me.
4. We ate all of them.
5. It is time for her to go.
6. They will help us today.
7. I thanked him for it.
8. You and I need to hurry.
9. Tomorrow we will go home.
10. This book came for him.
11. A package came for us.
12. You are a good sport.
13. He and I ate the apples.
14. Animals like them also.
15. It was very good.
16. How did she do?

Page 42

The Fourth of July is our nation's birthday. Another name for it is spelled out in the boxes of the puzzle. Finish the puzzle by writing the appropriate words from the firecrackers. You will not use all of the words.
Finaliza el crucigrama escribiendo las palabras apropiadas de los cohetes en los espacios en blanco.

Firecracker words: nickel, field, either, startle, death, breath, tongue, sandal, medal, worth, sprinkle, stroke, clumsy, ankle, shuffle, whether, guard, partner, plural, mumble, burglar, quarter, prompt, scramble, rather, greedy, daughter, couple

Puzzle answers:
- f**I**eld
- to**N**gue
- **D**eath
- br**E**ath
- s**P**rinkle
- a**N**kle
- me**D**al
- wh**E**ther
- part**N**er
- s**C**ramble
- quarter
- gree**D**y
- s**A**ndal
- clums**Y**

Bugs, Bugs, and More Bugs. The world has so many different kinds of bugs, but there's always room for one more. Create a brand new type of bug. Describe it. Where does it live? What does it do? What does it eat? How does it survive? Who are its friends or enemies?
Crea un nuevo tipo de insecto. Descríbelo.

Story will vary. *Drawing will vary.*

Page 43

Multiplying with tens and hundreds is fast and fun.
Multiplicación con decenas y centenas.

1. 4 × 10 = **40**
2. 600 × 6 = **3600**
3. 7 × 800 = **5,600**
4. 30 × 8 = **240**
5. 5 × 20 = **100**
6. 800 × 5 = **4,000**
7. 8 × 90 = **720**
8. 50 × 6 = **300**
9. 600 × 5 = **3,000**
10. 4 × 100 = **400**
11. 7 × 80 = **560**
12. 7 × 500 = **3,500**
13. 900 × 7 = **6,300**
14. 600 × 4 = **2,400**
15. 900 × 4 = **3,600**
16. 8 × 900 = **7,200**
17. 800 × 2 = **1,600**
18. 7 × 900 = **6,300**
19. 3 × 10 = **30**
20. 700 × 6 = **4,200**
21. 3 × 800 = **2,400**
22. 7 × 40 = **280**
23. 9 × 10 = **90**
24. 10 × 100 = **1,000**
25. 4 × 60 = **240**
26. 80 × 2 = **160**
27. 500 × 4 = **2,000**
28. 7 × 700 = **4,900**
29. 30 × 8 = **240**
30. 800 × 6 = **4,800**
31. 9 × 500 = **4,500**
30. 9 × 300 = **2,700**
33. 300 × 5 = **1,500**

Pronouns such as I, you, he, she, it, we, and they can be the subject of a sentence. Read these sentences. The subject is underlined. Rewrite the sentences and use a subject pronoun in place of the underlined subject. Write in cursive.
Vuelve a escribir estas oraciones. Utiliza un pronombre subjetivo en el lugar del sujeto subrayado.

1. Jim and I went fishing with our dad.
   We went fishing with our dad.
2. The weather was sunny and warm.
   It was sunny and warm.
3. Ann and Sue can help us with the bait.
   They can help us with the bait.
4. Mr. Jack broke his leg.
   He broke his leg.
5. Kathy is going to New York on a vacation.
   She is going to New York on a vacation.
6. Ryan will paint the scenery.
   He will paint the scenery.

Page 44

Categorize these words under one of the headings.
Hint: There can be eight words under each heading.
Remember: Categorizing words means to put them in groups that have something in common. One row of examples is given.
Categoriza estas palabras bajo uno de los encabezados.

Word list: interstate, add, region, colony, oxygen, solid, bacteria, city, hemisphere, stop, column, inch, debate, larva, yield, basin, hexagon, canal, environment, speed, equal, fossil, candidate, intersection, measure, insect, bay, caution, map, estimate, numerator, freedom, society, elevation, freeway, railroad, patriot, habitat, civilization, mineral, detour, quotient

Math Words	Geography Words	Transportation Words	Science Words	Social Studies Words
add	*region*	*interstate*	*bacteria*	*colony*
hexagon	hemisphere	caution	larva	debate
measure	bay	detour	insect	freedom
inch	map	intersection	solid	candidate
equal	basin	stop	oxygen	patriot
numerator	canal	speed	habitat	city
column	environment	yield	fossil	society
estimate	elevation	freeway	mineral	civilization

What about These Animals in Our Country? Buffalo, condors, and grizzly bears have all but disappeared from our country. The symbol of our country, the bald eagle, is very rare in most states. Bald eagles and bears live in mountainous regions. Prairie dogs and antelope live on the plains. Alligators live in marshy areas. Rattlesnakes live in the desert. Wild turkeys can be found in wilderness areas. These are all animals found in our country. There are also many others. Choose one of the following to do on a separate piece of paper.
Elige una de estas actividades para hacer en papel aparte.

1. Choose and draw a picture of an animal from our country. Place it in the correct habitat. Color it accurately. What other interesting animals do you think might belong in this area? Draw them. What other important information does your picture show?
2. If you choose not to draw a picture about an animal, write a paragraph about one. Use the same type of information that the picture would portray.

What animal(s) did you choose? _____

Answers will vary.

Page 45

Addition and multiplication are related. Answer the addition problems and then write the related multiplication problem.
Resuelve los problemas de adición y luego escribe problemas de multiplicación relacionados.

EXAMPLE: 10 + 10 + 10 + 10 + 10 = 50 or 5 × 10 = 50

1. 20 + 20 + 20 = __60__   __3__ × __20__ = __60__
2. 9 + 9 + 9 + 9 + 9 + 9 = __54__   __6__ × __9__ = __54__
3. 100 + 100 + 100 + 100 = __400__   __4__ × __100__ = __400__
4. 8 + 8 + 8 + 8 + 8 + 8 + 8 + 8 = __64__   __8__ × __8__ = __64__
5. 12 + 12 + 12 + 12 = __48__   __4__ × __12__ = __48__
6. 75 + 75 + 75 = __225__   __3__ × __75__ = __225__
7. 35 + 35 + 35 + 35 + 35 + 35 = __210__   __6__ × __35__ = __210__
8. 51 + 51 + 51 + 51 + 51 = __255__   __5__ × __51__ = __255__

Use the pronouns me, her, him, it, us, you, and them after action verbs. Use I and me after the other nouns or pronouns. Circle the correct pronoun in each sentence.
Encierra en un círculo el pronombre correcto para cada oración.

1. Lily and (**I**, me) like to visit museums.
2. (**They**, Them) were very juicy oranges.
3. He helped her and (I, **me**).
4. (**We**, Us) tried not to fall as much this time.
5. Miss Green gave a shovel and bucket to (he, **him**).
6. (**I**, Me) wanted a new horse for Christmas.
7. Rick asked (she, **her**) to come with us.
8. Jason went with (they, **them**) to the mountain.
9. Mother asked (I, **me**) to fix the dinner.
10. Carla got some forks for (we, **us**).
11. Please, teach that trick to Lisa and (I, **me**).
12. She and (**I**, me) swam all day.

Page 46

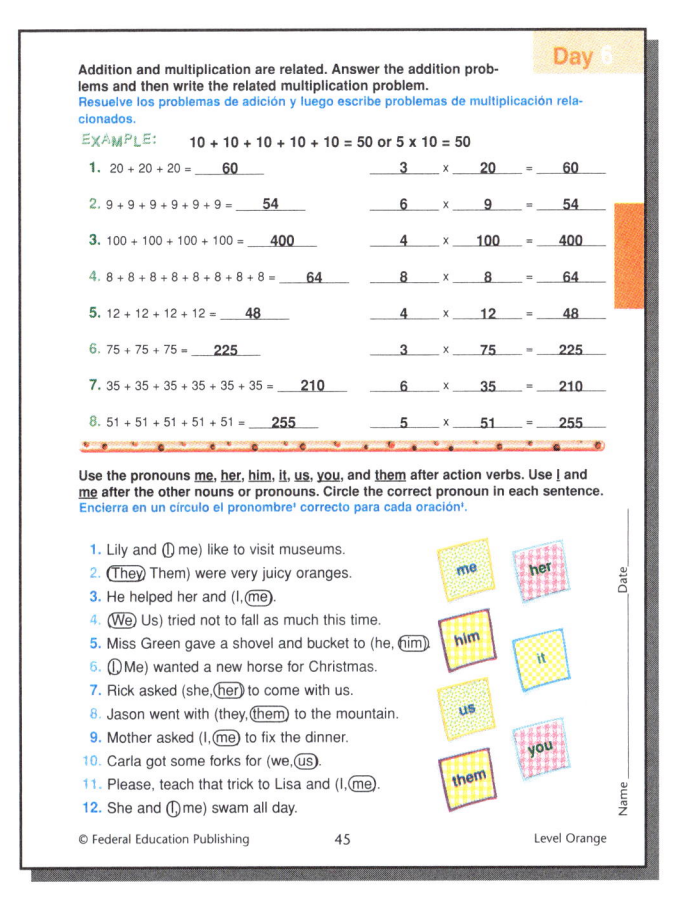

Study this table about trees, and use it to answer the questions below. Can you identify the trees around you?
Utiliza esta tabla sobre árboles para contestar las preguntas a continuación.

Tree	Bark	Wood	Leaves
Elm	brown and rough	strong	oval-shaped, saw-toothed edges, sharp points
Birch	creamy white, peels off in layers	elastic, won't break easily	heart-shaped or triangular with pointed tips
Oak	dark gray, thick, rough, deeply furrowed	hard, fine-grained	round, finger-shaped lobes
Willow	rough and broken	brown, soft, light	long, narrow, curved at tips
Maple	rough gray	strong	grow in pairs and are shaped like your open hand
Hickory	loose, peels off	white, hard	shaped like spearheads
Christmas Holly	ash colored	hard and fine-grained	glossy, sharp-pointed

1. Which tree has heart-shaped leaves? __Birch__
Hand-shaped? __Maple__
2. How many trees have hard wood? __three__
3. Which trees have sharp-pointed leaves? __Elm, Birch, Christmas Holly__
4. Which tree has wood like a rubber band? __Birch__
5. How many different colors of bark does the table show? __four__
Name them __gray, white, ash, brown__
6. Which tree do you think we get syrup from? __Maple__
7. Which tree bark do you think Indians used to cover their canoes? __Birch__
8. Which wood do you think is best for making furniture? __Willow (wicker furniture)__, __Oak__, and __Maple__
9. Why do you think the holly tree is called Christmas Holly? __Answers will vary.__
10. Look around your yard and neighborhood. Can you identify any of the trees from the table? If so, which ones? __Answers will vary.__

Page 47

Complete this multiplication table.
Completa esta tabla de multiplicación.

×	10	20	30	40	50	60	70	80	90
1	10	20	30	40	50	60	70	80	90
2	20	40	60	80	100	120	140	160	180
3	30	60	90	120	150	180	210	240	270
4	40	80	120	160	200	240	280	320	360
5	50	100	150	200	250	300	350	400	450
6	60	120	180	240	300	360	420	480	540
7	70	140	210	280	350	420	490	560	630
8	80	160	240	320	400	480	560	640	720
9	90	180	270	360	450	540	630	720	810

How does multiplying by hundreds differ from multiplying by tens?
__Answers will vary, as there is more than one way to do it.__
Could you change this table to show multiplying by hundreds? __Yes__
How? __By adding a zero to each number (except for those on the left side).__

Using Its, It's, Your, and You're. It's and you're are contractions. Its and your are possessive pronouns. Fill in the blanks with it's, its, your, or you're.
Completa los espacios en blanco con it's, its, your, o you're.

1. I hope __you're__ coming to my barn dance.
2. The dance will be for __your__ friends also.
3. Do you think __it's__ too cold for a barn dance?
4. __Its__ starting time is eight o'clock.
5. Will __your__ family come to the dance with you?
6. __Its__ floor is long and wide.
7. __You're__ coming early, aren't you?
8. I think I will need __your__ help.
9. __It's__ going to last about four hours.
10. __It's__ bound to be a lot of fun.

Write a sentence of your own for each word.
Escribe una oración con cada palabra.

11. it's __Sentences will vary.__
12. its
13. you're
14. your

Page 48

Read this crazy story. Every time you come to an underlined word, write the abbreviation for it.
Cuando te encuentres con una palabra subrayada, escribe la abreviatura.

Last January __Jan.__ we moved from Georgia __GA.__ to New York __N.Y.__. It was a very long trip. We had to walk most of the way because the car broke down. We left on Monday __Mon.__, March __Mar.__ 10 and didn't get there until five years __yrs.__ later.

On the trip I had to learn how to measure. One day I measured gallons __gals.__, inches __ins.__, yards __yds.__, and grams __g.__. I also learned about science __sci.__, adverbs __advs.__, and adjectives __adjs.__. It was a boring trip!

We only traveled about two miles per hour __mph__. That's why it took us so long. Also, we stopped at a number __no.__ of relatives' places and stayed for months __mos.__ on end.

Next time let's fly!

Name an animal or insect that begins with the letters given. If there is not one that begins with that letter, leave it blank or put an X in the box.
Nombra un animal o insecto que comience con las letras dadas. Si no encuentras uno, coloca una X en el recuadro.

	s	d	r	t
insects				
birds				
reptiles				
rodents				
spiders				
zoo animals				
wild animals				
farm animals				
ocean animals				
dinosaurs				

Answers will vary.

Page 49

Day 8

What about Time? You know that 60 seconds = 1 minute, 60 minutes = 1 hour, 24 hours = 1 day, 7 days = 1 week, 52 weeks = 1 year, 12 months = 1 year, and 365 days = 1 year (except leap year, which has 366 days).

Use what you know to complete the following.
Aplica lo que sabes sobre el tiempo para completar los espacios en blanco.

1. Phillip is in the fourth grade. He is 10 __years__ old.
2. There are 30 __days__ in June.
3. Nancy's baby brother started to walk at the age of 11 __months__.
4. We have 48 __hours__ in 2 days.
5. Nick's swimming lesson is 25 __minutes__ long.
6. It took Leslie 10 __minutes__ to comb her hair.
7. Mother's Day is celebrated once a __year__.
8. Many children get about 3 __months__ summer vacation.
9. It takes about 1 __second__ to blink your eyes.
10. Most children go to school 5 __days__ a week.
11. There are 30 __seconds__ in half a minute.
12. It took Monica 2 and a half __hours__ to do all her chores.

Write these words in alphabetical order. Be sure to look at the third or fourth letters.
Ordena estas palabras en orden alfabético.

1. events, evening, every, eventually
   __evening__ __events__ __eventually__ __every__
2. tremendous, treatment, tree, treasure
   __treasure__ __treatment__ __tree__ __tremendous__
3. coast, coconut, coal, collect, color
   __coal__ __coast__ __coconut__ __collect__ __color__
4. entrance, entry, end, enthusiasm, enough
   __end__ __enough__ __enthusiasm__ __entrance__ __entry__
5. grandfather, graph, grain, grateful, grab, graduated
   __grab__ __graduated__ __grain__ __grandfather__ __graph__ __grateful__

© Federal Education Publishing — 49 — Level Orange

Page 50

Day 8

What Does It Really Mean? Write what you think these idiomatic expressions mean.
Escribe lo que crees que significan estas frases idiomáticas.

1. She was really pulling my leg. __not telling the truth__
2. Do you think we'll be in hot water? __be in trouble__
3. If you don't button your lip, I'll scream! __be quiet__
4. Sonny, please get off my back! __leave me alone__
5. When you are having fun, time flies. __goes fast__
6. You've hit it on the head, Andrew. __got it right__
7. Ryan will lend a hand tomorrow. __help__
8. In the winter, my bedroom is like an icebox. __very cold__
9. Mrs. Tune always has beautiful flowers; she must have a green thumb. __takes good care of plants__
10. My brother's stomach is a bottomless pit. __eats a lot__

A Litter Graph. Go on a "litter" walk. In a plastic bag, gather up litter as you go. Only pick up safe litter. Do not pick up anything marked hazardous waste, needles, or litter you are unsure of. When you are finished, bring it home. Categorize what you have found and display it in a bar graph.
Recoge basura cuando hagas una caminata. Solamente recoje basura segura. No recojas nada peligroso. Categoriza lo que encuentres y ponlo en una gráfica de barras.

Type of Litter	1	2	3	4	5	6	7	8	9	10	more than 10

Answers will vary.

Level Orange — 50 — Bridges™

Page 51

Day 9

Place Value Division Patterns. We know that 8 ÷ 2 = 4, so 80 ÷ 2 = 40, and 800 ÷ 2 = 400. Do the following division patterns.
Resuelve los siguientes patrones de división.

1. 9 ÷ 3 = __3__   90 ÷ 3 = __30__   900 ÷ 3 = __300__
2. 8 ÷ 2 = __4__   80 ÷ 2 = __40__   800 ÷ 2 = __400__
3. 12 ÷ 4 = __3__   120 ÷ 4 = __30__   1,200 ÷ 4 = __300__
4. 6 ÷ 3 = __2__   60 ÷ 3 = __20__   600 ÷ 3 = __200__
5. 30 ÷ 6 = __5__   300 ÷ 6 = __50__   3,000 ÷ 6 = __500__
6. 72 ÷ 8 = __9__   720 ÷ 8 = __90__   7,200 ÷ 8 = __900__
7. 32 ÷ 8 = __4__   320 ÷ 8 = __40__   3,200 ÷ 8 = __400__
8. 49 ÷ 7 = __7__   490 ÷ 7 = __70__   4,900 ÷ 7 = __700__
9. 56 ÷ 8 = __7__   560 ÷ 8 = __70__   5,600 ÷ 8 = __700__
10. 25 ÷ 5 = __5__   250 ÷ 5 = __50__   2,500 ÷ 5 = __500__
11. 40 ÷ 8 = __5__   400 ÷ 8 = __50__   4,000 ÷ 8 = __500__
12. 63 ÷ 9 = __7__   630 ÷ 9 = __70__   6,300 ÷ 9 = __700__

Look up the word meet in a dictionary. At the end of each sentence, write what part of speech (noun or verb) meet is. Then write the number for the meaning of the word meet.
Busca la palabra meet en un diccionario. Al final de cada oración¹ escribe si meet es un sustantivo⁰ o un verbo¹. Luego escribe el número del significado que aparece en el diccionario.

EXAMPLE: I will meet you at three.   *Verb – 2*

Numbers will vary.

1. Tomorrow we are going to have a track meet. __Noun__
2. I hope he doesn't meet with disaster. __Verb__
3. We need to meet the plane at seven P.M. __Verb__
4. He will have to meet the payments every month. __Verb__
5. It was nice to meet and talk with you yesterday. __Verb__
6. Are you going to meet your friends later? __Verb__

© Federal Education Publishing — 51 — Level Orange

Page 52

Day 9

Someone or Something with Power. What is power? Choose something or someone with power. How do they have power? How did they get it? Could they lose it? Do they use it? How? Why? Do you have power? Yes you do! What are some of the powers that you have? What are some that you don't have that you would like to have?
Elige algo o alguien con poder y escribe sobre él.

Answers will vary.

Level Orange — 52 — Bridges™

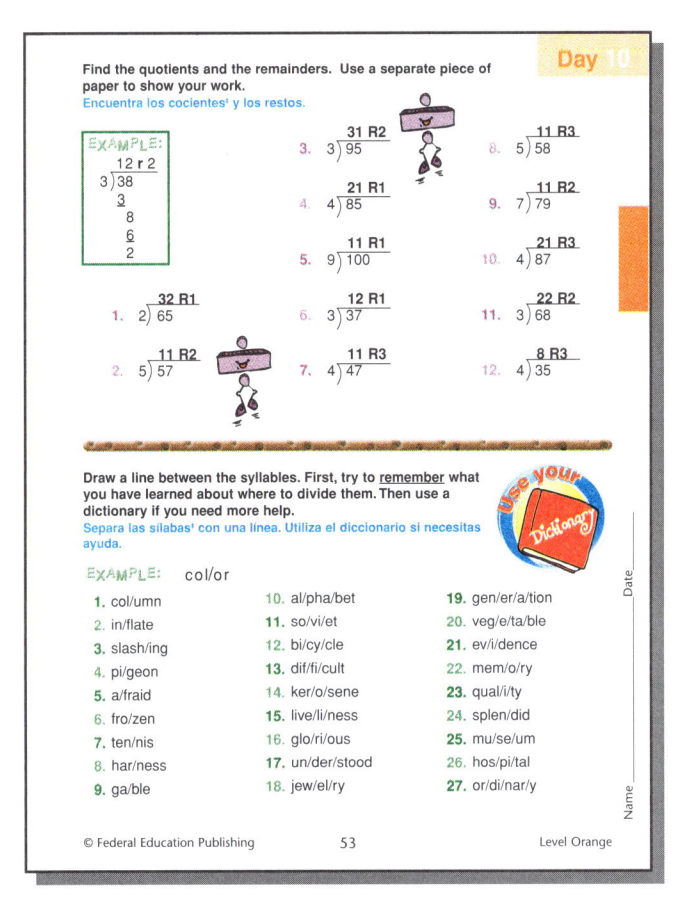

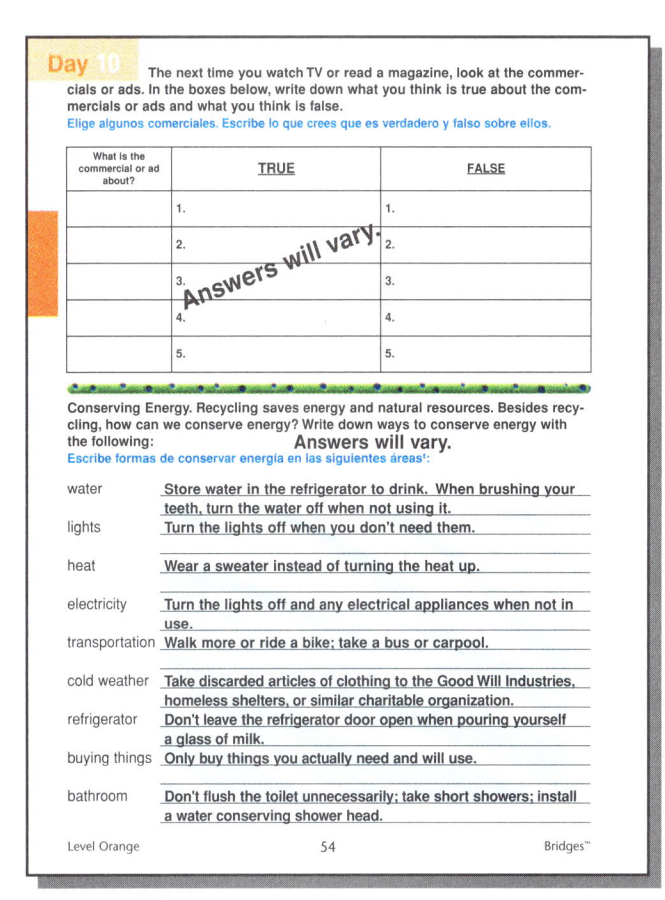

Page 53

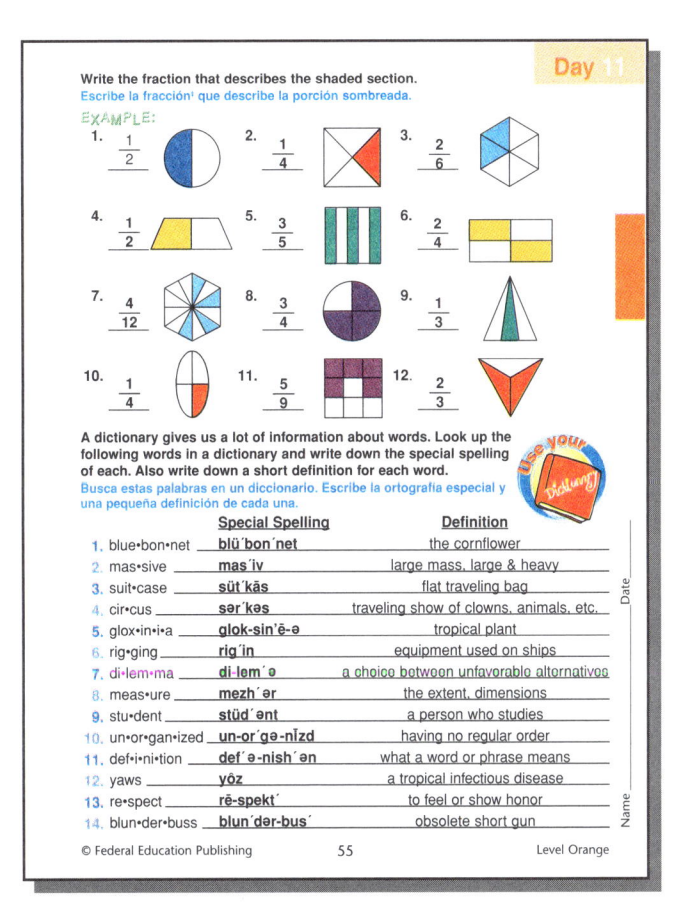

Find the quotients and the remainders. Use a separate piece of paper to show your work.
Encuentra los cocientes¹ y los restos.

EXAMPLE:
```
   12 r 2
3)38
   3
   ―
   8
   6
   ―
   2
```

1. 2)65 = 32 R1
2. 5)57 = 11 R2
3. 3)95 = 31 R2
4. 4)85 = 21 R1
5. 9)100 = 11 R1
6. 3)37 = 12 R1
7. 4)47 = 11 R3
8. 5)58 = 11 R3
9. 7)79 = 11 R2
10. 4)87 = 21 R3
11. 3)68 = 22 R2
12. 4)35 = 8 R3

Draw a line between the syllables. First, try to <u>remember</u> what you have learned about where to divide them. Then use a dictionary if you need more help.
Separa las sílabas¹ con una línea. Utiliza el diccionario si necesitas ayuda.

EXAMPLE: col/or

1. col/umn
2. in/flate
3. slash/ing
4. pi/geon
5. a/fraid
6. fro/zen
7. ten/nis
8. har/ness
9. ga/ble
10. al/pha/bet
11. so/vi/et
12. bi/cy/cle
13. dif/fi/cult
14. ker/o/sene
15. live/li/ness
16. glo/ri/ous
17. un/der/stood
18. jew/el/ry
19. gen/er/a/tion
20. veg/e/ta/ble
21. ev/i/dence
22. mem/o/ry
23. qual/i/ty
24. splen/did
25. mu/se/um
26. hos/pi/tal
27. or/di/nar/y

Page 54

The next time you watch TV or read a magazine, look at the commercials or ads. In the boxes below, write down what you think is true about the commercials or ads and what you think is false.
Elige algunos comerciales. Escribe lo que crees que es verdadero y falso sobre ellos.

What is the commercial or ad about?	TRUE	FALSE
1.	1.	1.
2.	2.	2.
3.	3.	3.
4.	4.	4.
5.	5.	5.

Answers will vary.

Conserving Energy. Recycling saves energy and natural resources. Besides recycling, how can we conserve energy? Write down ways to conserve energy with the following: **Answers will vary.**
Escribe formas de conservar energía en las siguientes áreas¹:

water — Store water in the refrigerator to drink. When brushing your teeth, turn the water off when not using it.

lights — Turn the lights off when you don't need them.

heat — Wear a sweater instead of turning the heat up.

electricity — Turn the lights off and any electrical appliances when not in use.

transportation — Walk more or ride a bike; take a bus or carpool.

cold weather — Take discarded articles of clothing to the Good Will Industries, homeless shelters, or similar charitable organization.

refrigerator — Don't leave the refrigerator door open when pouring yourself a glass of milk.

buying things — Only buy things you actually need and will use.

bathroom — Don't flush the toilet unnecessarily; take short showers; install a water conserving shower head.

Page 55

Write the fraction that describes the shaded section.
Escribe la fracción¹ que describe la porción sombreada.

EXAMPLE:

1. 1/2
2. 1/4
3. 2/6
4. 1/2
5. 3/5
6. 2/4
7. 4/12
8. 3/6
9. 1/3
10. 1/4
11. 5/9
12. 2/3

A dictionary gives us a lot of information about words. Look up the following words in a dictionary and write down the special spelling of each. Also write down a short definition for each word.
Busca estas palabras en un diccionario. Escribe la ortografía especial y una pequeña definición de cada una.

		Special Spelling	Definition
1.	blue•bon•net	blü´bon´net	the cornflower
2.	mas•sive	mas´iv	large mass, large & heavy
3.	suit•case	süt´kās	flat traveling bag
4.	cir•cus	sėr´kəs	traveling show of clowns, animals, etc.
5.	glox•in•i•a	glok-sin´ē-ə	tropical plant
6.	rig•ging	rig´in	equipment used on ships
7.	di•lem•ma	di-lem´ə	a choice between unfavorable alternatives
8.	meas•ure	mezh´ər	the extent, dimensions
9.	stu•dent	stüd´ənt	a person who studies
10.	un•or•gan•ized	un-or´gə-nīzd	having no regular order
11.	def•i•ni•tion	def´ə-nish´ən	what a word or phrase means
12.	yaws	yóz	a tropical infectious disease
13.	re•spect	rē-spekt´	to feel or show honor
14.	blun•der•buss	blun´dər-bus´	obsolete short gun

Page 56

Practice writing and spelling these homonyms. Write in cursive. After you know how to spell them, have someone give you a test to see if you can spell them without looking. Write each word twice.
Practica escribir y deletrear estos homónimos¹.

Writing will vary.

way, weigh, base, bass, threw, through, scene, seen

sight, site, arc, ark, tide, tied, waist, waste, sore, soar, pare, pair, pear

Water in the Air. There is water in the air. How does it get there? Clouds and rain are made from water vapor in the air.
Try this to help explain how water gets into the air. Take 3 or more drinking glasses that are all about the same size. Fill the glasses almost full of water. Place them in different areas such as warm places, cool places, dark places, windy places, outside places, inside places, and other places of your choice. Watch them for 4 or 5 days or longer. Check the water levels. What happened to the water in the glasses? Where did it go? Explain in your own words where you think the water vapor in the atmosphere comes from and where it goes?
Trata de hacer este experimento. Escribe sobre los resultados.

Answers will vary.

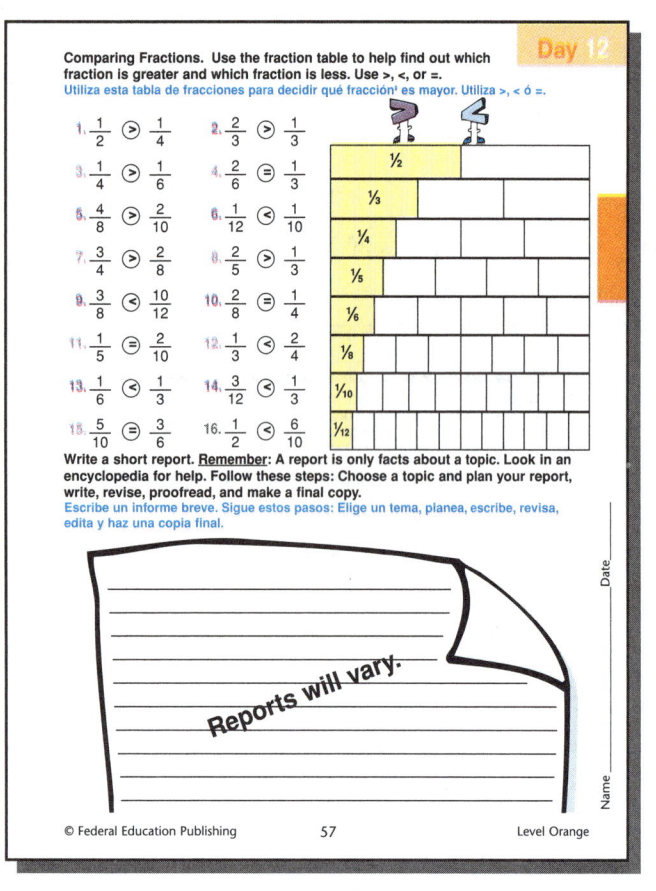

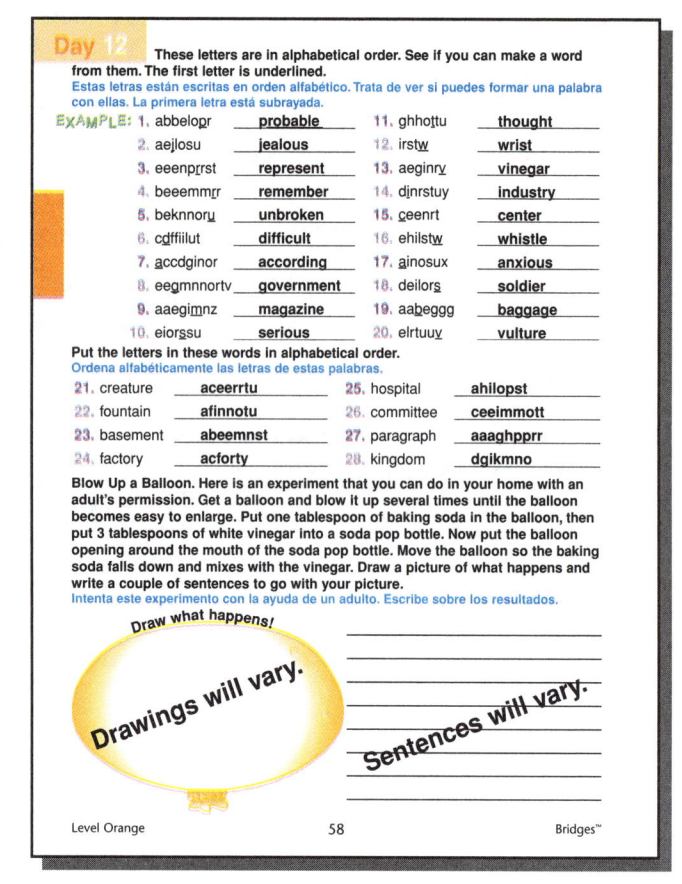

Page 57

Comparing Fractions. Use the fraction table to help find out which fraction is greater and which fraction is less. Use >, <, or =.
Utiliza esta tabla de fracciones para decidir qué fracción es mayor. Utiliza >, < ó =.

1. $\frac{1}{2}$ > $\frac{1}{4}$
2. $\frac{2}{3}$ > $\frac{1}{3}$
3. $\frac{1}{4}$ > $\frac{1}{6}$
4. $\frac{2}{6}$ = $\frac{1}{3}$
5. $\frac{4}{8}$ > $\frac{2}{10}$
6. $\frac{1}{12}$ < $\frac{1}{10}$
7. $\frac{3}{4}$ > $\frac{2}{5}$
8. $\frac{2}{5}$ > $\frac{1}{3}$
9. $\frac{3}{8}$ < $\frac{10}{12}$
10. $\frac{2}{8}$ = $\frac{1}{4}$
11. $\frac{1}{5}$ = $\frac{2}{10}$
12. $\frac{1}{3}$ < $\frac{2}{4}$
13. $\frac{1}{6}$ < $\frac{3}{3}$
14. $\frac{3}{12}$ = $\frac{1}{3}$
15. $\frac{5}{10}$ = $\frac{3}{6}$
16. $\frac{1}{2}$ > $\frac{6}{12}$

Write a short report. Remember: A report is only facts about a topic. Look in an encyclopedia for help. Follow these steps: Choose a topic and plan your report, write, revise, proofread, and make a final copy.
Escribe un informe breve. Sigue estos pasos: Elige un tema, planea, escribe, revisa, edita y haz una copia final.

Reports will vary.

Page 58

These letters are in alphabetical order. See if you can make a word from them. The first letter is underlined.
Estas letras están escritas en orden alfabético. Trata de ver si puedes formar una palabra con ellas. La primera letra está subrayada.

EXAMPLE:
1. abbelopr — probable
2. aejlosu — jealous
3. eeenprrst — represent
4. beeemmrr — remember
5. beknnoru — unbroken
6. cdffiilut — difficult
7. accdginor — according
8. eegmnnortv — government
9. aaegimnz — magazine
10. eiorssu — serious
11. ghhottu — thought
12. irstw — wrist
13. aeginry — vinegar
14. djnrstuy — industry
15. ceenrt — center
16. ehilstw — whistle
17. ainosux — anxious
18. deilors — soldier
19. aabeggg — baggage
20. elrtuuv — vulture

Put the letters in these words in alphabetical order.
Ordena alfabéticamente las letras de estas palabras.

21. creature — aceerrtu
22. fountain — afinnotu
23. basement — abeemnst
24. factory — acforty
25. hospital — ahilopst
26. committee — ceeimmott
27. paragraph — aaaghpprr
28. kingdom — dgikmno

Blow Up a Balloon. Here is an experiment that you can do in your home with an adult's permission. Get a balloon and blow it up several times until the balloon becomes easy to enlarge. Put one tablespoon of baking soda in the balloon, then put 3 tablespoons of white vinegar into a soda pop bottle. Now put the balloon opening around the mouth of the soda pop bottle. Move the balloon so the baking soda falls down and mixes with the vinegar. Draw a picture of what happens and write a couple of sentences to go with your picture.
Intenta este experimento con la ayuda de un adulto. Escribe sobre los resultados.

Draw what happens!
Drawings will vary.
Sentences will vary.

Page 59

Multiplying 3-digit Numbers by 1-digit Numbers
Multiplica estos números de 3 dígitos por números de 1 dígito.

EXAMPLE: 6 x 3 = 18   3 x 80 = 240   3 x 100 = 300   or $\begin{array}{r}21\\186\\\times 3\\\hline 558\end{array}$
18 + 240 + 300 = 558

1. 162 × 5 = 810
2. 398 × 2 = 796
3. 904 × 8 = 7,232
4. 329 × 5 = 1,645
5. 240 × 7 = 1,680
6. 432 × 6 = 2,592
7. 412 × 8 = 3,296
8. 542 × 9 = 4,878
9. 506 × 5 = 2,530
10. 554 × 6 = 3,324
11. 473 × 9 = 4,257
12. 257 × 8 = 2,056

Put commas in the following sentences to separate words in a series.
Coloca las comas en estas oraciones para separar las palabras de las series.

1. Nan, Tom, Julie, and James are going to a movie.
2. Anne took her spelling, reading, and math books to school.
3. The snack bar is only open on Monday, Tuesday, Friday, and Saturday.
4. Our new school flag is blue, green, yellow, black, and orange.
5. Women, men, children, and pets enjoy sledding.
6. Have you ever seen baby kittens, piglets, or goslings?
7. Carla and Mark bought postcards, film, candy, and souvenirs.

Now write four sentences of your own. Name at least three people, sports, or foods in a series. Be sure to put in the commas.
Escribe cuatro oraciones propias. Nombra por los menos personas, deportes o comidas en una serie. Asegúrate de agregar las comas.

Answers will vary.

Page 60

Parents and Family. What do you think your parents and family have in mind for your life? What do they want you to accomplish? What would they like to see you do? How do you feel about it? Think and write about it.
Piensa y escribe sobre lo que tus padres desean que logres.

Story will vary.

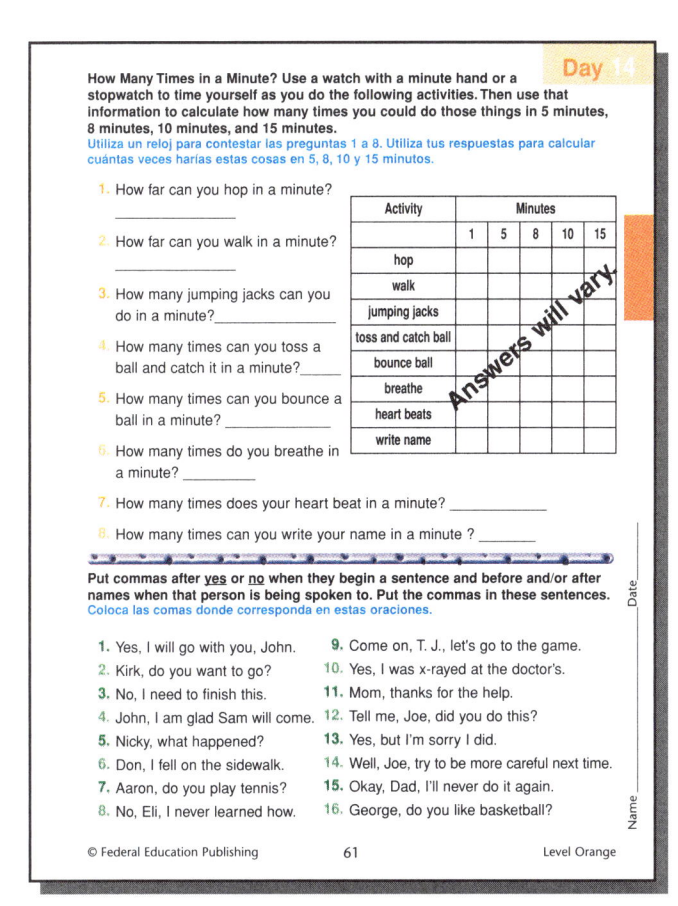

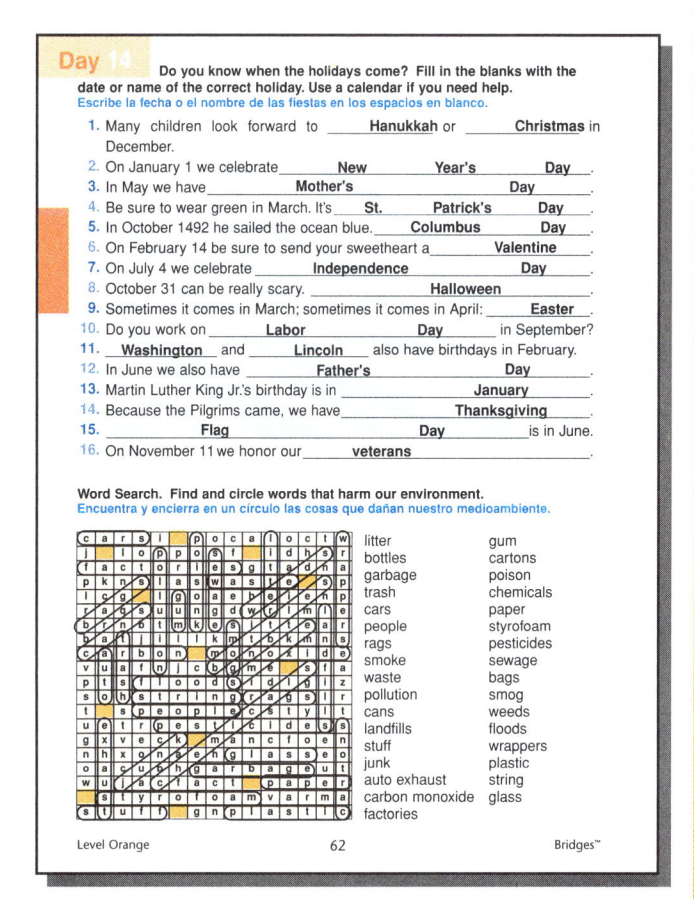

Page 61

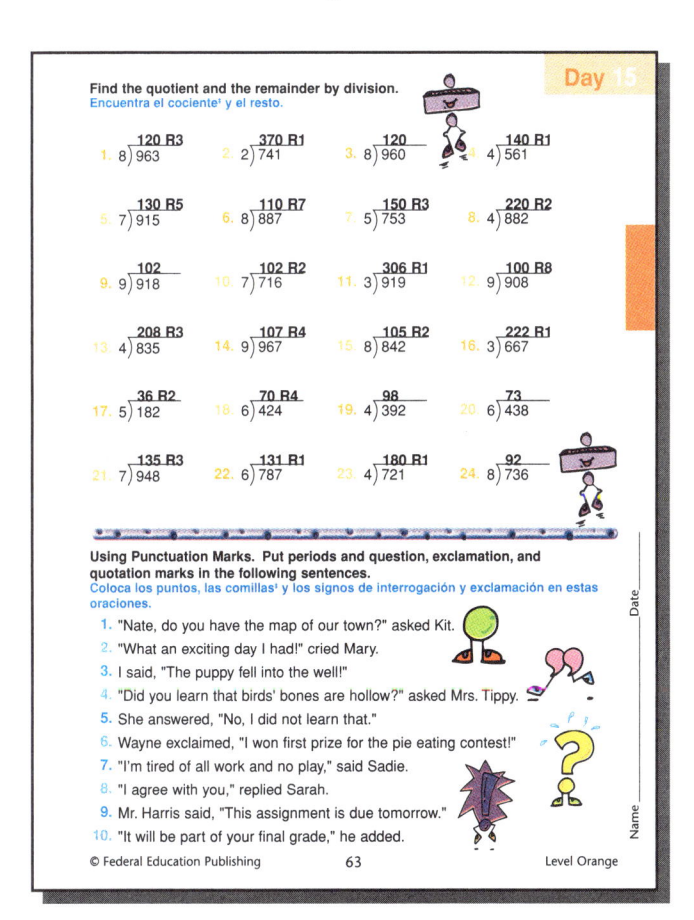

How Many Times in a Minute? Use a watch with a minute hand or a stopwatch to time yourself as you do the following activities. Then use that information to calculate how many times you could do those things in 5 minutes, 8 minutes, 10 minutes, and 15 minutes.
Utiliza un reloj para contestar las preguntas 1 a 8. Utiliza tus respuestas para calcular cuántas veces harías estas cosas en 5, 8, 10 y 15 minutos.

1. How far can you hop in a minute? _____
2. How far can you walk in a minute? _____
3. How many jumping jacks can you do in a minute? _____
4. How many times can you toss a ball and catch it in a minute? _____
5. How many times can you bounce a ball in a minute? _____
6. How many times do you breathe in a minute? _____
7. How many times does your heart beat in a minute? _____
8. How many times can you write your name in a minute? _____

Activity	Minutes				
	1	5	8	10	15
hop					
walk					
jumping jacks					
toss and catch ball					
bounce ball					
breathe					
heart beats					
write name					

Answers will vary.

Put commas after yes or no when they begin a sentence and before and/or after names when that person is being spoken to. Put the commas in these sentences.
Coloca las comas donde corresponda en estas oraciones.

1. Yes, I will go with you, John.
2. Kirk, do you want to go?
3. No, I need to finish this.
4. John, I am glad Sam will come.
5. Nicky, what happened?
6. Don, I fell on the sidewalk.
7. Aaron, do you play tennis?
8. No, Eli, I never learned how.
9. Come on, T. J., let's go to the game.
10. Yes, I was x-rayed at the doctor's.
11. Mom, thanks for the help.
12. Tell me, Joe, did you do this?
13. Yes, but I'm sorry I did.
14. Well, Joe, try to be more careful next time.
15. Okay, Dad, I'll never do it again.
16. George, do you like basketball?

Page 62

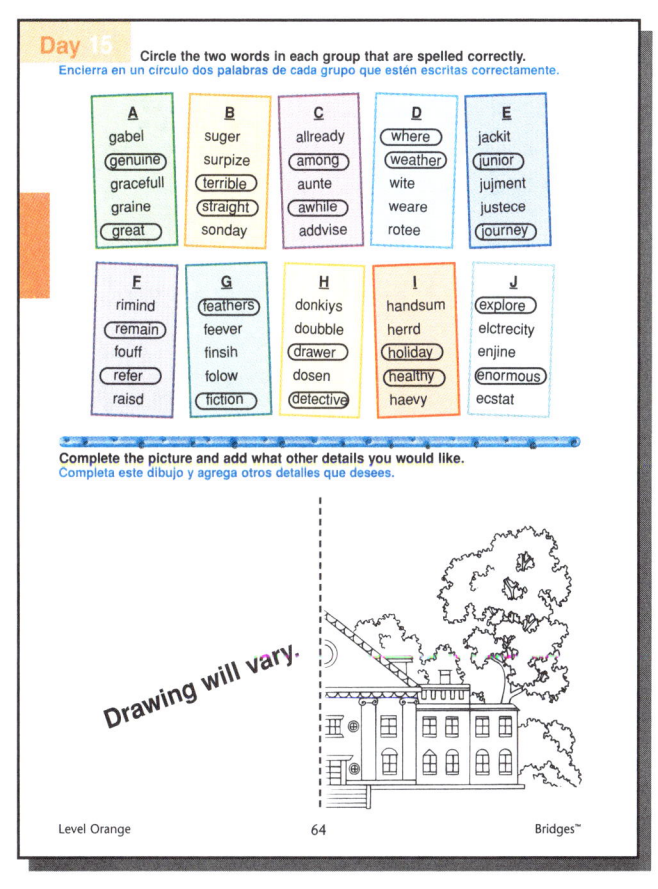

Do you know when the holidays come? Fill in the blanks with the date or name of the correct holiday. Use a calendar if you need help.
Escribe la fecha o el nombre de las fiestas en los espacios en blanco.

1. Many children look forward to __Hanukkah__ or __Christmas__ in December.
2. On January 1 we celebrate __New Year's Day__.
3. In May we have __Mother's Day__.
4. Be sure to wear green in March. It's __St. Patrick's Day__.
5. In October 1492 he sailed the ocean blue. __Columbus Day__.
6. On February 14 be sure to send your sweetheart a __Valentine__.
7. On July 4 we celebrate __Independence Day__.
8. October 31 can be really scary. __Halloween__.
9. Sometimes it comes in March; sometimes it comes in April: __Easter__.
10. Do you work on __Labor Day__ in September?
11. __Washington__ and __Lincoln__ also have birthdays in February.
12. In June we also have __Father's Day__.
13. Martin Luther King Jr.'s birthday is in __January__.
14. Because the Pilgrims came, we have __Thanksgiving__.
15. __Flag Day__ is in June.
16. On November 11 we honor our __veterans__.

Word Search. Find and circle words that harm our environment.
Encuentra y encierra en un círculo las cosas que dañan nuestro medioambiente.

litter	gum
bottles	cartons
garbage	poison
trash	chemicals
cars	paper
people	styrofoam
rags	pesticides
smoke	sewage
waste	bags
pollution	smog
cans	weeds
landfills	floods
stuff	wrappers
junk	plastic
auto exhaust	string
carbon monoxide	glass
factories	

Page 63

Find the quotient and the remainder by division.
Encuentra el cociente y el resto.

1. 963 ÷ 8 = 120 R3
2. 741 ÷ 2 = 370 R1
3. 960 ÷ 8 = 120
4. 561 ÷ 4 = 140 R1
5. 915 ÷ 7 = 130 R5
6. 887 ÷ 8 = 110 R7
7. 753 ÷ 5 = 150 R3
8. 882 ÷ 4 = 220 R2
9. 918 ÷ 9 = 102
10. 716 ÷ 7 = 102 R2
11. 919 ÷ 3 = 306 R1
12. 908 ÷ 9 = 100 R8
13. 835 ÷ 4 = 208 R3
14. 967 ÷ 9 = 107 R4
15. 842 ÷ 8 = 105 R2
16. 667 ÷ 3 = 222 R1
17. 182 ÷ 5 = 36 R2
18. 424 ÷ 6 = 70 R4
19. 392 ÷ 4 = 98
20. 438 ÷ 6 = 73
21. 948 ÷ 7 = 135 R3
22. 787 ÷ 6 = 131 R1
23. 721 ÷ 4 = 180 R1
24. 736 ÷ 8 = 92

Using Punctuation Marks. Put periods and question, exclamation, and quotation marks in the following sentences.
Coloca los puntos, las comillas y los signos de interrogación y exclamación en estas oraciones.

1. "Nate, do you have the map of our town?" asked Kit.
2. "What an exciting day I had!" cried Mary.
3. I said, "The puppy fell into the well!"
4. "Did you learn that birds' bones are hollow?" asked Mrs. Tippy.
5. She answered, "No, I did not learn that."
6. Wayne exclaimed, "I won first prize for the pie eating contest!"
7. "I'm tired of all work and no play," said Sadie.
8. "I agree with you," replied Sarah.
9. Mr. Harris said, "This assignment is due tomorrow."
10. "It will be part of your final grade," he added.

Page 64

Circle the two words in each group that are spelled correctly.
Encierra en un círculo dos palabras de cada grupo que estén escritas correctamente.

A: (gabel) (genuine) gracefull graine (great)
Correct: genuine, great

B: suger surpize (terrible) (straight) sonday

C: (allready) (among) aunte (awhile) addvise

D: (where) (weather) wite weare rotee

E: jackit (junior) jujment justece (journey)

F: rimind (remain) fouff (refer) raisd

G: (feathers) feever finsih folow (fiction)

H: donkiys (doubble) (drawer) dosen (detective)

I: handsum herrd (holiday) (healthy) haevy

J: (explore) elctrecity enjine (enormous) ecstat

Complete the picture and add what other details you would like.
Completa este dibujo y agrega otros detalles que desees.

Drawing will vary.

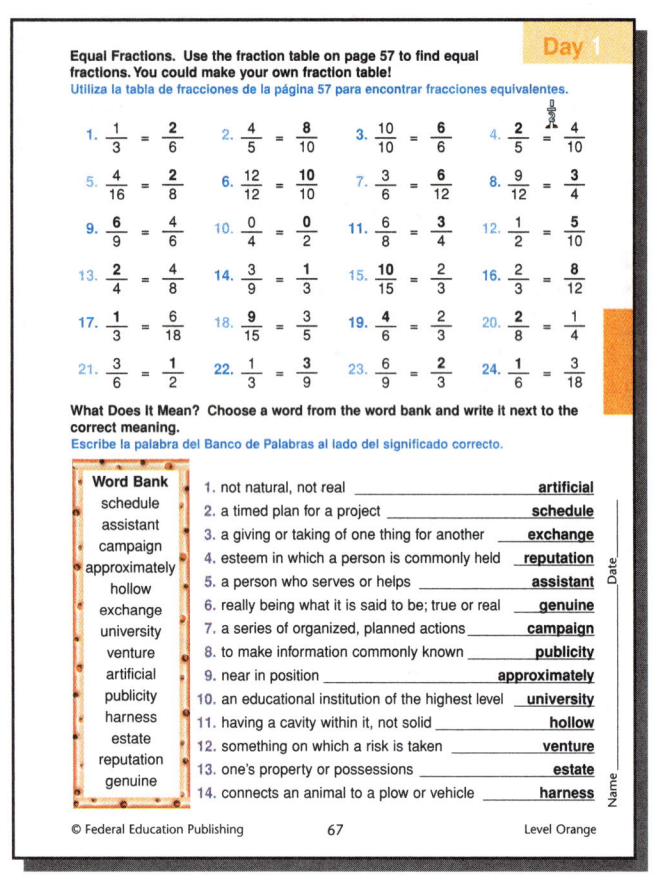

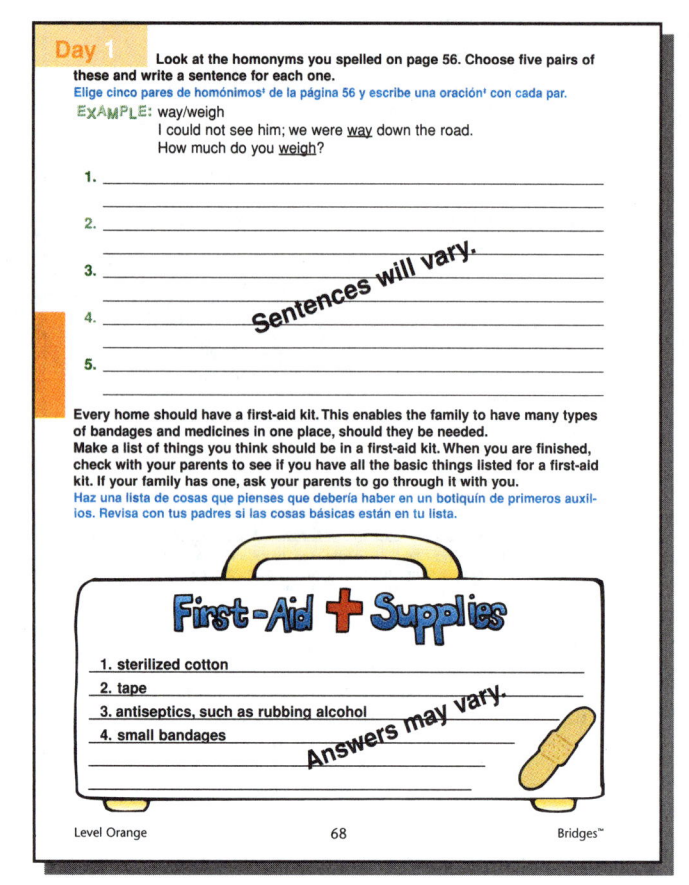

Page 67

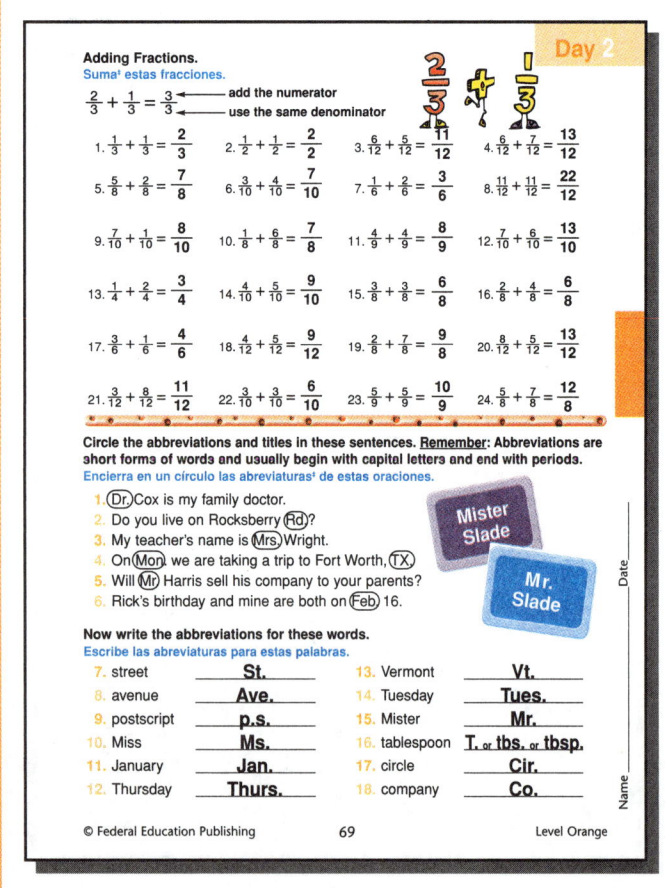

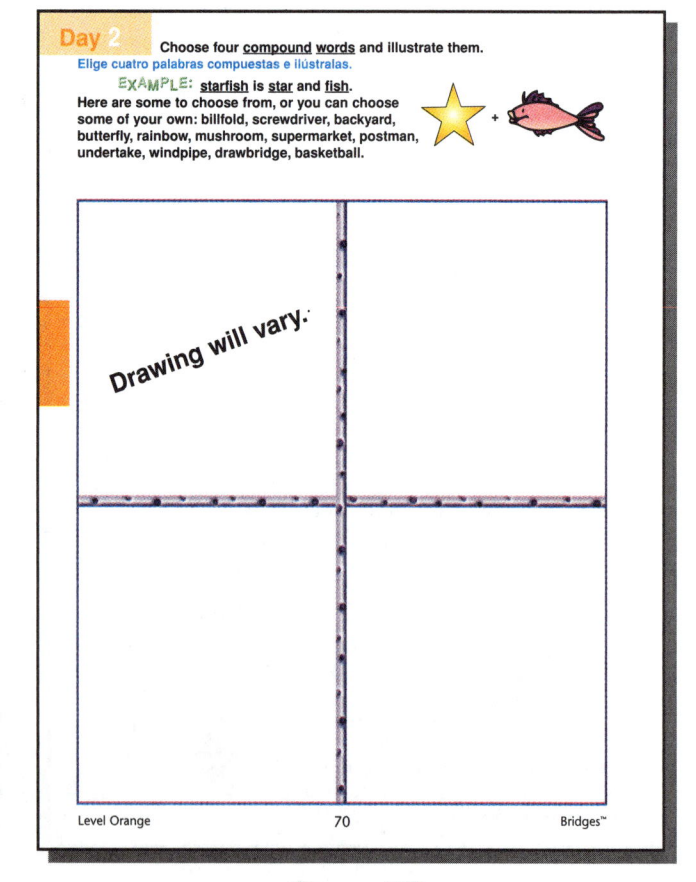

Equal Fractions. Use the fraction table on page 57 to find equal fractions. You could make your own fraction table!
Utiliza la tabla de fracciones de la página 57 para encontrar fracciones equivalentes.

1. $\frac{1}{3} = \frac{2}{6}$
2. $\frac{4}{5} = \frac{8}{10}$
3. $\frac{10}{10} = \frac{6}{6}$
4. $\frac{2}{5} = \frac{4}{10}$
5. $\frac{4}{16} = \frac{2}{8}$
6. $\frac{12}{12} = \frac{10}{10}$
7. $\frac{3}{6} = \frac{6}{12}$
8. $\frac{9}{12} = \frac{3}{4}$
9. $\frac{6}{9} = \frac{4}{6}$
10. $\frac{0}{4} = \frac{0}{2}$
11. $\frac{6}{8} = \frac{3}{4}$
12. $\frac{1}{2} = \frac{5}{10}$
13. $\frac{2}{4} = \frac{4}{8}$
14. $\frac{3}{9} = \frac{1}{3}$
15. $\frac{10}{15} = \frac{2}{3}$
16. $\frac{4}{6} = \frac{8}{12}$
17. $\frac{1}{3} = \frac{6}{18}$
18. $\frac{9}{15} = \frac{3}{5}$
19. $\frac{4}{6} = \frac{2}{3}$
20. $\frac{2}{8} = \frac{1}{4}$
21. $\frac{3}{6} = \frac{1}{2}$
22. $\frac{1}{3} = \frac{3}{9}$
23. $\frac{6}{9} = \frac{2}{3}$
24. $\frac{1}{6} = \frac{3}{18}$

What Does It Mean? Choose a word from the word bank and write it next to the correct meaning.
Escribe la palabra del Banco de Palabras al lado del significado correcto.

Word Bank
schedule, assistant, campaign, approximately, hollow, exchange, university, venture, artificial, publicity, harness, estate, reputation, genuine

1. not natural, not real — **artificial**
2. a timed plan for a project — **schedule**
3. a giving or taking of one thing for another — **exchange**
4. esteem in which a person is commonly held — **reputation**
5. a person who serves or helps — **assistant**
6. really being what it is said to be; true or real — **genuine**
7. a series of organized, planned actions — **campaign**
8. to make information commonly known — **publicity**
9. near in position — **approximately**
10. an educational institution of the highest level — **university**
11. having a cavity within it, not solid — **hollow**
12. something on which a risk is taken — **venture**
13. one's property or possessions — **estate**
14. connects an animal to a plow or vehicle — **harness**

Page 68

Day 1 Look at the homonyms you spelled on page 56. Choose five pairs of these and write a sentence for each one.
Elige cinco pares de homónimos de la página 56 y escribe una oración con cada par.

EXAMPLE: way/weigh
I could not see him; we were <u>way</u> down the road.
How much do you <u>weigh</u>?

1. _____
2. _____
3. _____
4. _____
5. _____

Sentences will vary.

Every home should have a first-aid kit. This enables the family to have many types of bandages and medicines in one place, should they be needed.
Make a list of things you think should be in a first-aid kit. When you are finished, check with your parents to see if you have all the basic things listed for a first-aid kit. If your family has one, ask your parents to go through it with you.
Haz una lista de cosas que pienses que debería haber en un botiquín de primeros auxilios. Revisa con tus padres si las cosas básicas están en tu lista.

First-Aid Supplies
1. sterilized cotton
2. tape
3. antiseptics, such as rubbing alcohol
4. small bandages

Answers may vary.

Page 69

Adding Fractions.
Suma estas fracciones.

$\frac{2}{3} + \frac{1}{3} = \frac{3}{3}$ ← add the numerator, use the same denominator

1. $\frac{1}{3} + \frac{1}{3} = \frac{2}{3}$
2. $\frac{1}{2} + \frac{1}{2} = \frac{2}{2}$
3. $\frac{6}{12} + \frac{5}{12} = \frac{11}{12}$
4. $\frac{6}{12} + \frac{7}{12} = \frac{13}{12}$
5. $\frac{5}{8} + \frac{2}{8} = \frac{7}{8}$
6. $\frac{3}{10} + \frac{4}{10} = \frac{7}{10}$
7. $\frac{1}{6} + \frac{2}{6} = \frac{3}{6}$
8. $\frac{11}{12} + \frac{11}{12} = \frac{22}{12}$
9. $\frac{7}{10} + \frac{1}{10} = \frac{8}{10}$
10. $\frac{1}{8} + \frac{6}{8} = \frac{7}{8}$
11. $\frac{4}{9} + \frac{4}{9} = \frac{8}{9}$
12. $\frac{7}{10} + \frac{6}{10} = \frac{13}{10}$
13. $\frac{1}{4} + \frac{2}{4} = \frac{3}{4}$
14. $\frac{4}{10} + \frac{5}{10} = \frac{9}{10}$
15. $\frac{3}{8} + \frac{3}{8} = \frac{6}{8}$
16. $\frac{2}{8} + \frac{4}{8} = \frac{6}{8}$
17. $\frac{3}{6} + \frac{1}{6} = \frac{4}{6}$
18. $\frac{4}{12} + \frac{5}{12} = \frac{9}{12}$
19. $\frac{2}{8} + \frac{7}{8} = \frac{9}{8}$
20. $\frac{8}{12} + \frac{5}{12} = \frac{13}{12}$
21. $\frac{3}{12} + \frac{8}{12} = \frac{11}{12}$
22. $\frac{3}{10} + \frac{3}{10} = \frac{6}{10}$
23. $\frac{5}{9} + \frac{5}{9} = \frac{10}{9}$
24. $\frac{5}{8} + \frac{7}{8} = \frac{12}{8}$

Circle the abbreviations and titles in these sentences. Remember: Abbreviations are short forms of words and usually begin with capital letters and end with periods.
Encierra en un círculo las abreviaturas de estas oraciones.

1. (Dr.) Cox is my family doctor.
2. Do you live on Rocksberry (Rd.)?
3. My teacher's name is (Mrs.) Wright.
4. On (Mon.) we are taking a trip to Fort Worth, (TX).
5. Will (Mr.) Harris sell his company to your parents?
6. Rick's birthday and mine are both on (Feb.) 16.

Now write the abbreviations for these words.
Escribe las abreviaturas para estas palabras.

7. street — **St.**
8. avenue — **Ave.**
9. postscript — **p.s.**
10. Miss — **Ms.**
11. January — **Jan.**
12. Thursday — **Thurs.**
13. Vermont — **Vt.**
14. Tuesday — **Tues.**
15. Mister — **Mr.**
16. tablespoon — **T. or tbs. or tbsp.**
17. circle — **Cir.**
18. company — **Co.**

Page 70

Day 2 Choose four <u>compound</u> <u>words</u> and illustrate them.
Elige cuatro palabras compuestas e ilústralas.

EXAMPLE: <u>starfish</u> is <u>star</u> and <u>fish</u>.
Here are some to choose from, or you can choose some of your own: billfold, screwdriver, backyard, butterfly, rainbow, mushroom, supermarket, postman, undertake, windpipe, drawbridge, basketball.

Drawing will vary.

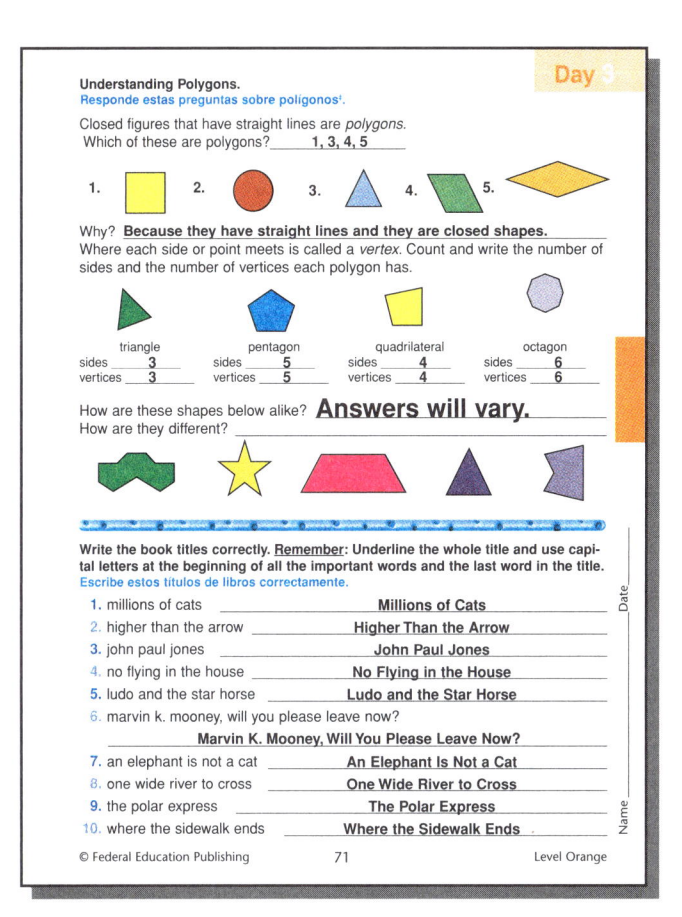

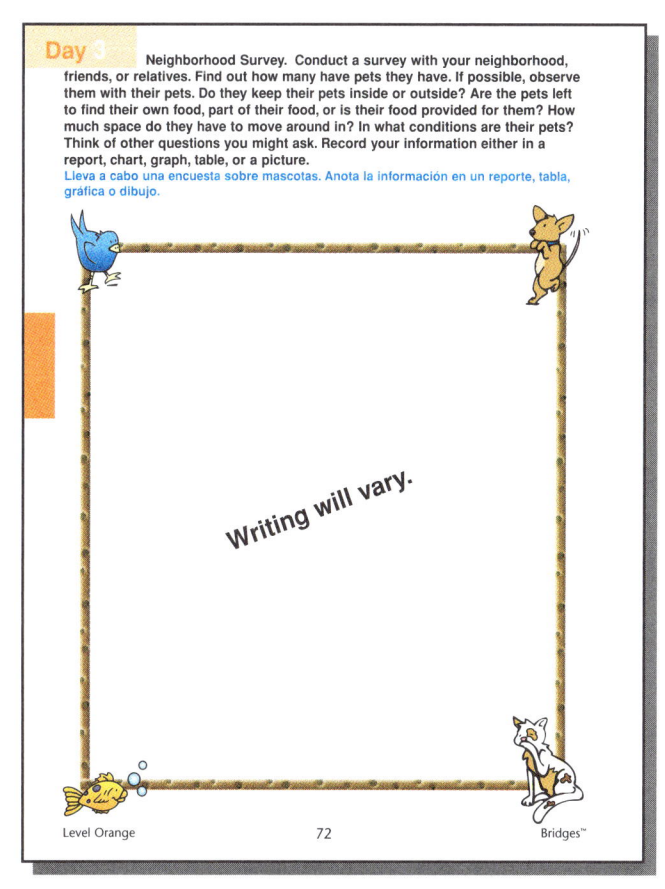

Page 71

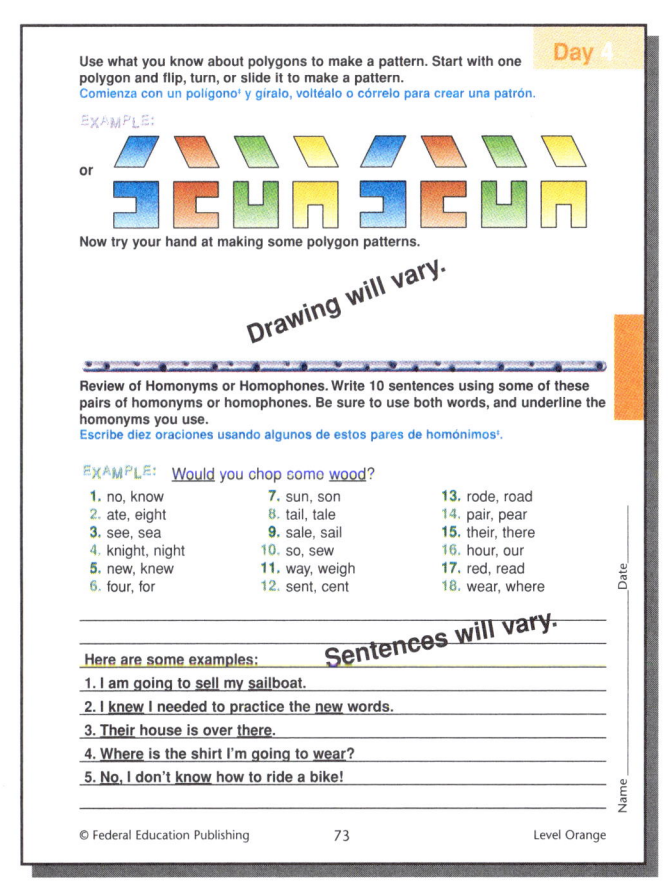

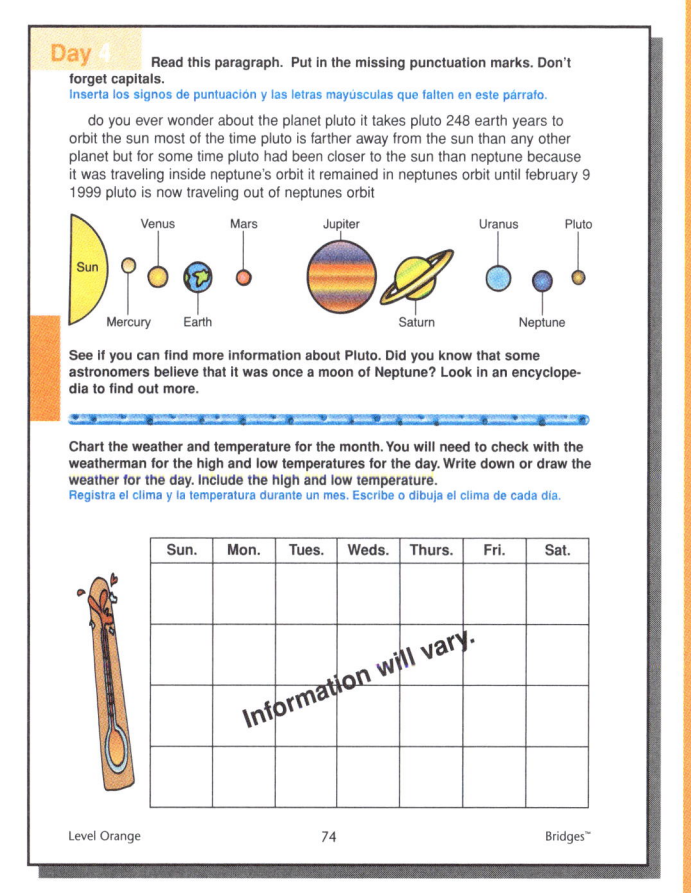

Understanding Polygons.
Responde estas preguntas sobre polígonos.

Closed figures that have straight lines are *polygons*.
Which of these are polygons? __1, 3, 4, 5__

1. (yellow square) 2. (red circle) 3. (blue triangle) 4. (green square) 5. (yellow rhombus)

Why? __Because they have straight lines and they are closed shapes.__
Where each side or point meets is called a *vertex*. Count and write the number of sides and the number of vertices each polygon has.

triangle	pentagon	quadrilateral	octagon
sides 3	sides 5	sides 4	sides 6
vertices 3	vertices 5	vertices 4	vertices 6

How are these shapes below alike? __Answers will vary.__
How are they different? _____

Write the book titles correctly. **Remember:** Underline the whole title and use capital letters at the beginning of all the important words and the last word in the title.
Escribe estos títulos de libros correctamente.

1. millions of cats — Millions of Cats
2. higher than the arrow — Higher Than the Arrow
3. john paul jones — John Paul Jones
4. no flying in the house — No Flying in the House
5. ludo and the star horse — Ludo and the Star Horse
6. marvin k. mooney, will you please leave now? — Marvin K. Mooney, Will You Please Leave Now?
7. an elephant is not a cat — An Elephant Is Not a Cat
8. one wide river to cross — One Wide River to Cross
9. the polar express — The Polar Express
10. where the sidewalk ends — Where the Sidewalk Ends

Page 72

Day 3

Neighborhood Survey. Conduct a survey with your neighborhood, friends, or relatives. Find out how many have pets they have. If possible, observe them with their pets. Do they keep their pets inside or outside? Are the pets left to find their own food, part of their food, or is their food provided for them? How much space do they have to move around in? In what conditions are their pets? Think of other questions you might ask. Record your information either in a report, chart, graph, table, or a picture.
Lleva a cabo una encuesta sobre mascotas. Anota la información en un reporte, tabla, gráfica o dibujo.

Writing will vary.

Page 73

Day 4

Use what you know about polygons to make a pattern. Start with one polygon and flip, turn, or slide it to make a pattern.
Comienza con un polígono y gíralo, voltéalo o córrelo para crear una patrón.

EXAMPLE:

Now try your hand at making some polygon patterns.

Drawing will vary.

Review of Homonyms or Homophones. Write 10 sentences using some of these pairs of homonyms or homophones. Be sure to use both words, and underline the homonyms you use.
Escribe diez oraciones usando algunos de estos pares de homónimos.

EXAMPLE: Would you chop some wood?

1. no, know
2. ate, eight
3. see, sea
4. knight, night
5. new, knew
6. four, for
7. sun, son
8. tail, tale
9. sale, sail
10. so, sew
11. way, weigh
12. sent, cent
13. rode, road
14. pair, pear
15. their, there
16. hour, our
17. red, read
18. wear, where

Sentences will vary.

Here are some examples:
1. I am going to sell my sailboat.
2. I knew I needed to practice the new words.
3. Their house is over there.
4. Where is the shirt I'm going to wear?
5. No, I don't know how to ride a bike!

Page 74

Day 4

Read this paragraph. Put in the missing punctuation marks. Don't forget capitals.
Inserta los signos de puntuación y las letras mayúsculas que falten en este párrafo.

do you ever wonder about the planet pluto it takes pluto 248 earth years to orbit the sun most of the time pluto is farther away from the sun than any other planet but for some time pluto had been closer to the sun than neptune because it was traveling inside neptune's orbit it remained in neptunes orbit until february 9 1999 pluto is now traveling out of neptunes orbit

(Solar system diagram: Sun, Mercury, Venus, Earth, Mars, Jupiter, Saturn, Uranus, Neptune, Pluto)

See if you can find more information about Pluto. Did you know that some astronomers believe that it was once a moon of Neptune? Look in an encyclopedia to find out more.

Chart the weather and temperature for the month. You will need to check with the weatherman for the high and low temperatures for the day. Write down or draw the weather for the day. Include the high and low temperature.
Registra el clima y la temperatura durante un mes. Escribe o dibuja el clima de cada día.

Sun.	Mon.	Tues.	Weds.	Thurs.	Fri.	Sat.

Information will vary.

© Federal Education Publishing — 123 — Level Orange

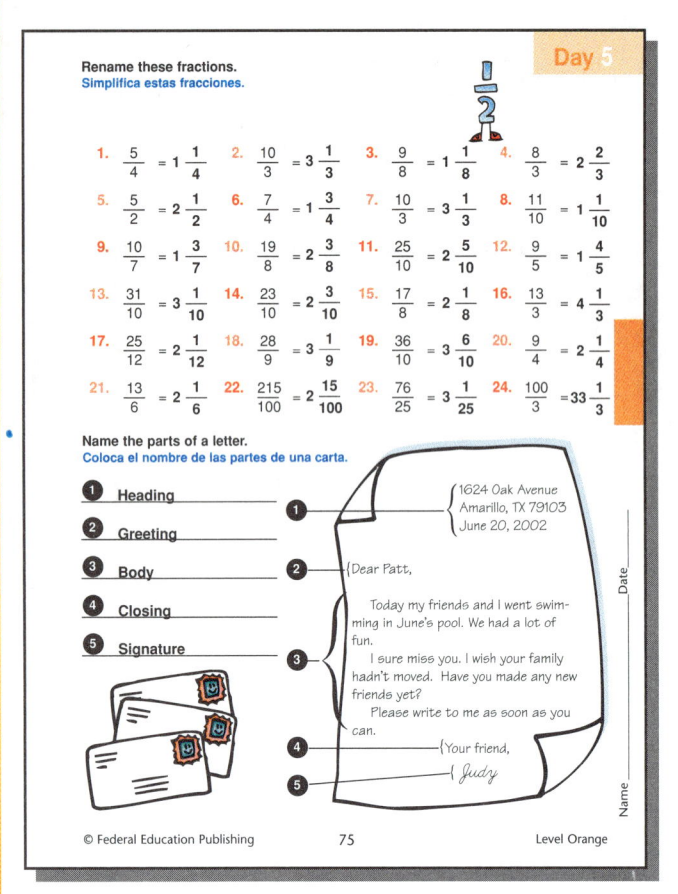

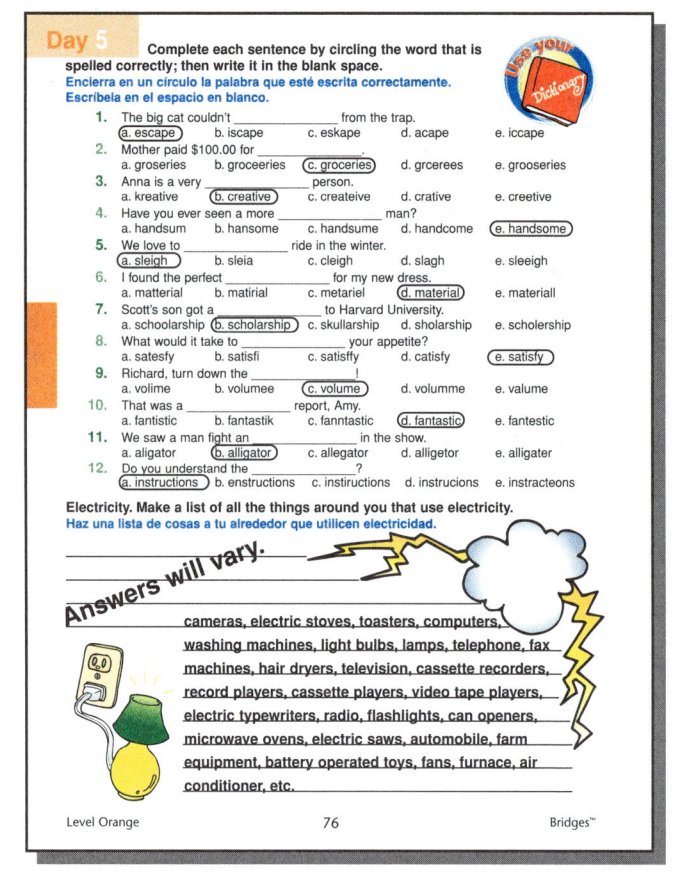

Page 75

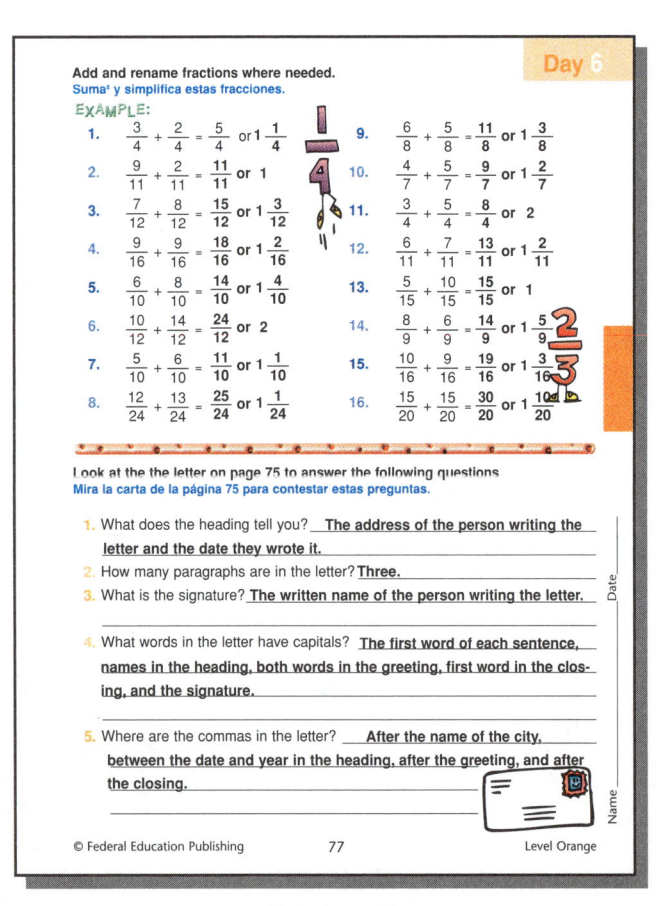

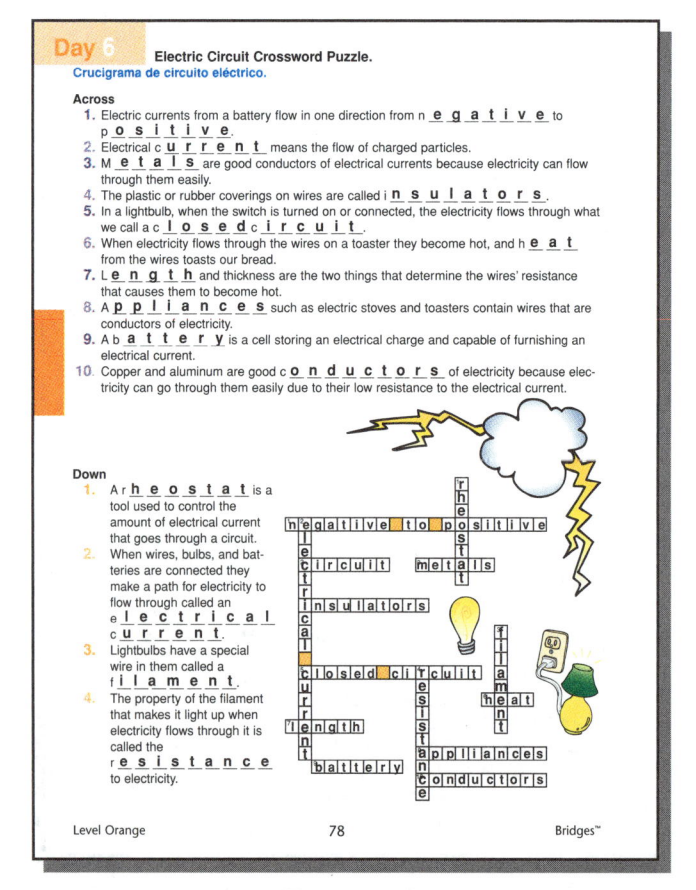

Rename these fractions.
Simplifica estas fracciones.

1. $\frac{5}{4} = 1\frac{1}{4}$
2. $\frac{10}{3} = 3\frac{1}{3}$
3. $\frac{9}{8} = 1\frac{1}{8}$
4. $\frac{8}{3} = 2\frac{2}{3}$
5. $\frac{5}{2} = 2\frac{1}{2}$
6. $\frac{7}{4} = 1\frac{3}{4}$
7. $\frac{10}{3} = 3\frac{1}{3}$
8. $\frac{11}{10} = 1\frac{1}{10}$
9. $\frac{10}{7} = 1\frac{3}{7}$
10. $\frac{19}{8} = 2\frac{3}{8}$
11. $\frac{25}{10} = 2\frac{5}{10}$
12. $\frac{9}{5} = 1\frac{4}{5}$
13. $\frac{31}{10} = 3\frac{1}{10}$
14. $\frac{23}{10} = 2\frac{3}{10}$
15. $\frac{17}{8} = 2\frac{1}{8}$
16. $\frac{13}{3} = 4\frac{1}{3}$
17. $\frac{25}{12} = 2\frac{1}{12}$
18. $\frac{28}{9} = 3\frac{1}{9}$
19. $\frac{36}{10} = 3\frac{6}{10}$
20. $\frac{9}{4} = 2\frac{1}{4}$
21. $\frac{13}{6} = 2\frac{1}{6}$
22. $\frac{215}{100} = 2\frac{15}{100}$
23. $\frac{76}{25} = 3\frac{1}{25}$
24. $\frac{100}{3} = 33\frac{1}{3}$

Name the parts of a letter.
Coloca el nombre de las partes de una carta.

1. Heading
2. Greeting
3. Body
4. Closing
5. Signature

Letter:
1. 1624 Oak Avenue, Amarillo, TX 79103, June 20, 2002
2. Dear Patt,
3. Today my friends and I went swimming in June's pool. We had a lot of fun. I sure miss you. I wish your family hadn't moved. Have you made any new friends yet? Please write to me as soon as you can.
4. Your friend,
5. Judy

Page 76

Complete each sentence by circling the word that is spelled correctly; then write it in the blank space.
Encierra en un círculo la palabra que esté escrita correctamente. Escríbela en el espacio en blanco.

1. The big cat couldn't _____ from the trap. (a. escape)
2. Mother paid $100.00 for _____. (c. groceries)
3. Anna is a very _____ person. (b. creative)
4. Have you ever seen a more _____ man? (e. handsome)
5. We love to _____ ride in the winter. (a. sleigh)
6. I found the perfect _____ for my new dress. (d. material)
7. Scott's son got a _____ to Harvard University. (b. scholarship)
8. What would it take to _____ your appetite? (e. satisfy)
9. Richard, turn down the _____! (c. volume)
10. That was a _____ report, Amy. (d. fantastic)
11. We saw a man fight an _____ in the show. (b. alligator)
12. Do you understand the _____? (a. instructions)

Electricity. Make a list of all the things around you that use electricity.
Haz una lista de cosas a tu alrededor que utilicen electricidad.

Answers will vary.

cameras, electric stoves, toasters, computers, washing machines, light bulbs, lamps, telephone, fax machines, hair dryers, television, cassette recorders, record players, cassette players, video tape players, electric typewriters, radio, flashlights, can openers, microwave ovens, electric saws, automobile, farm equipment, battery operated toys, fans, furnace, air conditioner, etc.

Page 77

Add and rename fractions where needed.
Sumaª y simplifica estas fracciones.

EXAMPLE:
1. $\frac{3}{4} + \frac{2}{4} = \frac{5}{4}$ or $1\frac{1}{4}$
2. $\frac{9}{11} + \frac{2}{11} = \frac{11}{11}$ or 1
3. $\frac{7}{12} + \frac{8}{12} = \frac{15}{12}$ or $1\frac{3}{12}$
4. $\frac{9}{16} + \frac{9}{16} = \frac{18}{16}$ or $1\frac{2}{16}$
5. $\frac{6}{10} + \frac{8}{10} = \frac{14}{10}$ or $1\frac{4}{10}$
6. $\frac{10}{12} + \frac{14}{12} = \frac{24}{12}$ or 2
7. $\frac{5}{10} + \frac{6}{10} = \frac{11}{10}$ or $1\frac{1}{10}$
8. $\frac{12}{24} + \frac{13}{24} = \frac{25}{24}$ or $1\frac{1}{24}$
9. $\frac{6}{8} + \frac{5}{8} = \frac{11}{8}$ or $1\frac{3}{8}$
10. $\frac{4}{7} + \frac{5}{7} = \frac{9}{7}$ or $1\frac{2}{7}$
11. $\frac{3}{4} + \frac{5}{4} = \frac{8}{4}$ or 2
12. $\frac{6}{11} + \frac{7}{11} = \frac{13}{11}$ or $1\frac{2}{11}$
13. $\frac{5}{15} + \frac{10}{15} = \frac{15}{15}$ or 1
14. $\frac{8}{9} + \frac{6}{9} = \frac{14}{9}$ or $1\frac{5}{9}$
15. $\frac{10}{16} + \frac{9}{16} = \frac{19}{16}$ or $1\frac{3}{16}$
16. $\frac{15}{20} + \frac{15}{20} = \frac{30}{20}$ or $1\frac{10}{20}$

Look at the letter on page 75 to answer the following questions
Mira la carta de la página 75 para contestar estas preguntas.

1. What does the heading tell you? **The address of the person writing the letter and the date they wrote it.**
2. How many paragraphs are in the letter? **Three.**
3. What is the signature? **The written name of the person writing the letter.**
4. What words in the letter have capitals? **The first word of each sentence, names in the heading, both words in the greeting, first word in the closing, and the signature.**
5. Where are the commas in the letter? **After the name of the city, between the date and year in the heading, after the greeting, and after the closing.**

Page 78

Electric Circuit Crossword Puzzle.
Crucigrama de circuito eléctrico.

Across
1. Electric currents from a battery flow in one direction from n**egative** to p**ositive**.
2. Electrical c**urrent** means the flow of charged particles.
3. M**etals** are good conductors of electrical currents because electricity can flow through them easily.
4. The plastic or rubber coverings on wires are called i**nsulators**.
5. In a lightbulb, when the switch is turned on or connected, the electricity flows through what we call a c**losed circuit**.
6. When electricity flows through the wires on a toaster they become hot, and h**eat** from the wires toasts our bread.
7. L**ength** and thickness are the two things that determine the wires' resistance that causes them to become hot.
8. A**ppliances** such as electric stoves and toasters contain wires that are conductors of electricity.
9. A b**attery** is a cell storing an electrical charge and capable of furnishing an electrical current.
10. Copper and aluminum are good c**onductors** of electricity because electricity can go through them easily due to their low resistance to the electrical current.

Down
1. A r**heostat** is a tool used to control the amount of electrical current that goes through a circuit.
2. When wires, bulbs, and batteries are connected they make a path for electricity to flow through called an e**lectrical** c**urrent**.
3. Lightbulbs have a special wire in them called a f**ilament**.
4. The property of the filament that makes it light up when electricity flows through it is called the r**esistance** to electricity.

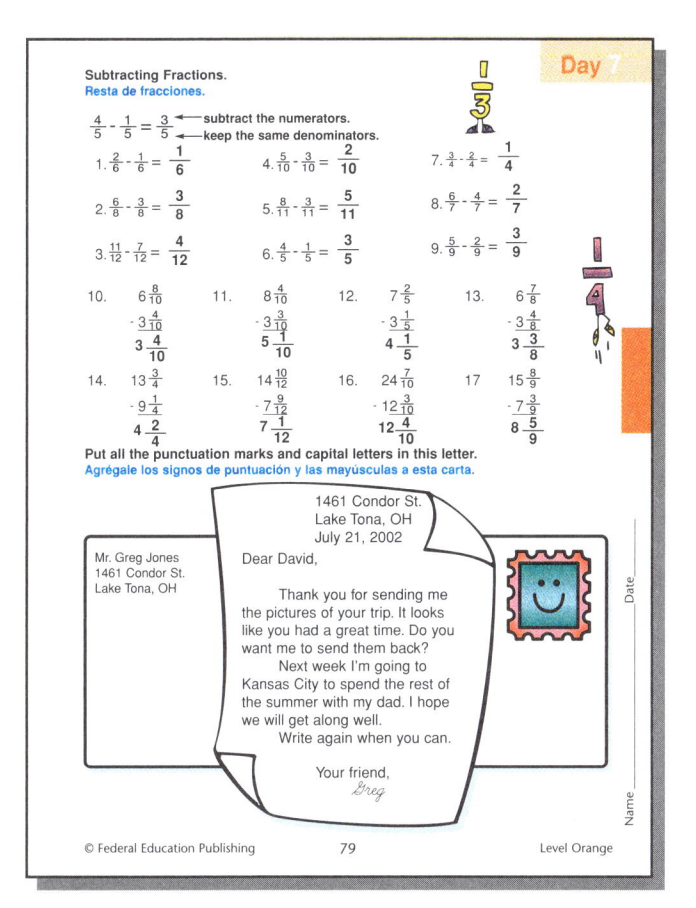

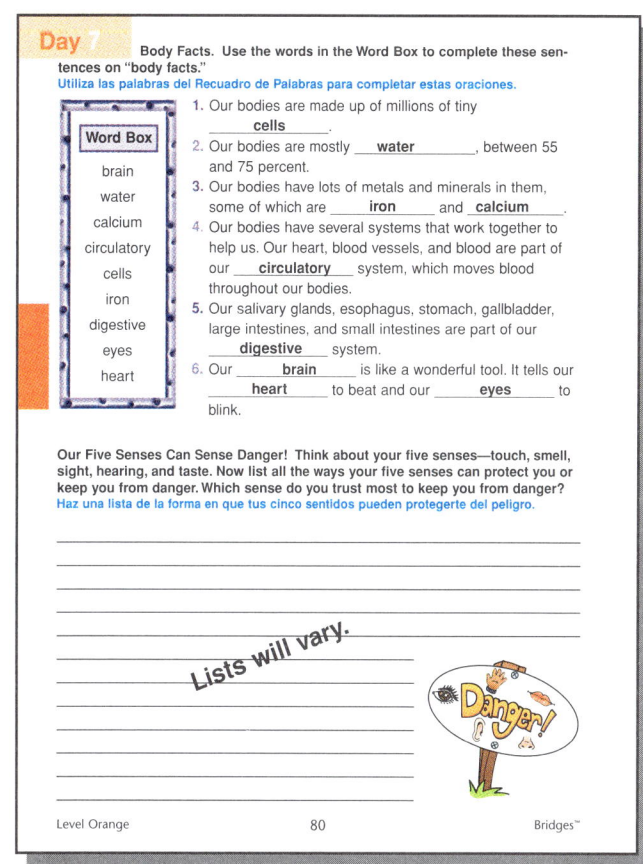

Page 79

Subtracting Fractions.
Resta de fracciones.

$\frac{4}{5} - \frac{1}{5} = \frac{3}{5}$ ← subtract the numerators.
← keep the same denominators.

1. $\frac{2}{6} - \frac{1}{6} = \frac{1}{6}$
2. $\frac{6}{8} - \frac{3}{8} = \frac{3}{8}$
3. $\frac{11}{12} - \frac{7}{12} = \frac{4}{12}$
4. $\frac{5}{10} - \frac{3}{10} = \frac{2}{10}$
5. $\frac{8}{11} - \frac{3}{11} = \frac{5}{11}$
6. $\frac{4}{5} - \frac{1}{5} = \frac{3}{5}$
7. $\frac{3}{4} - \frac{2}{4} = \frac{1}{4}$
8. $\frac{6}{7} - \frac{4}{7} = \frac{2}{7}$
9. $\frac{5}{9} - \frac{2}{9} = \frac{3}{9}$

10. $6\frac{8}{10} - 3\frac{4}{10} = 3\frac{4}{10}$
11. $8\frac{4}{10} - 3\frac{3}{10} = 5\frac{1}{10}$
12. $7\frac{5}{5} - 3\frac{1}{5} = 4\frac{1}{5}$
13. $6\frac{7}{8} - 3\frac{4}{8} = 3\frac{3}{8}$
14. $13\frac{3}{4} - 9\frac{1}{4} = 4\frac{2}{4}$
15. $14\frac{10}{12} - 7\frac{3}{12} = 7\frac{7}{12}$
16. $24\frac{7}{10} - 12\frac{3}{10} = 12\frac{4}{10}$
17. $15\frac{8}{9} - 7\frac{3}{9} = 8\frac{5}{9}$

Put all the punctuation marks and capital letters in this letter.
Agrégale los signos de puntuación y las mayúsculas a esta carta.

Mr. Greg Jones
1461 Condor St.
Lake Tona, OH

1461 Condor St.
Lake Tona, OH
July 21, 2002

Dear David,
    Thank you for sending me the pictures of your trip. It looks like you had a great time. Do you want me to send them back?
    Next week I'm going to Kansas City to spend the rest of the summer with my dad. I hope we will get along well.
    Write again when you can.

        Your friend,
        Greg

Page 80

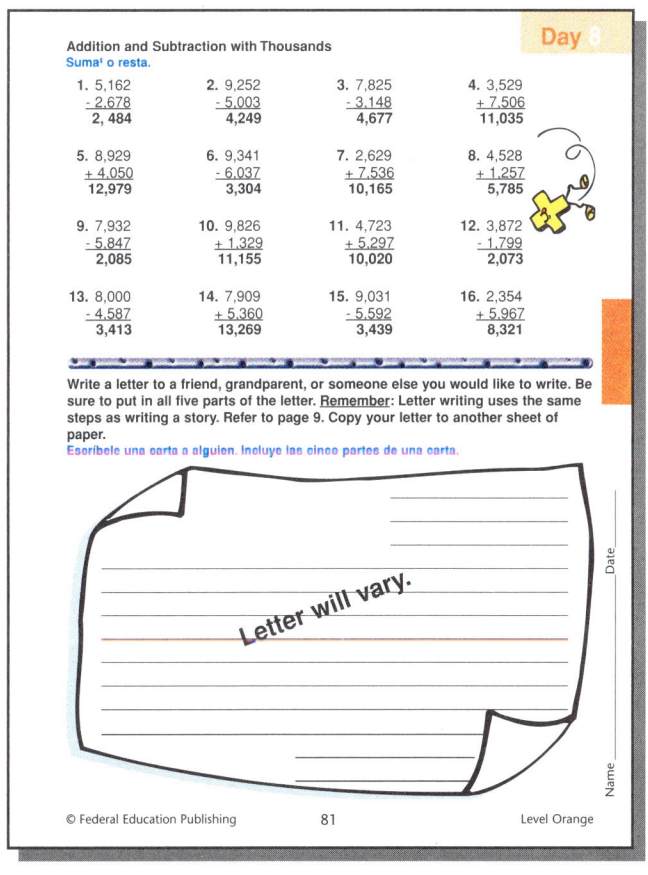

Body Facts. Use the words in the Word Box to complete these sentences on "body facts."
Utiliza las palabras del Recuadro de Palabras para completar estas oraciones.

Word Box: brain, water, calcium, circulatory, cells, iron, digestive, eyes, heart

1. Our bodies are made up of millions of tiny **cells**.
2. Our bodies are mostly **water**, between 55 and 75 percent.
3. Our bodies have lots of metals and minerals in them, some of which are **iron** and **calcium**.
4. Our bodies have several systems that work together to help us. Our heart, blood vessels, and blood are part of our **circulatory** system, which moves blood throughout our bodies.
5. Our salivary glands, esophagus, stomach, gallbladder, large intestines, and small intestines are part of our **digestive** system.
6. Our **brain** is like a wonderful tool. It tells our **heart** to beat and our **eyes** to blink.

Our Five Senses Can Sense Danger! Think about your five senses—touch, smell, sight, hearing, and taste. Now list all the ways your five senses can protect you or keep you from danger. Which sense do you trust most to keep you from danger?
Haz una lista de la forma en que tus cinco sentidos pueden protegerte del peligro.

Lists will vary.

Page 81

Addition and Subtraction with Thousands
Suma o resta.

1. 5,162 − 2,678 = 2,484
2. 9,252 − 5,003 = 4,249
3. 7,825 − 3,148 = 4,677
4. 3,529 + 7,506 = 11,035
5. 8,929 + 4,050 = 12,979
6. 9,341 − 6,037 = 3,304
7. 2,629 + 7,536 = 10,165
8. 4,528 + 1,257 = 5,785
9. 7,932 − 5,847 = 2,085
10. 9,826 + 1,329 = 11,155
11. 4,723 + 5,297 = 10,020
12. 3,872 − 1,799 = 2,073
13. 8,000 − 4,587 = 3,413
14. 7,909 + 5,360 = 13,269
15. 9,031 − 5,592 = 3,439
16. 2,354 + 5,967 = 8,321

Write a letter to a friend, grandparent, or someone else you would like to write. Be sure to put in all five parts of the letter. **Remember:** Letter writing uses the same steps as writing a story. Refer to page 9. Copy your letter to another sheet of paper.
Escríbele una carta a alguien. Incluye las cinco partes de una carta.

Letter will vary.

Page 82

Below are the stressed syllables of some spelling words. Write the other syllables and then write the words in cursive. Each blank stands for a letter.
Debajo se encuentran las sílabas tónicas de algunas palabras. Escribe las otras sílabas y luego escribe las palabras en cursiva. Cada espacio en blanco representa una letra.

Word Box: favor, amount, busy, accept, violin, paddle, piano, begin, dial, bacon, several, salad, wonderful, unlock, vegetable, ~~parent~~, library, limit, into, depend

1. par´ **ent** — *parent*
2. li´ _ _ _ — **library**
3. lim´ _ _ — **limit**
4. in´ _ _ — **into**
5. _ _ pend´ — **depend**
6. ba´ _ _ — **bacon**
7. di´ _ _ — **dial**
8. _ _ gin´ — **begin**
9. _ _ a´ _ — **piano**
10. pad´ _ _ — **paddle**
11. sev´ _ _ _ — **several**
12. sal´ _ _ — **salad**
13. won´ _ _ _ _ — **wonderful**
14. _ _ lock´ — **unlock**
15. veg´ _ _ _ _ _ — **vegetable**
16. _ _ lin´ — **violin**
17. _ cept´ — **accept**
18. bus´ _ — **busy**
19. _ mount´ — **amount**
20. fa´ _ _ _ — **favor**

Self-Portrait Poem.
Sigue las instrucciones para escribir un poema sobre ti mismo.

1. Write your name.
2. Write two words that tell about you.
3. Write three words that tell what you like to do.
4. Write two more words that describe you.
5. Write your name again.

Try writing another "portrait poem" about a favorite person or pet in your life.

Writing will vary.

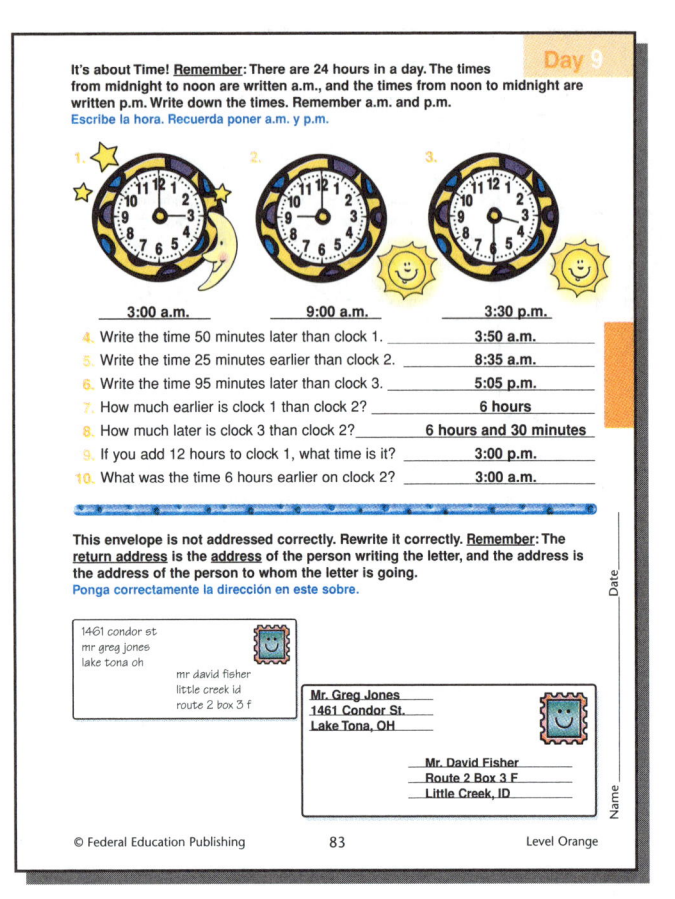

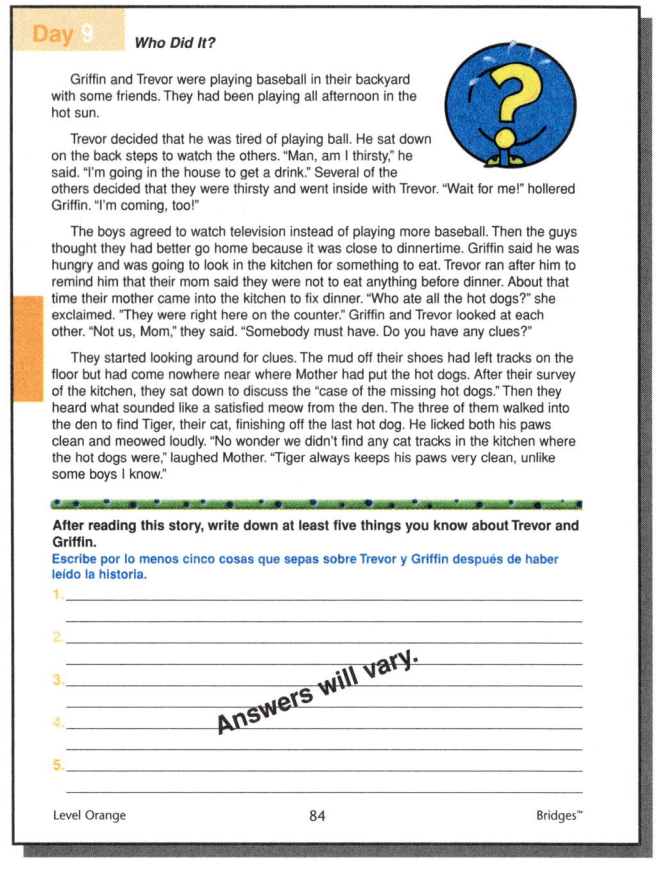

Page 83

Day 9

It's about Time! Remember: There are 24 hours in a day. The times from midnight to noon are written a.m., and the times from noon to midnight are written p.m. Write down the times. Remember a.m. and p.m.
Escribe la hora. Recuerda poner a.m. y p.m.

1. 3:00 a.m.
2. 9:00 a.m.
3. 3:30 p.m.

4. Write the time 50 minutes later than clock 1. _____ 3:50 a.m.
5. Write the time 25 minutes earlier than clock 2. _____ 8:35 a.m.
6. Write the time 95 minutes later than clock 3. _____ 5:05 p.m.
7. How much earlier is clock 1 than clock 2? _____ 6 hours
8. How much later is clock 3 than clock 2? _____ 6 hours and 30 minutes
9. If you add 12 hours to clock 1, what time is it? _____ 3:00 p.m.
10. What was the time 6 hours earlier on clock 2? _____ 3:00 a.m.

This envelope is not addressed correctly. Rewrite it correctly. Remember: The return address is the address of the person writing the letter, and the address is the address of the person to whom the letter is going.
Ponga correctamente la dirección en este sobre.

1461 condor st
mr greg jones
lake tona oh

mr david fisher
little creek id
route 2 box 3 f

Mr. Greg Jones
1461 Condor St.
Lake Tona, OH

Mr. David Fisher
Route 2 Box 3 F
Little Creek, ID

Page 84

Day 9 — Who Did It?

Griffin and Trevor were playing baseball in their backyard with some friends. They had been playing all afternoon in the hot sun.

Trevor decided that he was tired of playing ball. He sat down on the back steps to watch the others. "Man, am I thirsty," he said. "I'm going in the house to get a drink." Several of the others decided that they were thirsty and went inside with Trevor. "Wait for me!" hollered Griffin. "I'm coming, too!"

The boys agreed to watch television instead of playing more baseball. Then the guys thought they had better go home because it was close to dinnertime. Griffin said he was hungry and was going to look in the kitchen for something to eat. Trevor ran after him to remind him that their mom said they were not to eat anything before dinner. About that time their mother came into the kitchen to fix dinner. "Who ate all the hot dogs?" she exclaimed. "They were right here on the counter." Griffin and Trevor looked at each other. "Not us, Mom," they said. "Somebody must have. Do you have any clues?"

They started looking around for clues. The mud off their shoes had left tracks on the floor but had come nowhere near where Mother had put the hot dogs. After their survey of the kitchen, they sat down to discuss the "case of the missing hot dogs." Then they heard what sounded like a satisfied meow from the den. The three of them walked into the den to find Tiger, their cat, finishing off the last hot dog. He licked both his paws clean and meowed loudly. "No wonder we didn't find any cat tracks in the kitchen where the hot dogs were," laughed Mother. "Tiger always keeps his paws very clean, unlike some boys I know."

After reading this story, write down at least five things you know about Trevor and Griffin.
Escribe por lo menos cinco cosas que sepas sobre Trevor y Griffin después de haber leído la historia.

1. _____
2. _____
3. _____ Answers will vary.
4. _____
5. _____

Page 85

Day 10

Fractions to Tenths and the Decimal Equivalents for the Fraction
Remember: When working with fractions that have a denominator of 10, you can write them as fractions in tenths, or you can use the decimal equivalent. Do this activity by writing each both ways.
Escribe la fracción correcta y/o el decimal en los espacios en blanco.

1. 6/10 or .6
2. 3/10 or .3
3. 9/10 or .9
4. 7/10 or .7
5. 1/10 or .1
6. 5/10 or .5
7. 3/10 or .3
8. 1 7/10 or 1.7
9. 3 5/10 or 3.5
10. 1.9 or 1 9/10
11. .8 or 8/10
12. 3.4 or 3 4/10

On page 81, you wrote a letter to someone. Today, address an envelope and send the letter to them. Be sure to put your address in the upper left-hand corner and the address of the person to whom you're sending the letter in the center. Don't forget to put a stamp in the upper right-hand corner. Use the space below to practice.
Coloca la dirección a un sobre y envía la carta que has escrito en la página 81.

Envelopes will vary.

Page 86

Day 10 — Write an analogy to finish these sentences. Remember: An analogy is a comparison between two pairs of words. Try to think of the relationship between the two words given and then think of another word that has the same kind of relationship to the third word.
Escribe una analogía para finalizar estas oraciones.

EXAMPLE: Story is to read as song is to sing.

1. Brother is to boy as sister is to _____ girl _____.
2. Princess is to queen as prince is to _____ king _____.
3. Milk is to drink as hamburger is to _____ eat _____.
4. Arrow is to bow as bullet is to _____ gun _____.
5. Car is to driver as plane is to _____ pilot _____.
6. Ceiling is to room as lid is to _____ jar _____.
7. Paper is to tear as glass is to _____ break _____.
8. Large is to huge as small is to _____ tiny _____.
9. Wrist is to hand as ankle is to _____ foot _____.
10. Father is to uncle as mother is to _____ aunt _____.
11. Cupboard is to dishes as library is to _____ books _____.
12. Hard is to difficult as easy is to _____ simple _____.
13. Moon is to earth as earth is to _____ sun _____.
14. Time is to clock as date is to _____ calendar _____.

Exercising Parts of the Body. Make a list of 5 or 6 exercises. Some examples are running, hopping, sit-ups, jumping jacks, touching your toes, push-ups, jumping, skipping, playing sports, gymnastics, and swinging your arms. Try them. Which parts of the body are affected? Write down the results. Try this exercise. Take an ordinary spring-centered clothespin. Hold the ends between your thumb and one of your fingers. How many times can you open and close it in 30 to 40 seconds?
Haz una lista de 5 ó 6 ejercicios físicos. Trata de hacerlos. Escribe qué partes de tu cuerpo se ven afectadas.

Answers will vary.

Page 87

Day 11

Use what you know about fractions to tenths and their decimal equivalents to work with hundredths. Remember: When a whole object is divided into 100 equal parts, each part is one hundredth ($\frac{1}{100}$ or .01). Write the fraction as a decimal.
Escribe la fracción¹ como decimal.

1. $\frac{49}{100}$ = **.49**   2. $\frac{20}{100}$ = **.25**   3. $\frac{20}{100}$ = **.20**   4. $\frac{52}{100}$ = **.52**
5. $\frac{86}{100}$ = **.86**   6. $\frac{37}{100}$ = **.37**   7. $\frac{4}{100}$ = **.04**   8. $\frac{9}{100}$ = **.09**

Now write the mixed number as a decimal.
Escribe la fracción mixta como decimal.

9. $1\frac{93}{100}$ = **1.93**   10. $7\frac{15}{100}$ = **7.15**   11. $9\frac{13}{100}$ = **9.13**   12. $15\frac{47}{100}$ = **15.47**
13. $46\frac{89}{100}$ = **46.89**   14. $35\frac{6}{100}$ = **35.06**   15. $94\frac{7}{100}$ = **94.07**   16. $625\frac{12}{100}$ = **625.12**
17. $12\frac{5}{100}$ = **12.05**   18. $81\frac{1}{100}$ = **81.01**   19. $37\frac{87}{100}$ = **37.87**   20. $10\frac{11}{100}$ = **10.11**

Adjectives are words that tell about or describe nouns and pronouns. Circle the adjective(s) in these sentences. Write the noun(s) or pronoun(s) described at the end of the sentence.
Encierra en un círculo los adjetivos¹ de estas oraciones. Escribe los sustantivos¹ o pronombres¹ descritos.

1. A (beautiful) light flashed across the (cloudy) sky.   **light   sky**
2. Her (golden) hair was very (long).   **hair**
3. On the (tall) mountain we found (blue) and (yellow) flowers.
   mountain, flowers
4. He was (brave) after the accident.   **He**
5. It is (fun) but it is also (dangerous) to skydive.   **skydiving**
6. Our (brown) dog had (six) (cute) puppies.
   dog, puppies

Now fill in the blanks with adjectives.
Completa los espacios en blanco con adjetivos.

7. My _____ pencil is never in my desk.
8. The _____ students were having a _____ time.
9. Lions are _____ animals that we can see in the zoo.
10. The _____, _____ ride was making me sick.
11. My brother, Jack, sang a _____ song when we were camping.
12. _____, _____ snakes were wiggling around in the box.

Answers will vary.

Page 88

Day 11

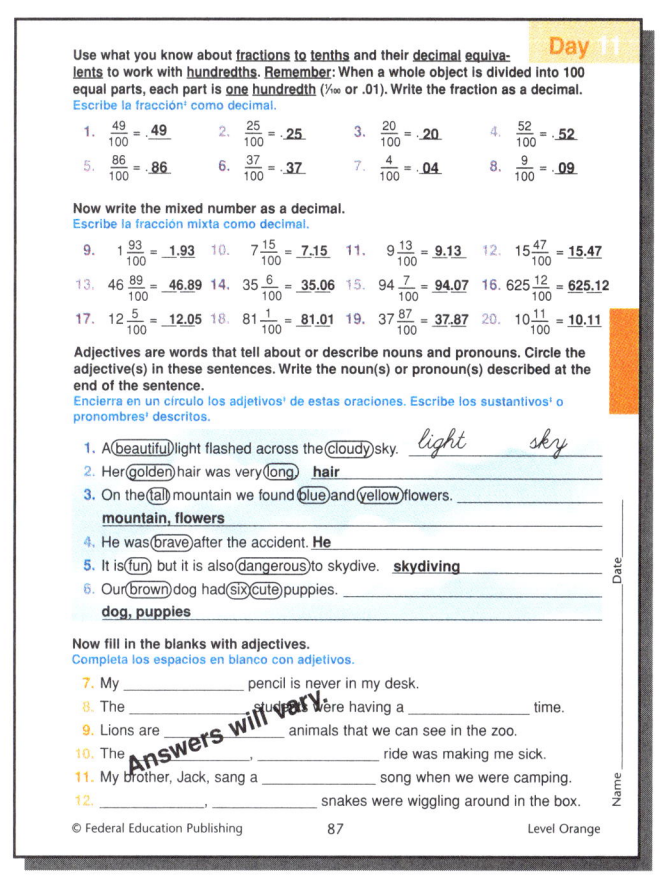

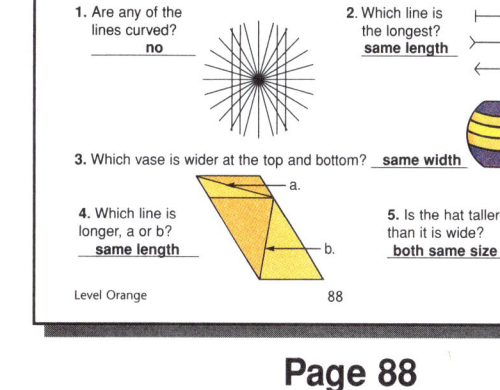

Fill in the blanks below with health terms from the box.
Completa los espacios en blanco con los términos sobre la salud del Recuadro de Palabras.

> nutrients, healthy, sleep, exercise, liquids, water, cleanliness, checkups, energy, food groups.

1. **Nutrients** are basic nourishing ingredients in good foods that we eat.
2. **Exercise** helps us to strengthen our muscles. It helps our heart and lungs grow, too.
3. **Checkups** help us prevent tooth decay and maintain good health.
4. Meat, fruits and vegetables, milk, and breads and cereals make up the basic four **food** **groups** that keep us healthy.
5. Being healthy means feeling good and having the **energy** to work and play.
6. Vitamins and minerals are kinds of **nutrients** that we get from food.
7. Being **healthy** means feeling good and not being sick.
8. Sugar, starch, and fats are **nutrients** that the body uses for fuel to give us **energy**.
9. We need to drink a lot of **liquid** because our body is approximately 60 to 70 percent **water**.
10. Plenty of **sleep** helps give our body time to grow and repair itself. Children need 10 to 11 hours of it because they are not finished growing.
11. **Cleanliness** is a way of fighting germs and staying healthy.
12. We need health **checkups** by a doctor or dentist at least once a year.

Are you confused?
¿Estás confundido?

1. Are any of the lines curved?   **no**
2. Which line is the longest?   **same length**
3. Which vase is wider at the top and bottom?   **same width**
4. Which line is longer, a or b?   **same length**
5. Is the hat taller than it is wide?   **both same size**

Page 89

Day 12

Decimals and Money. Remember: 100 pennies = 1 dollar. One penny is 1/100 of a dollar, or $.01, so 49 pennies = $.49. We can compute money by adding, subtracting, multiplying, and dividing—just watch the decimals. Look at the signs. Use a separate piece of paper to show your work.
Puedes calcular dinero sumando, restando multiplicando y dividiendo. Solamente observa los decimales.

EXAMPLE:

```
 $57.34        $62.89        $12.45              $3.95
+ 62.89       - 34.91        x    3         5 ) $19.75
--------      --------       -------            -15
$120.23        $27.98         $37.35             47
                                                -45
                                                 25
                                                -25
                                                  0
```

1. $409.75 − 249.83 = **$159.92**
2. $14.74 × 3 = **$44.22**
3. $492.00 − 349.50 = **$142.50**
4. 4) $12.92 = **$3.23**
5. $162.49 + 186.32 = **$348.81**
6. 7) $49.77 = **$7.11**
7. $601.89 + 403.23 = **$1,005.12**
8. $9.57 × 6 = **$57.42**
9. $668.45 + 171.63 = **$840.08**
10. $915.04 − 102.56 = **$812.48**
11. $741.13 × 8 = **$5,929.04**
12. 4) $29.48 = **$7.37**

Write nouns to go with these adjectives.
Escribe sustantivos¹ que concuerden con estos adjetivos¹.

1. two, red **apples**
2. fluffy, yellow **chicks**
3. cold, wet **day**
4. dark, strange **shadow**
5. wild, dangerous **beast**
6. black, furry **bear**
7. big, heavy **table**
8. fancy, little **dress**
9. pink, small **pigs**
10. smooth, green **frog**
11. fat, juicy **worms**
12. loud, shrill **sound**
13. fourteen, blue **gloves**
14. long, thick **neck**
15. cozy, warm **bed**
16. sharp, silver **knife**

Answers may vary.

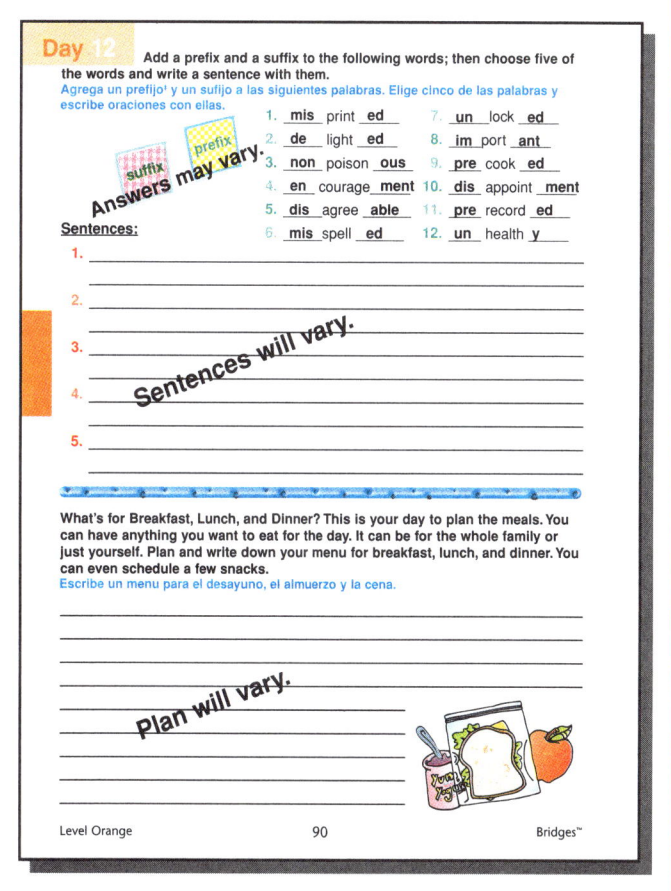

Page 90

Day 12

Add a prefix and a suffix to the following words; then choose five of the words and write a sentence with them.
Agrega un prefijo¹ y un sufijo a las siguientes palabras. Elige cinco de las palabras y escribe oraciones con ellas.

1. **mis** print **ed**
2. **de** light **ed**
3. **non** poison **ous**
4. **en** courage **ment**
5. **dis** agree **able**
6. **mis** spell **ed**
7. **un** lock **ed**
8. **im** port **ant**
9. **pre** cook **ed**
10. **dis** appoint **ment**
11. **pre** record **ed**
12. **un** health **y**

Answers may vary.

Sentences:
1.
2.
3.
4.
5.

Sentences will vary.

What's for Breakfast, Lunch, and Dinner? This is your day to plan the meals. You can have anything you want to eat for the day. It can be for the whole family or just yourself. Plan and write down your menu for breakfast, lunch, and dinner. You can even schedule a few snacks.
Escribe un menú para el desayuno, el almuerzo y la cena.

Plan will vary.

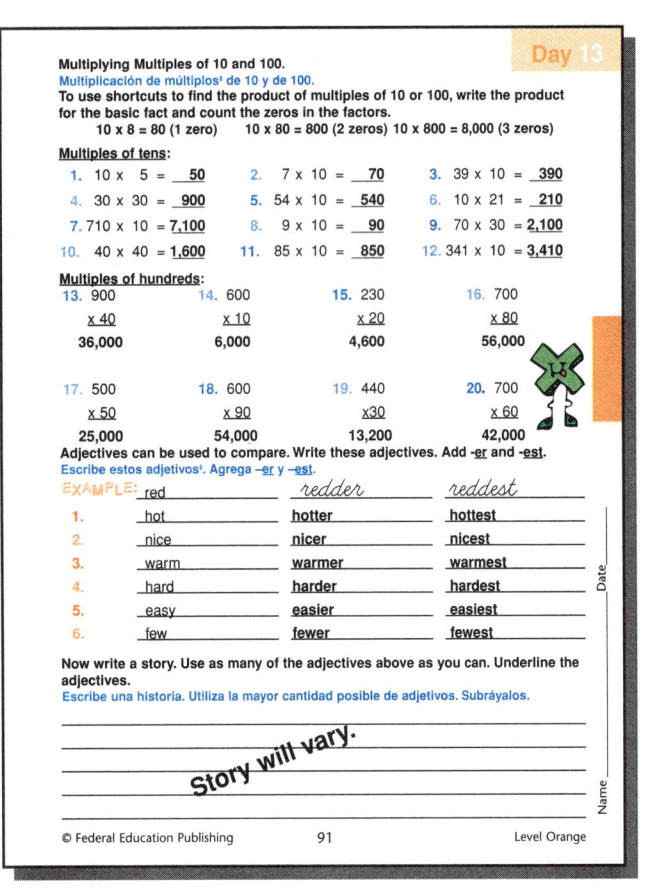

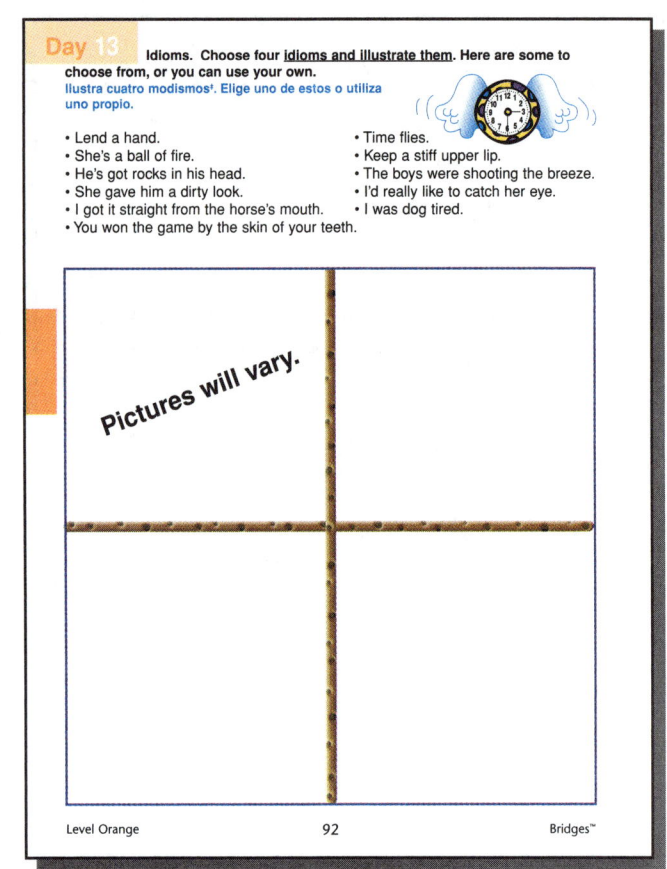

Page 91

Multiplying Multiples of 10 and 100. — Day 13
Multiplicación de múltiplos de 10 y de 100.
To use shortcuts to find the product of multiples of 10 or 100, write the product for the basic fact and count the zeros in the factors.
10 × 8 = 80 (1 zero)   10 × 80 = 800 (2 zeros)   10 × 800 = 8,000 (3 zeros)

Multiples of tens:
1. 10 × 5 = __50__
2. 7 × 10 = __70__
3. 39 × 10 = __390__
4. 30 × 30 = __900__
5. 54 × 10 = __540__
6. 10 × 21 = __210__
7. 710 × 10 = __7,100__
8. 9 × 10 = __90__
9. 70 × 30 = __2,100__
10. 40 × 40 = __1,600__
11. 85 × 10 = __850__
12. 341 × 10 = __3,410__

Multiples of hundreds:
13. 900 × 40 = 36,000
14. 600 × 10 = 6,000
15. 230 × 20 = 4,600
16. 700 × 80 = 56,000
17. 500 × 50 = 25,000
18. 600 × 90 = 54,000
19. 440 × 30 = 13,200
20. 700 × 60 = 42,000

Adjectives can be used to compare. Write these adjectives. Add -er and -est.
Escribe estos adjetivos. Agrega –er y –est.

EXAMPLE: red — redder — reddest
1. hot — hotter — hottest
2. nice — nicer — nicest
3. warm — warmer — warmest
4. hard — harder — hardest
5. easy — easier — easiest
6. few — fewer — fewest

Now write a story. Use as many of the adjectives above as you can. Underline the adjectives.
Escribe una historia. Utiliza la mayor cantidad posible de adjetivos. Subráyalos.

Story will vary.

Page 92

Idioms. Choose four idioms and illustrate them. Here are some to choose from, or you can use your own. — Day 13
Ilustra cuatro modismos. Elige uno de estos o utiliza uno propio.

- Lend a hand.
- She's a ball of fire.
- He's got rocks in his head.
- She gave him a dirty look.
- I got it straight from the horse's mouth.
- You won the game by the skin of your teeth.
- Time flies.
- Keep a stiff upper lip.
- The boys were shooting the breeze.
- I'd really like to catch her eye.
- I was dog tired.

Pictures will vary.

Page 93

Place Value. A place-value chart can help us read as well as figure out large numbers. — Day 14
Utiliza la tabla de valores posicionales para leer y escribir estos números.

Hundred Millions	Ten Millions	Millions	Hundred Thousands	Ten Thousands	Thousands	Hundreds	Tens	Ones
8	6	5	3	7	1	4	3	

Using the place-value chart to help you, read and write the following numbers.
1. Eighty-six million five hundred thirty-seven thousand one hundred forty-three __86,537,143__.
2. Seven hundred eighty-nine million four hundred ninety-six thousand three hundred twenty-one __789,496,321__.
3. One hundred sixty million seven hundred six thousand one hundred twenty-nine __160,706,129__.
4. Seventy-one million four hundred eleven thousand eight hundred ninety-nine __71,411,899__.
5. One hundred million three hundred seventy-five thousand __100,375,000__.
6. Ninety million two hundred fifty-seven thousand four hundred forty-three __90,257,443__.
7. 1,369,000 __One million, three hundred sixty-nine thousand.__
8. 375,403,101 __Three hundred seventy-five million, four hundred three thousand, one hundred one.__
9. 894,336,045 __Eight hundred ninety-four million, three hundred thirty-six thousand, forty-five.__
10. 284,300,070 __Two hundred eighty-four million, three hundred thousand, seventy.__

Overworked And. Rewrite the paragraph and leave out all the occurrences of and that you can. Write in cursive and be sure to put capitals and periods where they need to go.
Vuelve a escribir este párrafo. Elimina la palabra and todas las veces que sea posible.

Answers may vary.

My friend and I visited Cardiff, Wales, and we learned that Cardiff is the capital and largest port of Wales and the city lies on the River Taff near the Bristol Channel and Cardiff is near the largest coal mines in Great Britain and it is one of the great coal-shipping ports of the world.

My friend and I visited Cardiff, Wales. We learned that Cardiff is the capital and largest part of Wales. The city lies on the River Taff near the Bristol Channel. Cardiff is near the largest coal mines in Great Britain. It is one of the great coal-shipping parts of the world.

How many times were you able to leave and out of the paragraph? __Four__

Page 94

Day 14 — The following words are often misspelled. Write each word three times, then have someone give you a test on another piece of paper.
Escribe cada palabra tres veces y luego haz que alguien te evalúe.

EXAMPLE:
1. although — although although although
2. arithmetic — arithmetic arithmetic arithmetic
3. trouble — trouble trouble trouble
4. bought — bought bought bought
5. chocolate — chocolate chocolate chocolate
6. aunt — aunt aunt aunt
7. handkerchief — handkerchief handkerchief handkerchief
8. piece — piece piece piece
9. vacation — vacation vacation vacation
10. practice — practice practice practice
11. receive — receive receive receive
12. getting — getting getting getting
13. lessons — lessons lessons lessons
14. weather — weather weather weather
15. surprise — surprise surprise surprise

Categorizing the People in Your Family. Include some aunts, uncles, and cousins. Categorize them according to age, height, weight, hair color, hair length, eye color, etc. What do they have in common? What are some of their differences? Then draw a picture of them. Use another sheet of paper.
Categoriza a las personas de tu familia. ¿En qué se parecen? ¿En qué se diferencian?

family member	age	height	weight	hair color

Answers will vary.

Page 95

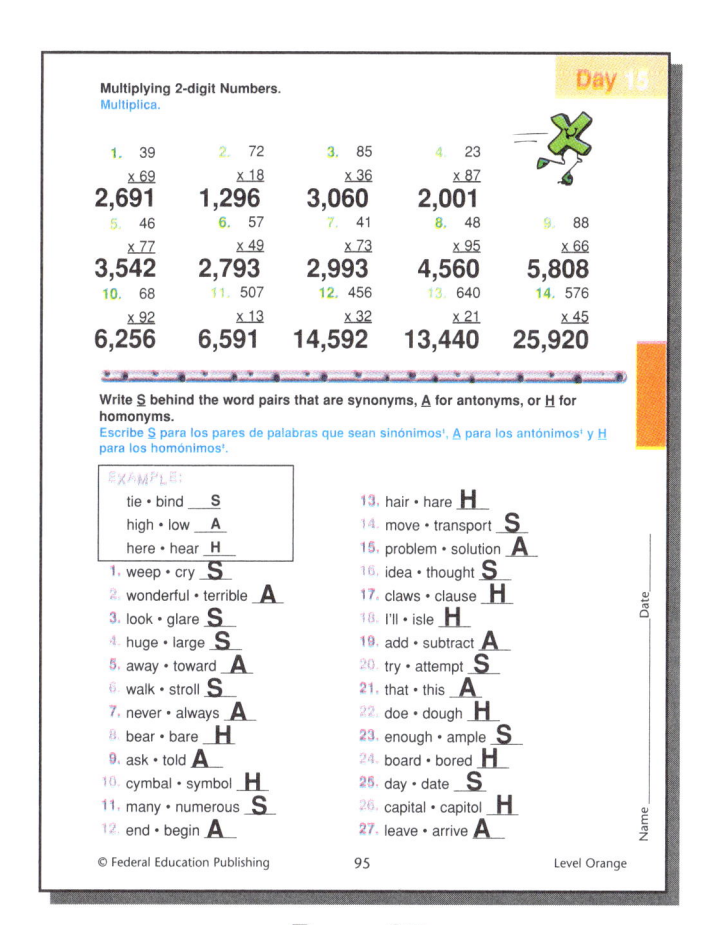

Multiplying 2-digit Numbers.
Multiplica.

1. 39 × 69 = **2,691**	2. 72 × 18 = **1,296**	3. 85 × 36 = **3,060**	4. 23 × 87 = **2,001**	
5. 46 × 77 = **3,542**	6. 57 × 49 = **2,793**	7. 41 × 73 = **2,993**	8. 48 × 95 = **4,560**	9. 88 × 66 = **5,808**
10. 68 × 92 = **6,256**	11. 507 × 13 = **6,591**	12. 456 × 32 = **14,592**	13. 640 × 21 = **13,440**	14. 576 × 45 = **25,920**

Write S behind the word pairs that are synonyms, A for antonyms, or H for homonyms.
Escribe S para los pares de palabras que sean sinónimos, A para los antónimos y H para los homónimos.

EXAMPLE:
- tie • bind __S__
- high • low __A__
- here • hear __H__

1. weep • cry __S__
2. wonderful • terrible __A__
3. look • glare __S__
4. huge • large __S__
5. away • toward __A__
6. walk • stroll __S__
7. never • always __A__
8. bear • bare __H__
9. ask • told __A__
10. cymbal • symbol __H__
11. many • numerous __S__
12. end • begin __A__
13. hair • hare __H__
14. move • transport __S__
15. problem • solution __A__
16. idea • thought __S__
17. claws • clause __H__
18. I'll • isle __H__
19. add • subtract __A__
20. try • attempt __S__
21. that • this __A__
22. doe • dough __H__
23. enough • ample __S__
24. board • bored __H__
25. day • date __S__
26. capital • capitol __H__
27. leave • arrive __A__

Page 96

Do this crossword puzzle. Read the clues to help you decide what words go in the boxes. Lee las pistas y decide qué palabras van en los recuadros.

Down
1. birds with webbed feet
2. plays the piano
3. gave money
5. holds up the gate
8. boards for building
9. frilly
11. do it again to a story
12. hair by the eye
13. another name for a mule

Across
2. red from the sun
4. won't bend easily
5. eat outside
6. beginning of a word
7. decay of food
10. very large; great
14. nothing in it
15. cook in

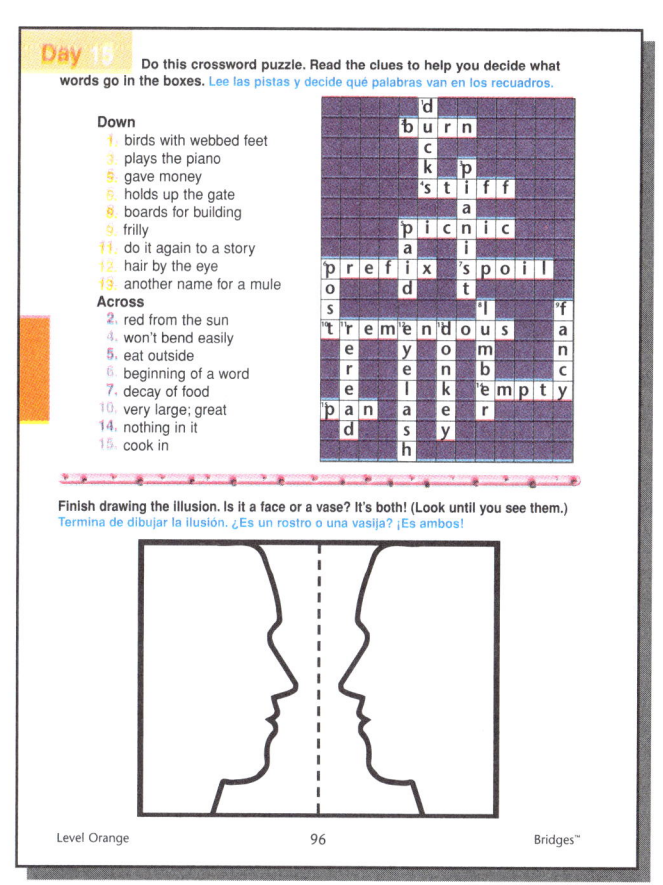

Finish drawing the illusion. Is it a face or a vase? It's both! (Look until you see them.)
Termina de dibujar la ilusión. ¿Es un rostro o una vasija? ¡Es ambos!

Notes

Five things I'm thankful for:

1. _____
2. _____
3. _____
4. _____
5. _____

Notes

Five things I'm thankful for:

1. _____
2. _____
3. _____
4. _____
5. _____

Multiplication and Division

Developing multiplication and division math skills can be a challenging experience for both parent and child.

- **Have a positive attitude.**
- **Relax and enjoy the learning process.**
- **Keep the learning time short and fun you will get better results.**
- **Review the cards with your child.**
- **Read the front of the card.**
- **Check your answer on the reverse side.**
- **Separate those he/she does not know.**
- **Review those he/she does know.**
- **Gradually work through the other cards.**

These steps will help build your child's confidence with multiplication and division. Enjoy the rewards!

"Teacher, Teacher"

Three or more players.
Each player takes a turn as "Teacher."
The Teacher mixes up the flashcards and holds one card up at a time.
First player to yell out "Teacher, Teacher,"
will have the first chance to give the answer.
If his/her answer is right he/she receives 5 points.
If his/her answer is wrong, he/she will not receive any points.
Move on to the next person until someone answers correctly.
The next round someone else is teacher.
Repeat each round.
Reward the different levels, everyone wins!

Time Challenge

Follow the directions for "Teacher, Teacher" and add a time to it.
Increase the point system to meet the Time Challenge.
Reward the different levels, everyone wins!

Level Orange

0	0	0	0
×0	×1	×2	×3
4	3	2	1

0	0	0	0
×4	×5	×6	×7
8	7	6	5

0	0	0	1
×8	×9	×10	×1
3	2	1	9

| 1)1̄ | 1)2̄ | 1)3̄ | 1)4̄ |
| 0 | 0 | 0 | 0 |

| 1)5̄ | 1)6̄ | 1)7̄ | 1)8̄ |
| 0 | 0 | 0 | 0 |

| 1)9̄ | 2)2̄ | 2)4̄ | 2)6̄ |
| 1 | 0 | 0 | 0 |

2×1	2×2	3×1	3×2
7	6	5	4

3×3	4×1	4×2	4×3
2	1	9	8

4×4	5×1	5×2	5×3
6	5	4	3

2)8	2)10	2)12	2)14
6	3	4	2

2)16	2)18	3)3	3)6
12	8	4	9

3)9	3)12	3)15	3)18
15	10	5	16

5 × 4	5 × 5	6 × 1	6 × 2
1	9	8	7
6 × 3	6 × 4	6 × 5	6 × 6
5	4	3	2
7 × 1	7 × 2	7 × 3	7 × 4
9	8	7	6

3)21 12	3)24 6	3)27 25	4)4 20
4)8 36	4)12 30	4)16 24	4)20 18
4)24 28	4)28 21	4)32 14	4)36 7

7 × 5 4	7 × 6 3	7 × 7 2	8 × 1 1
8 × 2 8	8 × 3 7	8 × 4 6	8 × 5 5
8 × 6 3	8 × 7 2	8 × 8 1	9 × 1 9

5)5	5)10	5)15	5)20
8	49	42	35

5)25	5)30	5)35	5)40
40	32	24	16

5)45	6)6	6)12	6)18
9	64	56	48

9 ×2	9 ×3	9 ×4	9 ×5
7	6	5	4

9 ×6	9 ×7	9 ×8	9 ×9
2	1	9	8

10 ×1	10 ×2	10 ×3	10 ×4
6	5	4	3

6)24 45	6)30 36	6)36 27	6)42 18
6)48 81	6)54 72	7)7 63	7)14 54
7)21 40	7)28 30	7)35 20	7)42 10

10 × 5 7	10 × 6 6	10 × 7 5	10 × 8 4
10 × 9 2	10 × 10 1	7)49 9	7)56 8
7)63 6	8)8 5	8)16 4	8)24 3

8)32	8)40	8)48	8)56
80	70	60	50

8)64	8)72	9)9	9)18
8	7	100	90

9)27	9)36	9)45	9)54
3	2	1	9

9)63	9)72	9)81	10)10
10)20	10)30	10)40	10)50
10)60	10)70	10)80	10)90

1)0	2)0	3)0	4)0
1	9	8	7

5)0	6)0	7)0	8)0
5	4	3	2

9)0	10)0		
9	8	7	6

Certificate of Completion
(Certificado de Cumplimiento)

Awarded to
(Otorgado a)

for the completion of *Bridges*
(por completar *Bridges*)

Parent's Signature
(Firma del Padre)

Teacher's Signature
(Firma del Maestro)

bridges